STRONG ENOUGH
FOR TWO

STRONG ENOUGH FOR TWO

How to Overcome Codependence and Other Enabling Behavior and Take Control of Your Life

DR. JIM MASTRICH
with BILL BIRNES

COLLIER BOOKS
Macmillan Publishing Company · New York
Collier Macmillan Canada · Toronto
Maxwell Macmillan International
New York · Oxford · Singapore · Sydney

Collier Books
Macmillan Publishing Company
866 Third Avenue, New York, NY 10022

Collier Macmillan Canada, Inc.
1200 Eglinton Avenue East, Suite 200
Don Mills, Ontario M3C 3N1

Library of Congress Cataloging-in-Publication Data
Mastrich, Jim.
Strong enough for two: how to overcome codependence
and other enabling behavior and take control of your
life/Jim Mastrich; with Bill Birnes.—1st Collier Books ed.
    p. cm.
Includes index.
ISBN 0-02-034520-8
    1. Codependency (Psychology)—Popular works. 2.
Codependents—Rehabilitation. I. Birnes, William J. II.
Title. III. Title: Strong enough for 2.
RC569.5.C63M37   1990
616.86—dc20   90-42239   CIP

Macmillan books are available at special discounts for
bulk purchases for sales promotions, premiums,
fund-raising, or educational use. For details, contact:

Special Sales Director
Macmillan Publishing Company
866 Third Avenue
New York, NY 10022

First Collier Books Edition 1990

10 9 8 7 6 5 4 3 2 1

Printed in the United States of America

This book is dedicated to my clients who over the years have mustered the courage to face themselves in the struggle to take charge of their lives. I am honored in working with these individuals who have decided that they can stand on their own and no longer need to be *Strong Enough for Two.*

Contents

Understanding Our Life Scripts

Four people sit across from one another in a mini–group therapy session. They sit on the edges of their chairs, legs tightly crossed, knuckles white with tension. At first they only stare at each other, sizing up the situation, mustering the courage to speak. Jeanne is first. She has taken care of others her entire life. If she had needs herself, she disregarded them and tended to those of her husband, her children, or her sisters. Mark has always put himself last. Born into the middle position of four other brothers, he learned to compromise, to lower his expectations and settle for the leftovers that nobody else wanted. Dot, on the other hand, was the family clown. She made herself the butt of every joke. In her family, when people lost their tempers, nobody ever got mad at Dot—nobody ever took her seriously. Carol feels used up and doesn't know why. She is only thirty-eight, but feels as if nothing is left for herself. Whatever she had is gone, and there is no point in going on with the rest of her life.

All four people are members of an enablers' support group. They talk about feeling empty and unfulfilled, frustrated and confused. They don't have the words to explain their situations, but they share a common feeling: an almost automatic response to the needs of other people. They can sniff out what other people want as if they were bloodhounds, even if those wants are subtle and unstated. They turn themselves inside out to satisfy those wants, sacrificing themselves and their own legitimate needs in the process. These people are enablers, individuals whose basic reaction in any relationship is to take care of the other person, even when it hurts themselves. Enablers perpetuate the drinking of alcoholics, provide for the needs of drug abusers, accommodate themselves to the cravings of compulsive overeaters, and help family members and friends continue their addictive and negative life-styles.

Enabling and Codependency Defined

Enabling is an adaptive form of behavior in which the actions of one person (the enabler) directly but inadvertently allow the irresponsible, dysfunctional, or destructive actions of another person (the abuser) to continue. Enabling is usually well-intentioned at first—it is even altruistic—but it eventually cements the dysfunction of the abuser to the need of the enabler to preserve the relationship at all costs. You can look at it as if it were an equation:

abuser's dysfunctional behavior + enabler's need to preserve
the relationship = dysfunctional relationship

Enabling is not a disease, but like the disease of alcoholism, it is progressive because what may start out as an altruistic impulse may lead to complete dependency. If enabling is not a disease, what is it? I define it as an adaptive form of behavior and attitude, a coping mechanism gone progressively awry until it becomes maladaptive. We'll expand this definition later on when we apply it to different types of relationships, but for the present, this working definition helps us to see why enabling is so difficult to identify in troubled relationships and why it can continue for years under the guise of helpfulness and companionship.

Enabling almost always masquerades beneath the camouflage of positive, supportive, nurturing, and socially acceptable behavior. But because it is inherently dysfunctional, the relationship does not change. The continuation of the behavior that initially was altruistic only locks the dysfunction into place. The relationship becomes progressively dysfunctional until it weakens both the abuser and the enabler. This is what makes enabling so insidious.

Codependents

When enablers act to sustain the addictions of drug abusers and alcoholics, they are commonly referred to as codependents. Codependency is a form of enabling behavior specific to chemical dependencies, substance abuse, and drug addictions in which the enabler, by perpetuating the addictive behavior, becomes equally dependent with the abuser on the abuser's continuing addiction. Codependency is so prevalent, it has become a national health problem. However, the term has been overused and misapplied to situations where there is no actual substance abuse involved. This has created all sorts of confusion and has even caused some psychologists and social commentators to complain that codependency is the big nonissue of the 1990s. As I intend to argue a bit later, nothing could be further from the truth. If we look at codependency as a form of enabling connected to the abuse of a substance, then we can truly say that the enabler is codependent upon the substance. However, when individuals simply help to perpetuate and support the negative behavior of another person, they are called enablers.

The Loving Confrontation

Enabling has its roots in nurturing and caring behavior. The difference between the two is the willingness and courage of the potential enabler to confront the abuser in a loving way. I call this the "loving confrontation," and I actively encourage couples to engage in it when tensions build in the relationship. Rather than deny the tensions, and in so doing cement negative behaviors into position, the enabler should confront the abuser about his or her behavior. Enablers need to set the ground rules of their participation in the relationship. They need to establish the basis of communication, assert their rights to challenge unhealthy or irresponsible behavior, set limits to their willingness to allow irresponsible behavior to continue, and test the mettle of the relationship against the silence of denial. Most enablers want to stop, but they don't know how. That is the purpose of this book.

The Life Script

For people raised in dysfunctional families, the past can act like leg irons, weighing them down and inhibiting their movements for the rest of their lives. The roles assigned to them as children, roles they learned to play in families that were scarred by alcoholism, drugs, trauma, abuse, or long-term emotional debilitation, often determine how these adult children will interact with others for the rest of their lives. They limit choices. They color perceptions. They become emotional scripts or psychological programs that dictate feelings, emotions, behavior, and responses to the outside world. Consequently, unless people confront their pasts and rewrite life scripts, they may be condemned to keep on replaying the roles assigned to them in those families of origin.

If you felt hopeless or insecure as a child, you might experience similar feelings of anxiety or hopelessness in each new adult relationship and wonder why things never change. If, because of physical or sexual abuse, you were fearful of adults, the behaviors you developed to protect yourself will keep on replaying themselves long after the source of that abuse is gone. If you learned that the way relationships work is for you to be the giver, then it is likely that similar one-way relationships will haunt you throughout your life unless you break the pattern. You enable other people to take advantage of you or to "use you up" until there is nothing more that you can give. Your adult relationships may turn sour or you may consciously or unconsciously push people away and never understand why. And the worst part of it might be the seeming instinctiveness of these actions: "I don't know why I do it; it's automatic. It just happens that way."

Does this sound familiar? If you have voiced similar complaints, you needn't feel guilty or ashamed. You belong to a very large group of people whose present lives have been compromised by the roles they've had to play as children. Most of you are enablers. You belong to a group of people who suffer because of someone else's addiction or dysfunction. You'd be surprised to know that there are millions of people who act out present roles because at sometime in the past they were handed an enabling script by their parents or close relatives. The most insidious part about enabling is that you don't stop the behavior simply because you've left your family of origin. The behavior keeps on repeating itself with every new situation, even though the situation does not require the enabling behavior. In this book, we'll show you how to rewrite that script and overcome that enabling behavior. You'll learn that you no longer have to shoulder someone else's burden, be the parent to your parent, or enable someone else to perpetuate his or her dysfunctional behavior. By virtue of having now become aware of your role in this pattern, you've already been freed. In this book we'll show you how to practice and enjoy your freedom.

Perhaps your friend, call her Mary, played the role of martyr or clown as a child. Perhaps, she believed, it was only her ability to defuse physically or emotionally threatening situations by turning laughter on herself that kept her alive. After all, someone who's laughing at you, is not beating you up, or worse. When Mary was a child her script was written for her. Now as an adult she plays it out over and over again in relationships, with friends, and even on the job. She feels herself acting out her script in the same types of situations time after time, even with people she's only just met. Why, she may ask herself in frustration, can't her situation ever change? Why does she always find herself repeating the same behavior? No matter how many resolutions she makes, no matter how many times she promises herself that she will change, she always plays out the same role, sees the same looks in the eyes of others, and hears herself saying the same lines for the umpteenth time. She knows she will always clown her way out of the promotion she believes she deserves, in an attempt to cover up her disappointment, all the while confirming to the world that she'll never get the kind of job responsibilities she knows she can handle. It's an endless loop.

In my own professional practice as a counselor and psychotherapist, I've encountered many people like Mary, and perhaps like yourself, who are locked into self-destructive life scripts. People who won't care for themselves, because they are absorbed by the needs of others. They take responsibility for other people, and by so doing, they can avoid responsibility for themselves. In trying to help enablers, I've found that there is a great need for a practical self-help book that can help people bridge the gap between their dysfunctional families of origin and the families they are in the process of creating. If I could, I'd hand my clients a book to help them link their pasts and presents and rewrite the scripts of their lives. Because I couldn't find a book like that, I decided to write one and dedicate it to the clients who have freely shared their stories with me so others can be helped by the insights they've bravely faced.

Snapshots of Three Enablers

The following anecdotes serve to illustrate some of the variety of contexts in which enabling occurs. These and all those presented in *Strong Enough for Two* are based on actual cases from my practice.

JANE

> I just can't take it. I don't know what decisions to make. I can't make them. I just want to be left alone.

Jane had snapped over the phone and now she was out of control. She'd been terribly confused for months during the protracted divorce proceedings. Now she'd had enough. Even the people outside her office were startled when they heard her scream into the receiver. They'd seen it coming, but were too afraid of her to ask what was wrong. Now she felt she was coming undone. Eight long years of a bitterly disappointing marriage were finally coming to an end. The property settlement, the painful negotiations to divide the assets seemed about to be concluded. The rest should have been simply mop-up work to nail down the final details so there'd be no loose ends dangling when she walked into the courthouse. With the hearing date scheduled for the following week, Jane found herself interrupted at work every fifteen minutes by seemingly insignificant phone calls from her lawyer. She couldn't hold a thought in her mind for more than thirty seconds before her phone beeped again and the soft, nasal insistence of her lawyer's voice pushed itself into her brain. Although he was only doing what he was being paid for, making sure that she was certain about the decisions he was helping her to make, it didn't stop her from flying off the handle when he called. In light of her normally calm exterior, this was very revealing.

Jane is very bright. Between the Xanax she was taking for her migraines and the Mylanta for her burning stomach, she had patched herself through the final period of her divorce. She had held onto her job as a successful midlevel personnel manager in a prominent multinational corporation at the same time she was raising her family. This in itself was no easy matter. She was a decision-maker. On the surface it seemed that the questions at hand about arranging for the sale of the house and the time frame for the actual divorce would be no big deal for her; in fact, one would think that she might be very relieved. However, Jane was on the edge of panic. Her stomach was churning in its own acid and she began to feel another migraine coming on. Moreover, she couldn't sleep at night without a heavy dose of her prescribed barbiturates. Not being one to ask for help or to shirk her responsibilities, Jane continued to try to get through each day's work as though she were on an assembly line. However, for a change, she was revealing the burden of the upset she was carrying by becoming impatient around the office. She was also making obvious mistakes. Jane rarely made mistakes. She always functioned in top form. Everyone could see her mistakes, especially her boss. Shame and inadequacy swept over her. It was this feeling of being out of control that brought her into counseling.

I don't know what's going on in me. When Bernie and I were dating I was so hopeful about life. I knew I had made some mistakes in my first marriage and I wanted so badly for this to work out. Looking back on it now it seems that I ignored some pretty obvious signs. I gave up my friends because Bernie felt uncomfortable around them; and I loved going to the ocean. Bernie knew that too, but we stopped going because he claimed the sun and wind bothered him. I wanted things to work out, and I would do anything for him, but when I found out he had been having an affair I knew the marriage was over. Unfortunately it's taken me over six years to get out. I must be pretty stupid.

Jane's problems had nothing to do with stupidity. She is a classic enabler. The daughter of a physically abusive and demanding mother and a passive father, Jane learned early in life that it was unrealistic to expect to get what she wanted from a loved one or, in fact, from any relationship. Furthermore, as the eldest of five sisters, she took it upon herself to protect them from the crazed outbursts of her mother. This would be a tall task for anyone, let alone a ten-year-old. Needless to say, she wasn't very successful at this and was often beaten for "interfering" and "causing trouble."

Jane's continual frustration of watching her younger siblings suffer at her mother's angry hands resulted in the development of a sense of powerlessness, a deep and subtle residue of anger, and an empathic concern for others less fortunate. As a result, in her adult life, Jane volunteers every Saturday morning to serve as a mediator between parents and their children in a court-sponsored program focusing on families experiencing domestic violence. By channeling her energies from her own abusive childhood, Jane is able to "try to make sure these kids don't have to go through what I did." This is constructive, cathartic, and healthy. Unfortunately she also channeled the results of her personal history into a continual pattern of negative, self-defeating behavior: enabling.

As we might expect, those in need often count on Jane's lending a helping hand. She tells of a standing joke among her friends that if there are any stray cats on the street they always seem to find their way to her door. As her current troop of felines reveals, she finds it difficult not to take in the cute, furry balls of neediness. "It's the eyes," she says. "I can't turn away once I see those eyes." Too many cats, however, is not Jane's problem. She has brought this same attitude to her relationships with men. She learned to gain a sense of fulfillment by taking care of them, too. This unleashed a chain of events in which she would put her own wants and needs second and eventually her mates would come to expect this. They also came to expect to lay exclusive claim to the central position in the relationship. It would get so that Jane would not even reveal her feelings and desires. Unfortunately for her she picked men who tended to be self-centered and consumed by their own neediness; consequently, the absence of her expressed wants wasn't even noticed. This cycle has continued in both her marriages, the first to a stray who was so inadequate and timid he was afraid of his own shadow; the second to an older tomcat who was only interested in preening himself and prowling the neighborhood for females. They both found their way to her door and Jane dutifully let them in.

Jane's actions never really get her what she wants, nor does her behavior ever heal the inadequacy and hurt in the other. Paradoxically Jane has fostered the script that she will never get what she wants and that those around her never have to be responsible for themselves and change. She is a bright, lovely, and caring woman who attempts to appease her sense of guilt and inadequacy by subordinating her wants and needs to those of the man in her life. Her challenge is to overcome the powerful effects of having grown up as the oldest child in a physically abusive household and in a culture where it is not only acceptable, but in fact desirable, for a female to deny her own needs, especially in deference to men.

FLORENCE

Florence's hopes abounded in the early years after World War II when so many young couples like she and Skip were buying houses in the burgeoning suburbs and beginning to start families. The feeling of promise and possibility that filled many in the nation at that time swept over Florence as well. Like Jane, Florence very badly wanted her dream of a happy home and family to come true, even if it meant overlooking some obvious problems.

Although it was during this period that Florence first noticed Skip's excessive drinking, she discounted it. She knew "Skip was a good man who didn't run around, always brought home the paycheck, and wasn't a bother to have around the house." He was no bother because he was slowly assuming his status as "the invisible man," as his adult children would eventually refer to him. The deeper Skip fell into his alcoholism, the less he was available for Florence and the children. In response, Florence reasoned that it was best not to complain—"I just wanted to keep the peace."

Florence is an archetypal enabler. Out of love for her husband and family she never allowed herself to place on Skip the reasonable demand that he stop his drinking and become a visible presence in the family. She enabled his drinking to continue. As part of this process Florence gradually took on more and more of the duties Skip was abdicating through his alcoholism. Skip continued to make it to work everyday and never failed to bring home the paycheck, but that was it. The closing of the front door upon his return home was almost simultaneous with the cracking of a flip-top. That first beer of the day began the daily decline in function regularly ending with Skip passed out in his chair in front of a blank television screen. With rare exceptions every day was the same. Florence and the children learned that if they wanted any meaningful dialogue with Skip, they'd better catch him as soon as he came home. Gradually the entire family stopped trying to talk with him almost altogether.

Florence's youngest son, Steve, even at age thirty, continued to live at home. That in itself didn't bother her. In fact, with Skip being the only other person at home, Florence appreciated having someone who might talk to her when she wanted to talk. She didn't even mind that Steve only paid his rent once in a while. She understood he was occasionally laid off from his construction job and felt sorry for him. She wished the job would work out better for him and that perhaps he'd meet a nice girl to take care of him. But Steve never seemed to go out on dates.

It got so that he hardly spoke at all, except to ask to borrow some money. He was almost as quiet as his father. Then there were those times, like Thanksgiving dinner, when he came down from his bedroom late and proceeded to chatter away. He didn't have much more than what a bird would eat. He seemed agitated and was offering his opinions in an obnoxious manner to everybody, including his grandmother! How was I to know he was addicted to cocaine?

Things seemed to get worse and worse with Steve. Soon he stopped playing sports altogether and began to run with a crowd Florence didn't know. Finally, at the urging of her other children, Florence agreed to go with them to counseling. It was there that she began to learn that she was acting as a codependent to Skip and Steve. Eventually, after she was trained with Steve's older siblings, a successful intervention was conducted with him. He completed a twenty-eight-day inpatient rehabilitation program, joined an aftercare program, and became active in Alcoholics

Anonymous. At the time of this writing Steve has been sober for fifteen months. His sobriety and Florence's newfound ability to confront the reality of her situation has also had a positive effect on Skip who, for the first time, is willing to look at his alcoholism as a disease.

Florence is not yet to the point that her codependent attitudes and behavior are fully behind her, but at least she was able to get them out of the way of helping her son. As things often come full circle, it is Steve who can be heard confronting his mother on her enabling tendencies. Florence, like many of us, still has work to do on herself.

Enabling behavior crops up in many forms. Florence, for instance, acted out the classic pattern of the codependent. In doing so she perpetuated the addictions of her loved ones: her husband Skip to alcohol and her son Steve to cocaine. Florence's behavior and attitudes inadvertently gave permission to these men to remain dependent on their drug of choice. This of course explains the addiction of Skip and Steve, but what about Florence? In codependency, as in any enabling relationship, the codependent or enabler is as locked into the pattern of dysfunctional behavior as the addict. For a number of reasons that were unique to her personal psychological history, Florence was also addicted to the poor communication and lack of intimacy that characterized relationships in her life, especially with those "closest" to her. Florence didn't know how to be close in relationships. She didn't know that it was her perfect right to make reasonable demands on her husband and son. And because of a deep and subtle fear of losing what she had, Florence couldn't allow herself to confront her loved ones. She may not have been happy in her relationship with Skip, but she was unwilling to risk losing it, or worse, find out that her urgent pleas would go unheeded. Rather than face the truth, Florence clouded the obvious and kept herself and Skip from facing it, pretending that if it were ignored it would simply go away. But no matter how hard we may try to deceive ourselves, the truth awaits us. And in facing the truth about any relationship we are inherently required to take responsibility for our actions. Codependent and enabling relationships by their very nature are designed so that we may attempt to skirt this responsibility.

Florence differs from Jane only insofar as her behavior is more classically codependent. Jane acts the part of the more broadly defined enabler. In Jane's case there was no addiction to an external substance, be it food, alcohol or other drugs, or gambling. Rather, her partner was an inadequate individual who propped himself up by being concerned only about himself. Jane's behavior toward Bernie literally enabled him to continue to ignore her wants and needs. If we take away the alcohol there is virtually no difference between the actions of these two women. As the following tale of Gary attests, enabling behavior is certainly not limited to the domain of "intimate" relationships.

GARY

Gary is tall and personable. He travels about the office with a smile on his face and usually a cute story or joke to tell. An all-American basketball star in college, he is far from being a wimp. Then how is it that a ninety-seven-pound young woman can push him around, seemingly at will? Gary may be a nice guy. Gary may be a rugged athlete. But as sure as the sun rises, Gary is an enabler.

> It's hard to imagine what to do with Carol. I mean she's a real wacko. I feel sorry for her and I don't know what's wrong with her, probably drugs or anorexia or maybe she's just nuts. She's always calling out sick and when she's here the office would be more productive if she weren't. My God can she talk. She disrupts everyone. She's constantly chattering on about partying the night before or her exploits with men. She's really revolting. Fortunately I can just close my door.

The fact is that Gary will never be successful at closing his door to Carol. The athlete in him may well understand that "You can run, but you can't hide," but as a supervisor of a dysfunctional employee, that's exactly what he's been trying to do.

Gary works as a department head within the financial division of a large corporation. This company has for years promoted a family image to both its employees and the public. Compassion for those who make their living there and a sense of responsibility to the community of which the company is a part are in fact written in as the cornerstone of its credo. In an effort to back up these words the company has established an employee assistance program (EAP). This program is available for employees and their family members to help them deal with any problems they may encounter, such as marital, parenting, substance abuse, financial, legal, or job-related difficulties. The EAP has even trained company supervisors in how to refer employees who are having difficulties in adequately performing their jobs. In the training Gary attended he was taught that a referral to EAP, in addition to being an example of sound management practices, is a compassionate way of addressing a job performance problem by offering help in lieu of disciplinary action.

Yet Gary "the nice guy" has never referred Carol to the EAP. He has spoken with her a couple of times about how it would be nice if she showed up to work on time and gives her an occasional "keep it down." But because he hasn't followed up and made her accountable for her actions, his efforts have been in vain. Instead, he engages in black humor about the situation with his peers. Instead of demanding adequate quality and quantity of work from her, he has given her less and less to do. By his inaction, Gary has also let her know it's OK to use profanity and disrupt the working atmosphere with loud talk and inappropriate comments. How does this happen? He's a bright, caring individual holding a secure supervisory position: What is Gary afraid of?

In essence it almost doesn't matter what Gary is afraid of. The nature of the employer-employee relationship demands that A be accountable to B and that B make his expectations clear to A. Should A not follow through, B should confront A about her behavior. Because of these clearly defined roles and rules, this type of relationship usually lends itself to less confusion. Gary, however, is confused, disarmed, and angry, and he hardly knows it. He covers his discomfort with humor and attempts to close his door on it.

Gary jokes about being raised a Catholic, altar boy, Boy Scout, a do-gooder of the highest order. But it is no joke. Gary learned that being a "good" person requires suppression of anger and denial that anything might be wrong. If something were wrong it would have to be confronted. Confrontation sometimes requires conflict, and because, in the world according to Gary, all confrontation is negative, rather than risk being seen as a bad person, he'd just as soon "stuff it."

Gary was taught by his parents and the nuns at Catholic school that they would withhold their approval of him unless he played his role and behaved only as a nice guy. However, he is no longer a child dependent on the sanction of these authorities and has yet to really learn that a sense of positive self-esteem can only come from within. He is an enabler, and in acting so is attempting to perpetuate the "nice guy" image. By letting his enabling behavior dominate his managerial style, Gary is perpetuating the illusion that he, the nice guy, doesn't get angry, and at the same time is becoming dysfunctional as a supervisor. Other employees see what Gary is allowing Carol to get away with and are becoming disgruntled. A corporate logo, not blood, binds this family together, but as in all dysfunctional families the impairment influences all members of the system. On the surface Carol is easily identified as the one with the problem, but we know she is not alone; Gary is her partner.

Just as it was for Florence, Gary needs as much help in coming to understand his dysfunctional behavior as does Carol. We've learned a great deal in helping the chemically dependent family come to identify and cope with its dysfunction. Both the treatment and lay communities are beginning to recognize more and more the need for the codependent to be treated for problems unique to him- or herself. Codependent individuals such as Florence have problems and issues that are separate from, yet inextricably linked to the alcoholic or addict. In the broader sense, overcoming all other types of enabling behavior—whether it be in a work setting, as is the case with Gary, or in a friendship or in a seemingly "normal" nonchemically dependent family—requires that the enabler face what it is that he or she uses to perpetuate these never-quite-win situations.

Nonresilient Family Structures

Jane, Florence, and Gary share common attitudes about themselves and others and react with the same patterns of behavior. Their inability to confront others directly, to establish boundaries, and to set limits with their partners and co-workers places them with a growing number of people who realize that their relationships are skewed or troubled. These people recognize their discomfort, and look for remedies to the pain. Their plight has become the subject of a great deal of commentary over the past two years, during which enabling behavior has been redefined so many times that the concept itself has come under some criticism. In book reviews, newspaper columns, and even in popular psychological magazines, writers have confused enabling with codependency and suggested that maybe everybody is codependent in one way or another. I disagree with that because I see enabling not as a disease in and of itself but as an emotional reaction to a set of conditions, a behavior mechanism that no longer serves its main purpose. Enabling is a way of tricking ourselves. By enabling, we create a feeling of control over events that may not be under our control. As a result, enabling may eventually become its own dysfunction, and this is where the general confusion about enabling lies.

People learn to be enablers in their families of origin. Therefore, in this book, I suggest that the root cause of most of the trouble lies in the family system. This is not an earth-shattering revelation, and I'm sure you've heard it from many other psychotherapists, substance abuse counselors, family therapists, or ministers. They've all told us that our families are in trouble. However, I've discovered that not only are our families in trouble, but the trouble is getting worse with every successive generation. Because human beings are social creatures who've survived the successive millennia by living and working collectively, children need to belong to large family or tribal networks for them to develop into normal, healthy, and resilient adults. Today's fractured family system does not address this need.

Originally—and I really mean originally—human beings evolved as a tribal species. The first tribes were probably little more than extended family units that roamed the land, shared the same network of caves or cliff dwellings, and banded together to hunt or resist common threats. Their extended families were large, perhaps loosely confederated into related cohorts or bands, and the social positions within the family units were clearly defined. The tribal-family unit had to have been a thoroughly resilient system that nurtured and protected its young. The structure of family units remained remarkably consistent during the subsequent social evolution, the majority of populations living on the land and cultivating family-oriented farms, and related families settled in neighboring communities. Even a hundred years ago, in our country, the rural farm community structure was the basis of family life, despite the rapid growth of the cities. Things were changing quickly, however. Families became smaller, children moved away from their hometowns and flocked to the cities, and the growth of large industrial factories provided workers with alternatives to farm labor. In other words, we were becoming an industrialized nation. As the means of production shifted to the cities and farm management passed from life-style to business, family farm ownership declined. The family unit became smaller and generations separated from one another. After the turn of the present century, this process accelerated. World War II kicked away the traditional underpinnings of American society and we experienced a period of rapid change and severe dislocation during which the entire structure of the family and society was changed.

Fifty years ago, grandparents lived with their children, and more often than not younger brothers or sisters lived in the same house with their married siblings. But in the course of fifty years, the nuclear family has evolved. And in the course of the past thirty years, the two-parent family has become a one-parent family. Today, more than half the children in our society grow up in single-parent homes. Also, a significant number of children are passed from parent to parent, family to family, and from families into the social welfare system. Accordingly, most, if not all, of the safeguards usually found in extended families are no longer available. For example, fifty years ago if Dad was a drinker you might have had an Uncle Joe or an Aunt Mary or even a grandparent to look to for solace and guidance. Individuals who might have been predisposed to specific addictions were, many times, helped by family members so that they did not become addicts. Today those buffers are no longer present and children and spouses are left on their own to survive.

A consequence of this circumstance today is that the coping skills most people may have developed in order to survive on their own now work as disadvantages as they encounter the world outside. You may have learned skills that helped you survive in your family, but which have left you ill prepared for encounters with the world outside. As a result, enabling has become more of a norm than an aberration.

Our Enabling Society

I don't want to belabor this point, but if you take the time to look around, you'll find that all of us live to some degree as codependents in an enabling society. In subsequent chapters you'll see how, just by the way products are marketed, we're told what to think, when to eat, what to drink, and how to disregard what our minds and bodies are telling us. We're encouraged to become obese, to consume more alcohol than is good for us, to equate overindulgence in food and drink with very unhealthy and demeaning forms of sexual experiences, and to distort our children's sensibilities so that they grow up to be dysfunctional consumers in a world overrun with insignificant products and awash in its own garbage. These are harsh statements, to be sure, but in my psychotherapy practice, I treat the victims of society who are poisoned by this garbage. I try to help them become detoxified. I try to help them make the choices between the things that are good for them and the things they think they want. I try to help them listen to their own voices. It isn't easy. As with all recovery, people need to be ready in order to really listen.

The biggest problems I have in explaining enabling and codependence to my clients are that:

1. Enabling has its roots in natural function. It begins from completely normal premises.

2. We live in a society of codependents and enablers. Because our family structures are failing, and along with them the well-defined social order, people are finding it easier and easier to fall into enabling relationships with other people.

3. Entire postwar generations of children have come of age in an America that has come to see "taking care" of others as a normal course of events. This kind of care-taking is not nurturing at all, but is in fact *dis*abling to both parties. Enabling and codependency has been practiced in our geopolitics and has been reinforced many hours every night in television sit-coms. Of course it comes so easily to us.

Since the end of the Second World War, the United States has become an "enabling nation." What was an accurate and appropriate perception at the close of the war—assuming as our burden the defense of Europe—is now no longer appropriate: In doing so we have sapped our resources, paid their bills, and enabled Europe to become a greater economic power than we are. By similarly burdening ourselves with the defense of the Pacific Rim, we must now stand idly by and watch Japan and other Pacific nations tap out the last of our manufacturing capabilities. We are becoming the weak link in the global metropolis of the new millennium because in the second half of the twentieth century the United States adopted enabling as a foreign and domestic policy. I know this sounds like an overly simplistic, reactionary and populist political speech, but I suggest that it has its own level of truth.

Getting a Handle on Your Enabling Behavior

Regardless of what your circumstance is, getting a handle on how enabling behavior may run and eventually ruin your life is essential. You may be an adult child of alcoholic (ACOA) parents or hail from a seemingly "perfect" family. It doesn't matter. Enabling is a learned pattern of thinking and behaving that knows no bounds in either its origin or in its manifestation. Some people are enablers when it comes to parenting, others in work situations, and still others only in love relationships. Whether you are an enabler in a work or a home situation doesn't matter. The reality is that at least one important area of your life is affected. And most people who are enablers generally have a hard time limiting it to just one sector. Usually it spreads into and permeates all vital life areas.

Paradoxically, enabling behavior is not treated by cutting it out, rather it is treated by recognizing and almost embracing it. This is much like the First Step of Alcoholics Anonymous and the other Twelve Step programs in that we must first recognize our sense of powerlessness over our impairment. Is there hope? Of course! In fact you have already begun the process of changing by choosing to read this book. Chances are you are already involved with other reading and self-help groups or are in the process of discovering yourself through counseling or psychotherapy. No changing can be done without first being willing to look with your eyes wide open and acknowledge that something is out of balance.

The Enabling Potential Test

Let's begin the process of change with a self-assessment and an acknowledgment. Indicate which of the following statements apply to you.

1. I usually feel guilty for asking for what I want.
2. I usually feel obligated when I am given something by another.
3. When I am given something, I often find myself wishing I would not "have to" get anything at all.
4. I try to avoid confrontations with others.
5. Usually it is hardest to deal with significant people in my life.
6. I worry about disappointing the other.
7. I usually feel the need to maintain control.
8. Deep inside, I secretly fear losing control.
9. I usually find myself assuming the role of caretaker in relationships.
10. It is my experience that people usually don't come through for me.
11. I often find myself trying to ignore my disappointment when I feel disappointed by others.
12. I usually don't reveal my disappointment to the person who disappointed me.
13. My attitude usually is that things (work, home, or relationships) will fall apart without my holding them together.
14. I complain about the burdens others make me carry.
15. I secretly like having so much control and responsibility.
16. Sometimes I feel and/or fear I am falling apart.
17. I usually have difficulty maintaining my boundaries (either physical or emotional) with others.
18. I sometimes feel shame for no reason.

19. I am honestly afraid of saying the truth for fear of its consequences.
20. I find it natural to carry other's burdens for them.
21. I usually have a difficult time detaching from others without severing all ties.
22. I sometimes find myself feeling responsible for *everything*.
23. I am very sensitive to what others think of me.
24. I often explain away my feeling that someone has let me down.
25. People can always rely on me, but there is usually no one there for me.

First of all, how did you feel while you were taking your enabling potential (EP)? Were you at all anxious? If so, can you explain why? What was the range of feelings you experienced? Can you identify the progression of feelings? Did you find yourself going numb? If so, can you guess why you might have chosen to distance yourself from your feelings? It is important to recognize right at the beginning that if you find yourself acting as an enabler there is nothing to feel guilty about. Remember, enabling is a coping mechanism, a defensive pattern of behavior usually set in place somewhere between early and middle childhood and often out of a need to fend off some very real emotional threats. You also learned very early that it was the way people interacted with each other in your family of origin. It probably no longer serves as the "adaptive" function it once was and that's why you want to exorcise it from your life. If you act like an enabler, you are an enabler. Nothing more and nothing less. At least now you are coming to know and understand it, and that is the only way that the process of change begins. By the way, if you found yourself either wanting to look good in how you answered the questions or began to be overly concerned about the "right" way to take your EP, you might as well consider these as additional indicators of your tendency to be an enabler.

If you found that you identified with seven or more of the items listed in the Enabling Potential Test this is a good indication that you tend to act as an enabler in relationships enough of the time to warrant concern. It also seems that your attitudes about yourself, like those of most enablers, reflect a sense of self-doubt and a tendency to have an external source of judgment. You are concerned about how others see you and you place an overemphasis on those outside of you for a judgment about your behavior.

If you scored under seven, you have less to worry about, but remember that because enabling behavior, like all aspects of emotional and mental health, is a continuum, everybody sooner or later acts at some point in the overly responsible, controlling way that we characterize as enabling or codependent. It is very rare for anyone to get less than three on the EP if they are really being honest and not self-deluding. This serves to remind us that enabling at its root is a normal behavior.

Your task should be to learn what you can do about changing your tendency to enable. While remembering the "normal" quality of enabling and its presence in almost every relationship, it is imperative that you come to understand the quality of what it feels like to be an enabler. After all, you don't enable just for the fun of it. Enablers and codependents are usually motivated and directed to act in these ways by the feelings that often subtly control their conscious thoughts and attitudes. Do you understand how your inner feelings and assumptions direct your enabling tendencies?

Empowerment

If you recognized your potential to enable another person's irresponsible behavior, you will have to focus on the affirmative. Empower yourself to control your own behavior by turning off the enabling switch. Let me help you to turn off the switch, to stop enabling other people. This is the basic premise of empowerment: I say that it's OK for you to *stop*. As of this moment, you are no longer an enabler. You can stop taking care of others, stop worrying about things you can't fix, and stop taking responsibility for keeping the world spinning on its axis. If you stop, the universe will *not* fall apart around you, the sun *will* rise tomorrow, and you will *not* be punished. I assure you of this. You have my guarantee. You are now officially empowered to:

1. Put yourself first
2. Not be responsible for the failures or shortcoming of others

3. Not carry around the burden of guilt because you have not done enough for your spouse or parent
4. Turn off that internal voice that keeps censuring everything you do
5. Activate yourself to create the life you've always wanted to live

By your very act of reading this page you have reached Step One of our Five-Step Program. You have acknowledged that your life has become unmanageable and that you are willing to change. You have begun the process. As for the voice inside of you that keeps you working for everybody but yourself, you can now turn it off. I now empower you to reach down inside yourself, throw the switch, and listen to the silence. That's the silence of freedom. You are becoming free.

By the end of the book, you will have realized that you had the power all along to shut off the enabling switch, to control your own destiny, and to let the chips that belong to others fall where they may. By the end of the book, you will believe, as I do, that the world really can be as your imagination and hope tells you it is. If you've convinced yourself, because you have been so conditioned, that you must be the safety net for everybody else, you are indeed the safety net. The world is as you say it is. If you can convince yourself not to be the safety net, to live life as you want to, then the world will be changed accordingly. That sounds very basic, but in real life, that's all it takes.

One of the requirements of this freedom is to understand the subtle payoff you receive from being the safety net in your significant relationships. You may not know it yet but you're already free from the intolerable burden of enabling and codependence. It's not that just my saying it makes it so, it's your willingness to stop playing the role of the savior of the world and just take care of your own needs. Perhaps just my saying it isn't enough. Perhaps it takes a Wizard of Oz to grant you a charter of emancipation from the world's responsibilities. If so, then our empowerment should serve as your charter. Cut it out of the book, write your name in the margin, and hang it on the wall where everyone can see it. If that's not enough, then maybe you need to explore the problems of enabling and codependency first and walk the Five Steps to freedom. By the end of the book we'll issue the very same proclamation again and you will have come a long way toward overcoming your problems with codependency and enabling. Reaching that point may be easier said than done, for you must truly be ready to take a radically different view of yourself and your relationships. Accordingly, you are invited to explore your past and the pasts of hundreds of thousands of enablers just like you who find themselves trapped in a vicious cycle of guilt, shame, and self-recrimination.

The Five Steps to Overcome Enabling Behavior

Our program is based on developing your ability to identify your behaviors and take positive action to remedy them. Because we know we have to take it in small steps, one day at a time, one success at a time, we've expressed the program in five simple steps. If you can master these steps, you have the power to change your entire life.

1. *Stop* the *denial* and acknowledge the dissatisfaction in your relationship with yourself and loved ones.
2. Recognize the *ways* in which you *enable*.
3. Understand what you feel *when* you *enable*.
4. Gain insight as to *how* you first developed your pattern of enabling behavior.
5. Begin to *practice* using attitudes and behavior that characterize *healthy* relationships.

Now begins the process of understanding how you initially developed enabling as a coping pattern. In the following chapters you will learn how to implement the five steps to controlling your tendency to enable. First we will explore the typical dynamics at play in a family that fosters enabling behavior. This will be followed in chapter 3 by a detailed exploration of codependency as a subset of enabling behavior. This is of particular importance to adult children of alcoholics and other survivors because we will illustrate how otherwise innocent victims may be drawn into an orbit around the abuser and be taught to function as enablers.

This first section will be concluded in chapter 4 with an examination of the forces that come to shape the behavior of an enabler. By learning how patterns of addiction and dysfunction are carried forward in families from generation to generation you will be arming yourself to let the buck stop where it should have stopped: in your family of origin. It is my hope that this book will serve as a valued resource by both reclaiming your life for *you* and preventing the legacy of enabling from being transmitted to the next generation.

2

The Making of an Enabler

Enablers aren't born, they're made. For most, their roles are fashioned in their dysfunctional families of origin. They adapt to the demands of their parents by learning to cope with the stress and trauma in their childhood. When the pressures of childhood finally ease, the coping mechanisms remain as relics—no longer fulfilling their function, but still the attitudes and behavior of adult children of dysfunctional families. Other enablers didn't learn enabling from their families of origin but rather acted it out as adults when a partner in a relationship began to act dysfunctionally. Perhaps your family may have taught you to value altruism, but despite your caring and concern, your partner's emotional irresponsibility or other dysfunction remains the same or may have gotten worse. It is now time for you, as well as your partner, to break what has become a bad habit. It is now clear that you can't control the actions of your partner, but you certainly can take charge of your own life. This chapter shows how enablers are made and how they still fight the battles of wars that may be long ended.

LAURA

Laura sits on the edge of her chair in group therapy. Her eyes dart around the room at the others, searching in their faces for any sign of disapproving looks. She'll often take a break to grab a cigarette in the hall, usually in the face of censure from the rest of the group who want her to quit chain-smoking. She's like a rabbit, always quick to jump at the first sign of any threat.

> I always knew Bill was hard on the kids. He doesn't often show his sensitive side but I know he loves them very much. He had it pretty hard growing up. His father was abusive to him and his mother. Fortunately for Bill she had the courage to take him under tow and move out when he was about five. Yet to this day he resents her. And she practically saved his life. Anyway, it's as if he's still angry and what bothers me is that the kids often take the brunt of it. And they're good kids too. It breaks my heart to see them get hurt. I always make sure I'm there to comfort them, but for the first ten years of our marriage I didn't think I could do anything about it.

Laura describes herself as a "loving mother" to her children and a "devoted wife to Bill." She makes sure that the rest of the group accepts her descriptions. She puts them first, she tells us, and her needs last—always. She can rarely talk about her own needs unless it's in the context of taking care of her husband and children. Like so many women in her position she is an enabler who fuels her dysfunctional pattern of behavior by her constant outward disclaimers of love and caring for her family. How can you blame her for loving her family and children, she asks. Isn't that what life's all about? Yet, at the same time, it's very puzzling and ironic that a person who says she cares so much for her family would allow her children to be the victims of a hurtful and abusive parent.

> Our children learned to be responsible very quickly. They were never behavior problems in school and always did their homework and chores. But when they would slip up, as kids are apt to do, Bill would berate them and oftentimes call them stupid or lazy.

Denying what she knew about child development and parenting, Laura stood by and watched Bill treat their children abusively. She knew someday that it would all crash around her, it was just a matter of time. When the time came, she would protect the children. But for the present, she would protect Bill. It was in fact this very assumption that served to perpetuate the draconian parenting methods used by Bill.

Assumptions

People like Laura can't slide into enabling behavior without a full complement of fundamental self-assumptions, most of which are false. Our self-assumptions operate like "great truths": basic attitudes and beliefs about ourselves and the world that we take for granted. They are the axioms: the two-plus-two-equal-fours that structure our entire framework of reality. Most of the time we don't even know they are operating.

Our assumptions control our thinking. They make us see things that aren't there and allow us to deny things that stare us in the face. They also control what we may come to think is possible. This was the case with Laura. She assumed that she couldn't or perhaps didn't have a right to ask Bill to act like a civilized human being who was supposed to raise his children instead of beat them into emotional submission. She refused to confront the damage he was doing to their children, hoping instead to make quiet repairs when he wasn't looking. She had pity and understanding for him, she claimed. She took into consideration his difficult childhood and this, coupled with her basic assumption that "men just aren't as sensitive as women," kept her from admitting what was really happening in her family. In other words, she enabled herself to become an enabler, which is a simplistic way of saying that Laura was also responsible for what was taking place in her family. She didn't realize, at first, that the basic missing assumption in her framework of reality was her own sense of herself. She had discounted her "self" to a point where it was hurting her children, crippling her husband, and destroying her marriage. Are we saying, therefore, that Laura-as-victim bears the majority of blame? That's the question she asked over and over again in group. And again and again others pointed out that assigning blame was one of the things that got her into this to begin with. By not assigning blame and simply accepting reality for what it is, she can, in a nonjudgmental way, break the cycle of enabling that has kept her self-esteem from asserting itself. Eventually Laura came to see that lack of self-esteem is an important factor in perpetuating enabling behavior. When she finally asked herself, "If I don't value myself, how can I ask another to?" she was able to understand the truth about her present family and her family of origin.

Enabling in the Nonaddictive Family

All families have several different members and each may serve as the enabler for the dysfunction of another. Because the term *enabling* comes out of the addiction literature we are often prone to consider chemical dependency as the likely dysfunction in a family member. However, as Laura can attest, that is not always the case. Although it has been estimated that alcoholics and people addicted to other drugs may affect the lives of over eighty million family members and loved ones in the United States alone, there are untold millions who live in nonaddictive families that operate with a secrecy exactly parallel to that of the chemically dependent family. Within these families there exists a denial that both binds its members together and strangles their individual senses of self. The dysfunctional member needn't be a father as Bill is, and the role of the enabler can be played by more than one person. The mother is only one of the many possible players. This is the case of Timmy.

TIMMY

Born into a lower-middle-class family, Timmy quickly learned to act the part of an enabler. The dysfunctional player in his family drama was his father; however the dysfunction was not manifested as harshness and insensitivity, as was the case with Bill, rather it was an obvious case of personal inadequacy. While completing his graduate work in engineering, Timmy eventually sought counseling in order to sort out the identity questions that grew out of his relationship with his father. In therapy, he poignantly recalled an early interaction with his father:

The first incident that I remember clearly happened Christmas morning when I was about six or seven. I had been given this big drum, the kind that's always in the painting of the three revolutionary war guys. You know *The Spirit of '76*. One guy's playing a drum, the other a fife, and the third holds a flag. I remember telling my parents how much I wanted the drum. At that age I was heavily into anything that had to do with war. So after I unwrapped it, my father insisted that he show me the "right" way to play it. What did I care? I was a kid and I just wanted to play with it. But he insisted and although even then I remember thinking this was kind of stupid, I went along. He showed me alright. He sat down, put it between his knees and promptly crushed it. So was I. I didn't even get a chance to play it. My older sister cried and started yelling at him. I didn't cry. I felt sorry for him. I didn't even say a word except "It's OK." He said he was sorry. He must have repeated it over fifty times that night. I now know he was more than sorry. He was pitiful. He didn't even have enough character to get me a replacement. I still remember the drum I didn't get.

This may have been the first incident Timmy could remember, but he had been "preparing" to be an enabler almost from the moment he could first understand the dynamics of his family. In his case Timmy modeled the behavior he saw in his mother and grandparents. It was subtle, but he was able to pick out the fragility and emptiness of his father and also the way the other significant adults in his life seemed to compensate for it. Timmy of course wasn't consciously aware of these dynamics, rather, like all children, he was just tuning into and picking up the signals being sent out around him. The assumptions and patterns of behavior that children learn are especially powerful, given that they are the first marks written on the blank slate.

All throughout his childhood Timmy never called his father on his inadequate behavior. Like his mother and grandparents, Timmy learned never to expect his father to come through. This, of course, didn't prevent him from wanting all the things that come with adequate and decisive fathering. Timmy's learning to not expect from his father was the coping strategy that salved his disappointment over the years and allowed his internal gyroscope to navigate him through childhood. However, as an adult, he had to learn to give up that coping strategy in favor of a more "normalized" view of the world. As a child, Timmy both wanted and needed his father to be there for him, to come through on the things fathers were supposed to. It wasn't as if his dad wasn't smart enough. He had a position of responsibility at the factory that demanded sound judgment and decision-making ability. In fact, his father was such a paradox that it was, and still is, hard for Timmy to understand who this man really is. Yet he continued into his early twenties to enable his father.

> I just started to feel as if I had had enough. I guess you could say I was pretty angry. That was another feeling I wasn't allowed to display in relation to my father. But I just stopped buying into his helplessness and doing stuff for him, like buying the water softener, getting the lawn mower repaired and selecting carpenters to put on the new roof. I had enough!

Timmy began to pull back and establish more reasonable boundaries and expectations with his father, but his father didn't change overnight. The patterns of dysfunctional behavior that enabling reinforces are so resistant to change that in most cases things get much worse before they get better. The trick is to hold your ground and maintain consistency in your behavior. You must, as Timmy did, keep forcing the issue until the person you've been enabling sees that there's no way out. That's just what happened in the early going between Timmy and his father: Things went from worse to even worse. After Timmy told his father he would metaphorically no longer tie his shoes for him, he was hit with a dose of inadequacy and guilt that sent him reeling and forced him to reevaluate what he was trying to accomplish. Timmy's father went through a period in which he felt compelled to check with Timmy and his sister on almost everything. "He seemed to need reassurance at every point more than ever before." Timmy was even getting pressure from his mother who pushed him to go back to the way it used to be. She was an enabler in the family as well. To his credit, Timmy stayed the course and by using the counseling process to help him remain focused, he was able to repel the temptation to bail his father out. He, like many "recovering" enablers, now feels much more at ease with himself and has begun to get in touch with a profound sense of personal freedom. As in an alcoholic's recovery, this doesn't mean that Timmy can relax and allow himself to slip back into shadows of his previous behavior. Recovery is a process that never ends. Timmy will have to remain consistent and vigilant. Most likely, so will you in your particular situation.

The Seeds of Enabling

There is no established pattern for who will manifest dysfunction in a family and who will "volunteer" to serve as the enabler. For the most part, the enabler functions as a kind of emotional valet to the person who is abdicating his or her duties as a responsible member of the family. It's almost natural to feel some form of sympathy for a person who's less than fully functional, especially if we understand alcoholism and other addictions to be diseases. However, what might start out as a feeling of genuine caring and concern for the dysfunctional person very quickly becomes a trap for both people. The person who is an enabler ends up completely taking care of an individual who is fully capable of performing his of her own life functions, asphyxiating that person's life and the enabler's life as well in the process. As much as any of us might fantasize about being taken care of, not having any responsibilities, this type of arrangement quickly proves to be suffocating for most emotionally healthy individuals. However, where a family member is very dysfunctional, the arrangement is more than satisfying, regardless of whether he or she is an alcoholic, cocaine addict, the victim of an inadequate and fragile personality, or a pathologically angry person. The last is the case of Nancy and her mother.

NANCY

Nancy grew up with her two younger sisters in a family that had a rather withdrawn and emotionally unavailable father and a mother who seemed forever fragile and on the edge of nervous collapse. From a very early age Nancy could see how easily her mother was hurt and upset. Nancy also came to learn that whenever mother felt disturbed, she was prone either to lashing out verbally or withdrawing into herself. Nancy remembered seeing her mother weeping alone in her chair many an afternoon.

> I would always try to comfort her. There I was, all of nine years old, attempting to parent my parent. She would talk to me about how unhappy her life was and how it was so hard to make my father happy. I would feel sorry for her. I still do. And I would try to fix things by listening and offering to help around the house. She liked that. And she liked me too. Only now do I realize she only seemed to value me when I was there for her. My needs never counted.

Nancy learned the value of acting "nice," pleasant, and caring: behaviors that have become fixed into her personality like autonomic reflexes. She became so accustomed to taking responsibility for the lives of others, she even chose a profession that would allow her to camouflage what was a dysfunction as a professional responsibility: She became a nurse. Although all nurses are not enablers, Nancy quickly incorporated her particular form of enabling into the daily routine of her profession. As a pediatrics nurse, Nancy is paid and praised for comforting infants and young children who must endure a stay in the hospital while they recover from surgery or illnesses. Unfortunately for Nancy, the very tendencies that serve her and her patients well at work set her up for repeated disappointments in her private life. Her relationships with men are often unhappy and unfulfilling.

Although Nancy is available for others and quick to identify and focus on their needs, she is also quick to smother other people with too much nurturing. At first, her nurturing serves her well in attracting men and addressing their interests in the early phases of a relationship. But those relationships don't last long because she turns herself into a nursemaid for the men she finds most attractive. It was this endless round of dead-end relationships that brought her into therapy. Where was she going wrong? Why was every relationship foundering on the same rocks? Why was she always feeling that it was her fault, that she wasn't caring enough? And, most importantly, where was all this pain she was feeling coming from?

In one of our first interviews, she revealed that she seemed to seek out men who wanted to be doted upon. Doting was something she could do. What she didn't see clearly until she began to analyze it for herself was that the men who were most interested in her doting were the ones who were least likely to reciprocate. These were the men to whom she found herself drawn. Sure they wanted attention, and Nancy exuded nothing if not personal warmth and the assurance that a guy could do a lot worse than be taken care of by her. However, those were exactly the type of men who tended to treat Nancy as a mother figure and take her for granted. The nicer and more accommodating she acted, the greater the pain when the relationship collapsed. "When you hear yourself saying the same things to guys over and over again," Nancy revealed at a group session, "and you have the same feelings of hopelessness when you stare into the darkness at four in the morning, you know you're in trouble."

Acting Nice

At first glance it appears that Nancy's propensity to act nice was simply one of the positive qualities of her personality. She was indeed a lovely and gentle person. However, her "acting nice" helped to perpetuate the myths that:

1. The way her mother dealt with her was just fine;
2. She thought it was alright if the important people in her life didn't give back to her; and
3. She wasn't hurt and angry.

I have a general rule of thumb that I often see validated in my psychotherapy practice. Simply put, there is a direct relationship between the intensity of a person's "acting nice" and the degree to which they are denying their anger and disappointment at not having been treated fairly and given the necessary and reasonable consideration that a healthy relationship requires. The enabler in Nancy used "acting nice" to cover up the fact that her wants and emotional needs were not being met. Nancy was truly a nice person. That was no act. But she was also a very disappointed and lonely person who was using "nice" as a way to deny her very real needs.

Enabling: Different Roles, Different Relationships

It is important to remember that the function of enabling behavior is to promote denial and by so promoting it to cover up the truthful but threatening facts underlying a relationship. It should be obvious, therefore, that the way to break the enabling pattern is to confront denial and embrace the truth. We must recognize that neither the nature of the particular dysfunction nor the identity of the family member covering it up are as important as the reality that an unhealthy relationship is perpetuating itself. The sad fact is that there is nothing inherently unhealthy about the nature of a relationship itself, it is only the underlying premises of the relationship—the denial and enabling—that make it unhealthy. Once these are addressed, if the relationship sustains the partners it will most likely continue on, stronger than it had been in the past. Paradoxically, enabling only serves to stifle a relationship even though it appears to allow it to continue. All enabling perpetuates is dysfunction. Once you understand and accept this, you will realize that you have nothing to gain by continuing the denial and perpetuating the dysfunction. Things only get worse.

We have already seen how two children enabled the behaviors of their same-sexed parents and in so doing continued to enable into their young adult years. These children developed this pattern of behavior early in their lives in response to a perceived sense that something important was missing from their relationships with their parents. That behavior became frozen and prevented them from establishing realistic boundaries as they grew up. This is often what happens when children enable their parents.

Parents Who Enable Their Children

Parents can also enable their children. Compulsive overeaters and chronically overweight individuals, for example, tend to reveal that one or both of their parents not only encouraged them to overeat, but encouraged them to use food as a compensation for shortcomings in other parts of their lives. Parental enabling and denial are also symptomatic of teenage drug addictions and teenage alcoholism. Often in these situations, a therapist will see some of the most complicated patterns of enabling: the subtle but ever powerful dynamics of the family system. The following example, the case of Lawrence Jr. and Lawrence Sr., clearly illustrates the making of an enabler over successive generations. Both the family genetic predisposition to alcoholism and the emotional affects of that alcoholism and codependency combine to fashion enablers and abusers in succeeding generations. If this dysfunctional cycle reminds you of your family, see where you might break the chain or rewrite your own script.

LAWRENCE

Lawrence was thirteen years old when he first sought counseling for help with his alcohol and marijuana problem. Asked when he first began to drink, Lawrence could not remember. This was very telling, considering he was a very intelligent young man with an otherwise firm memory.

> I haven't the slightest idea. All I know is that from the earliest time I have any memories I was drinking. I remember grabbing my mother's beer when she wasn't looking and guzzling it right down. I wasn't any older than five and I really liked the taste. I also loved driving her crazy. At other times I remember running over to the liquor cabinet and just grabbing any bottle and drinking it. It really got to my parents.

Despite the outwardly calm appearance of the intelligent, affluent Princeton teenager who sits in the easy chair at the far corner of my office, his pain gives him away. Lawrence likes to draw easily on his cigarette and take a long time before he graces me with an answer to a question. It's his way of exerting control. It's also the way most of the young men in his group behave when they feel they're under pressure. As a family therapist, you know from experience that you have to wait them out. Actually, they hate the silence more than you do.

I'd been working with Lawrence's family for many months,

listening over the phone to the panic in his mother's voice when the counselor called her to say they'd found drugs in his locker; consulting with his father who stays in Washington, D.C., during the week and only wanted me to "keep the lid on the thing" until he got home that Friday; fencing with Lawrence Jr. himself who kept on trying to reassure me that as soon as he decided to "lighten up" about his parents, he'd get off booze. Lawrence Jr. is a full-blown alcoholic. Though sober now, his recovery has been spotty and he has only just climbed back on the wagon. Although he was currently "dry," he was far from being truly sober. His family genogram reveals a pattern of alcoholism that stretches from generation to generation among the male members of his clan.

A genogram is a very helpful tool to see the connection between past and present within a family. This is a schematic of the family with significant information about each family member from generation to generation. If alcoholism is present, for example, we include those members who were diagnosed or hospitalized for alcohol-related problems. We also include references to the specific dynamics among family members, such as whether the maternal great-grandmother spent two years in a psychiatric hospital after the birth of her last child and whether the relationships between mothers and daughters have been marked by conflict. It is most helpful to go back several generations, because when there is dysfunction in a family it can usually be traced back through the generations. Enabling is one such behavior.

Genograms have been used primarily by family therapists as a means to quite literally picture the dynamics of families. It is a method of drawing a family tree that presents significant information about family members and their relationships. Genograms are most useful when information on at least three generations is provided. You might be very surprised by the pattern of information about your own family if you draw one. Most people find that the patterns displayed in so graphic a manner provide the basis for powerful insights as to how the family has operated for generations and how forms of dysfunction, such as alcoholism and enabling, have manifested themselves in the present generation.

The information presented in a genogram is particularly helpful if it is seen through the perspective of family systems theory. For our purposes here, a systems approach would consider the actions of each family member in relation to the other members. In this way an understanding of the individual in the context of the family can often provide for much deeper and more meaningful insight into the development of historical patterns of behavior. It is therefore imperative, for instance, that an examination of a genogram include information about life-cycle transitions, which may include births, deaths, divorces, and any other significant events that may mark the evolutionary pattern of the family. Although genograms arise from the family systems theory of Murray Bowen, M.D., and are used extensively by family therapists, they are of enormous use to any person who came from a family. And that means everyone.

In Lawrence Jr.'s case, his paternal grandfather, uncle, and great-grandfather were all alcoholics: an alcoholic in each generation. He is the family alcoholic of his generation. He's proud of it, he tells me, and he wears it like a varsity letter he might have earned in football. I tell him that there is a fair chance, given what we know from the research currently being conducted on the genetic predisposition of alcoholism, that Lawrence's brain and body were calling out for its fix of ethanol even before he was born. This seems to please him; it is just the kind of fatal flaw that he would like to indulge himself in. But I can't give away my pawn that easily. I explain that at first glance he might think that this serves as the entire explanation of what would eventually give rise to his compulsive use of alcohol and marijuana and his other irresponsible behavior. But there are other influences acting on him that we can't overlook. In other words, his problems are not entirely of his own making, but it's not just a question of his designer genes. The big picture in Lawrence's family is the insidious influence of alcoholism in affecting the emotional well-being of the nonalcoholic and often codependent family members.

Lawrence's father fits this role in his family of origin. Lawrence Sr. was never himself an alcoholic; however, he was deeply scarred by his father's alcoholism. Many a night when he came home from work, his father would emotionally and sometimes physically abuse him. His mother was codependent and, given the prevailing societal attitudes, she also put up with her share of abuse. It was in this setting that Lawrence Sr. learned how to behave in relationships with others. In particular he learned the ways men and women communicate, or not, with each other. He learned something about conflict resolution and the expression of feelings. And through all that he learned there was one overriding theme: don't express your feelings, don't let them get anything on you, and, above all, don't trust. Many children of alcoholic parents learn these same lessons.

As a consequence of this unhealthy family life, when Lawrence Sr. met and married Anne he brought along the emotional baggage from his family of origin. This was to be expected. We all do this because it is through our families of origin that we learn how to relate in family situations. However, our hope is that we were lucky enough to have been dealt a healthy and loving family in the lottery that goes on at birth. Lawrence Sr., clearly, was not so fortunate and began a difficult relationship with a woman who wanted emotional contact and direct expression of feelings. Lawrence Sr. couldn't understand this and responded by either taking flight, which he did most of the time, turning anger on himself and lapsing into silence, or by becoming rageful toward his wife and children. It is this dance away from health and intimacy that has been played around Lawrence Jr. for all of his sixteen years. It's still going on, and although he is now in his second year of sobriety and attends meetings of Alcoholic's Anonymous very frequently, he still finds it difficult not to act in other self-destructive ways.

> I blew off my job the other day. I can't stand my boss. I do all the work and he gets all the credit, and gives me no thanks. So I took the money my parents told me to save for car insurance and took the bus to New York and bought a guitar. When I got home that night my father got mad. He called me all sorts of names and threw me out. I ended up sleeping in the back of my friends pickup *(laughter)*. I don't know what's going to happen to me.

Lawrence Jr. has obvious issues with authority figures. He is a teenager at risk in school and ultimately, I believe, within the juvenile justice system unless he continues to abstain while on the road to living a truly sober life. From conflicts with his boss at work to fights with his teachers at school, the real conflict is with his parents. There is something wrong at home and his continued irresponsible behavior is his calling out for help. He wants to have the problem addressed at all cost and goes to any lengths to call attention to himself. Fortunately, through all the upset and drama in Lawrence's life, he tries to put his sobriety first, attends his AA meetings, and maintains a good relationship with his sponsor. Despite his regular attendance at Alcoholics Anonymous, however, Lawrence is still in trouble. He is not drinking or smoking marijuana and that is good. However, his sobriety is at risk because of his pattern of irresponsibility. And to the extent that he goes around "shooting himself in the foot" by not going to school or showing up late for work we can also consider him acting in an unsober fashion. It is the parents of this sixteen-year-old who are acting in ways that enable him to continue.

LAWRENCE SR.

I don't know what we're going to do with him. Sometimes he makes me so mad I could just strangle him. He doesn't do his school work, he wants to quit his job, *again*, and he constantly uses profanity to his mother. I'm beginning to think that we shouldn't have let him go to France on the school trip. He breaks every rule we set up.

Of course Lawrence breaks every rule his parents set up. He knows he's not going to face any meaningful consequences at home, and he hasn't yet felt the brick wall that he's surely walking into. Not only is Lawrence Jr. allowed to get away with everything he does, he's subtly encouraged to do so by the lack of outside discipline. Even though his parents complain, they never put their foot down in an appropriate way. By just getting angry and being verbally abusive toward Lawrence, his parents merely bring their oblique communication with him to yet a lower point. Furthermore, by responding to Lawrence's "fuck you both" with more of the same, Lawrence Sr. and Anne are in effect challenging him to a battle of wills. It's as if they are playing "who's in control," which is a game that is difficult to win with any teenager.

All teenagers must challenge their parents and institutional authority. It's part of the growing-up process, part of the way adolescents become adults. They first challenge the rules of the pack to assess their independence. They internalize those rules that are useful to them and a kind of synthesis occurs. They then become the enforcers of the rules. As parents, by encouraging your teenagers to challenge the rules while at the same time setting reasonable limits on their behavior and encouraging them to bring their problems to you for nonjudgmental discussion, you can navigate your children through this difficult but exciting period of their lives. However, by throwing down the gauntlet and forcing your adolescent children to pick it up, you are only setting the stage for a meaningless battle that won't abate until somebody gives in or the children leave the nest. The resulting damage can affect your lives and theirs for years. This was the case in Lawrence Jr.'s family.

Lawrence Jr.'s parents enabled his drug and alcohol abuse by not enforcing the established rules. They enabled him to act irresponsibly by not allowing him to experience the consequences of his actions. They are not alone. Their behavior is mirrored in hundreds of thousands of middle-class households across the country in which parents gravitate between lax enforcement of basic rules on the one hand and no-win confrontations over insignificant issues on the other. Their children push against the rules, looking for a sign that their parents are interested in them as human beings, but find only silence. Eventually, they push through the curtain and find themselves in over their heads as substance abusers or addicts. Those parents who are still not aware of the seriousness of the situation may become codependents, part of the alcoholic or addicted family syndrome.

Unfortunately, enabling parents have a willing support system in the majority of our public schools. In many affluent communities, such as Princeton where Lawrence Jr. is a student, the school systems often serve as enablers as well. I've seen it played out in public, private country day schools, and prep schools. The chief disciplinarian, typically the vice-principal, in response to a child's smoking marijuana, drinking beer, skipping classes, tearing up the football field in a four-wheel drive vehicle, or any other similarly imaginative adventure, threatens to suspend, make the problem a part of the child's permanent record, not let the student graduate, or some other unenforceable punishment. Most of the time the threat cannot possibly be carried out because if it were, the punishment would only reinforce the negative behavior. If students are bored in school and create disciplinary problems, throwing them out of school for a few days merely rewards them by giving them what they wanted in the first place.

In this way, Lawrence, just like countless other adolescents, has been enabled to continue his dysfunctional behavior by the inaction of both his parents and the administrators of his high school. They have been teaching him that being irresponsible does not necessarily entail facing a serious consequence. By being inconsistent in their respective roles as parents and disciplinarians, they have inadvertently taught Lawrence that it's merely a matter of bad luck if as the result of skipping school, for example, he has to pay the piper. Sometimes you're lucky and sometimes your not. Needless to say, this is not ample preparation for the world of work and college.

What makes Lawrence's case so illustrative of the enabling synergy of genetics and adaptive behavior is that it involves a complicated pattern of family dynamics. Lawrence is a teenage alcoholic and abuser of marijuana in recovery. His grandfather and uncle were alcoholics. His father is codependent in regard to both his own father and his son. His father is also emotionally stifled, noncommunicative, and distrustful. Lawrence's parents are most unhappy. Lawrence Sr. continually withdraws from the emotional demands of Anne. It is no coincidence that Lawrence Sr. has a job in Washington, D.C., requiring him to maintain a separate apartment there for his stays during the work week. Why should he intervene in the affairs of his wife and children when he has a completely separate life? It has been seven years since he acquired that job. And for seven years, with a few exceptions, he returns to Princeton only on the weekends. He's merely a visitor in his own house with none of the day-to-day responsibilities as comanager of the household. He's dumped that job entirely on his wife's shoulders. And his wife has allowed it to happen. By having permitted this arrangement to go on for so long, Lawrence Sr. and Anne have also been practicing enabling behavior with themselves. She enables him to be emotionally distant and he enables her to maintain a passivity in regard to her own emotional needs. Neither has to face a consequence for their actions. Unfortunately for Lawrence Jr., his parents are playing out the same dysfunctional pattern on him. What they fail to see, however, is that their son's irresponsibility is, in fact, the consequence for their abdication of parental responsibilities and enabling. This is why I see this family as prototypical of the way enablers are made and not born.

Enabling: Learned and Adaptive

Enabling behavior is both learned and adaptive. It is learned in much the same way a child picks up habits based on the daily observation of his or her parents. The more limited the child's exposure to the outside world, the more the child relies on what he or she sees at home as the basis of normalcy. Accordingly, children may come to judge certain behaviors as normal, never knowing, for instance, that emotional intrusiveness, family violence, incest, or drunkenness are unhealthy and destructive. It is the same way with the less dramatic dynamics in other dysfunctional families. Timmy saw the inadequate way his father behaved and observed the behavior of his mother and grandparents which, in essence, said, "Timmy, never expect your father to stand on his own two feet. Grow up quick so you can help take care of him." Timmy learned by example and observation to become a surrogate parent for his own father. Enabling behavior is thus passed on to children along with the family recipe for apple pie. It is something that is hardly ever questioned. In fact the reason why enabling is so difficult to arrest is that we never got to know how we acquired it in the first place.

As I already pointed out, although the majority of enabling behavior is learned in our families of origin, it may also be developed in order to deal with a particular relationship or set of relationships. In this sense it is adaptive. Perhaps it is even a transient coping mechanism that results from a particular occasion, such as an accident or illness. It functions as a way, albeit unhealthy, to maintain the stability of a relationship. For example, Anne may have come from a reasonably healthy family and entered into a relationship with Bob. Let's say that at some point in this relationship Bob begins to manifest a dysfunction. It doesn't matter what the nature of the dysfunction is, for the dynamics play out in similar fashions. Bob may have been a closet alcoholic who is getting worse, or a noncommunicative person, or perhaps he has developed a pattern of not following through with commitments. Although when Anne met Bob there were no obvious signs of the dysfunction, it only required time and the pressures of modern living to sprout. For whatever the reason, the seed of dysfunction germinated and slowly developed from something that Anne didn't know was there into something of annoyance or genuine concern. If Anne chooses not to confront Bob or is unsuccessful in getting Bob to alter the behavior in question, Anne is then faced with making a decision: challenge it and risk upsetting the equilibrium of the relationship or live with it and deny it, adapting to the relationship as it gradually deteriorates. This is not an easy choice, for Anne is now at the crossroads of her relationship. Anne can opt to confront Bob or decide not to "rock the boat" and put up with the problem. If she chooses the latter, she will begin to adapt to Bob's dysfunction. By accommodating him, she enables him and perpetuates the objectionable behavior, negative attitudes, or dysfunction.

Bob can be anybody: a father, brother, son, boss, co-worker, or employee. Bob can even be a Barbara who is a mother, sister, wife, or daughter. The point is, regardless of whatever specific dysfunction may be at issue, it remains a pattern of attitudes and/or behavior that interfere with the development of a normal, healthy relationship. If we choose to adapt to the dysfunction of another, we are beginning to live in the world of the unreal. We are beginning to be dishonest with the central person in our life: ourself.

Enabling and Gender Roles

Enabling is subtly learned and subtly passed on from generation to generation, becoming intricately linked to gender roles within the family dynamic. Scripts like "women belong in the kitchen," "a boy baby is more special than a girl," and "men don't cook or do laundry" are assumptions that form the basis of certain kinds of enabling relationships. Both girls and boys growing up in this atmosphere are preparing to go out into the world and play out these basic assumptions in their own generations. Their families set them on automatic pilot which in turn points them directly toward others whose dysfunction matches theirs. Codependents from alcoholic families usually wind up in relationships with alcoholics; enabler daughters who were surrogate parents to their fathers usually find irresponsible mates who need parenting as well, and boys who might have "mothered" their own mothers often bond with persons who require a great deal of mothering. Enablers and addicts fit together like tongue-in-groove from generation to generation. Along the way, individuals who may challenge one's dysfunctional worldview are screened out. This screening process is often unconscious, and the adult child of a dysfunctional family finds only partners and friends who are willing to dance the dance taught by the process of growing up in the family.

This routine of mate selection is a normal process that all of us go through in seeking companions or spouses. There is absolutely nothing wrong with using our family of origin as the springboard for establishing other relationships; in fact, that's where we learn the first sets of rules that teach us how to behave and what to expect. The problem, of course, is that because we all tend to carry on the traditions of our families, it becomes crucial that there not be too much baggage to drag along behind us. The reality is that all families have some sort of emotional baggage that is bestowed upon its children. There is no perfect family. We each are charged with doing the best we can with what we've been given. Ideally, the burdens won't be too great. We know, of course, that in the presence of increased types and levels of dysfunction, that task is all the more difficult. The worst-case scenarios are adult children who must cope with having been raised in an alcoholic, violent, incestuous, and/or otherwise emotionally intrusive household. This level of neglect passes on to children the legacy of having difficulty establishing and maintaining healthy relationships.

Boundaries

Distortions of personal boundaries fundamentally affect the ways children can develop into enabling adults. In fact, one of the most difficult burdens adult children of dysfunctional families have to bear is the establishment of healthy interpersonal boundaries when their own boundaries were violated as children. Jane's story, from chapter 1, shows how the dysfunction within the family of origin can lead to problems with boundaries in adult relationships. As an overcompensation to the harsh and neglectful way she and her sisters were parented, Jane began her early adult relationships by using little discrimination and attempted to accommodate to the wants and needs of friends and lovers. Without conscious volition, Jane, as a prototypical enabler, sought those who would take from her without giving in return. She found exactly what she wanted and was a too willing victim to the emotional abuse she endured. After two broken marriages she finally reacted by forging personal boundaries of iron that keep all potential intruders out.

> I don't care. I just want to be alone with my cats. People are always a hassle. They're always complaining. You can't go anywhere without having to worry about them. Are they enjoying the movie? Is the food all right? Who needs it?

In order to rewrite the script of how relationships have to be, Jane, like all of us, will have to face the fear that binds her to her role as an enabler. She will also have to face the distrust she feels toward people as well as the distrust she feels toward herself for seeming to be unable to regulate how far she lets people in when she opens the door. Bolting the door, however, is not the only solution. The Five Steps will be a helpful tool for her to use.

The establishment of boundaries is one of the most important ongoing events that take place during childhood. It stands to reason, therefore, that an adult's assault on the child's boundaries seriously distorts its subsequent development and sets the stage for repeated disappointments and abuse in later life. As adults without the protection of boundaries, we are unable to know and understand who we are in relation to others. We are also more apt to violate the territory of others. Rigid boundaries afford some temporary protection, but like the beech tree, they will eventually splinter in a heavy wind. Weak boundaries wave like a bed of kelp with the tides; they constantly change in the shifting currents. Adults with a weakened sense of personal boundaries are constantly vacillating, accommodating themselves to demands from the outside. In contrast you will find that a clear sense of boundary, which you can achieve with the use of the Five Steps, will free you to operate in a world with your own understanding of what is expected of you and what you can expect of others. You can decide who to let into your universe and how far they may come. This is not only your right, it is your personal responsibility in living a free and healthy life.

Denial: The Conspiracy of Silence

Denial of truth is a primary ingredient in the making of an enabler. Once you participate in a conspiracy not to admit the truth about your family, the abuser in your family, or yourself, you become as dependent upon the lie as the abuser. To admit the truth means to admit the necessity of change. To admit the truth in an addicted or alcoholic family means the abuser will have to acknowledge that he or she is no longer in control of his or her own life—and that is Step One of recovery. To admit the truth in a dysfunctional family means that there is something causing pain. From truth must come change.

However, in enabling families there exists a general agreement not to speak the truth. This in fact is one of the essential components of perpetuating the myth that "we are all right" and that "you're fine the way you are" and that it doesn't matter anyway because "I'm strong enough for the two of us." In order for any family or relationship to exist in a codependent or an enabling manner, there must exist a conspiracy of silence about the problem. We must all agree not to talk about it because if we did, it would cause disruption of our equilibrium. It doesn't matter that the equilibrium may be destructive, we assure ourselves, any equilibrium is better than the chaos of truth, even if the truth can eventually lead to a positive and satisfying change.

Accordingly, if you are wondering whether your family of origin or if your current relationship could be characterized as enabling, you might ask yourself what it is that you and your partner are *not* talking about. Generally if something is not being said it is a good sign that there is enabling going on. For instance if I realize that I am holding back from sharing the concern I feel about your gambling, about your drinking, about how you never remember my birthday when I always acknowledge yours, then perhaps—although I may not want it to—the wise person inside me knows that something is wrong. I may wish I didn't notice your gambling, but the fact is that I do. It is this inner wise person who can provide the right direction for us. We all have this inner wisdom. In enabling families, however, we were constantly trained to ignore and eventually dismiss it. Whatever the secret, enabling families assume that it can't stand the light of day. The truth is feared for it may disrupt the homeostatic relationship that we have grown accustomed to. If I am afraid that our relationship is too fragile to handle the truth, then I must do whatever I can to preserve it. I must keep it running at all costs, hoping that somehow everything will work itself out in the end. It never does, but that is what enablers hope for. The assumption about my or your fragility is often faulty, but nevertheless the conspiracy of silence keeps us together. It is this false illusion that makes us afraid to face the truth and afraid to heal the damage in our dysfunctional families.

Protection of Each Other

In order for the conspiracy of silence to continue, it must be refueled along the way. One of the propellants for this engine of denial is the myth that I must protect you. Often times this myth is not very conscious, but it nonetheless operates quite pervasively. It sounds like this:

> I may not be sure who I am trying to protect. I oftentimes act like it's you, but perhaps it is really me. I may not be sure what I'm trying to fend off by means of the protection. I usually act as if the truth that I know and keep from you may be too much for you. I think you can't handle it. I feel sorry for you.
> But perhaps it is me who isn't ready to risk speaking the truth. Perhaps it is me who feels fragile. If our relationship were to dissolve perhaps it is me who is afraid of standing on my own two feet.

There is usually always some altruism mixed in with this tendency for "protection." This is why family members and significant others comprise the majority of enablers. This is what makes enabling behavior so tragic. Regardless of whether the dysfunctional member is an addict on the edge of violence, a drunk who is out of control when not sedated by alcohol, or a person who feigns emotional wreckage whenever true feelings are revealed, the supposed envelope of protection that the enabler provides is really a perpetuation of the dysfunction. This is raw enabling, complete with a lot of denial thrown in. Only by speaking the truth, not the angry truth, but the whole truth, can we ever hope to remediate the dysfunctional behavior. This means speaking the truth about you and me. The dilemma is that while A "protects" B from the truth about B's gambling, A is enabling himself as well. How do you stop lying? It has been said many times among the Twelve Step community: Simply tell the truth. But in enabling families, the truth is almost always hidden. It is not hidden to protect anyone, but rather to perpetuate the denial of true and healthy feelings and thoughts. This is why children often act out in these families. They haven't learned yet how to dampen their spirit and cover up their feelings in order to perpetuate the status quo.

Unhealthy Expression of Feelings

Enabling is the stifling of expression, the suppression of feelings. In dysfunctional families where enabling behaviors are forged, there is no normal, healthy exchange of feelings. The conspiracy of silence requires that there be no real protection, rather the introduction of suppression. If there were real, healthy protection, each person's boundaries would be respected. Everyone in the family would be seen as a separate individual complete with unique and valuable thoughts and feelings worthy of dignity. The patriarch as well as the two-year-old and everyone in between would be seen as his or her own person, each with something to say. There would be no one right way to be or to think.

In enabling families, however, this healthy respect for one another's individual boundaries and feelings falls far short. Instead, there is either a nonexpression of feelings, a dampening of emotional expressiveness, or, if feelings are expressed, it is usually done in an awkward and unhealthy manner. When feelings are unexpressed, there is often a pervasive silence, an unstated acknowledgment that things are being left unsaid. People often aren't aware that they are feeling and if they know, they may not know what they're feeling. An example of this sort of thinking is revealed in the expressions commonly used in describing another who has cried at the loss of a loved one or at the breakup of a marriage. Phrases like he "broke down" or "fell apart" are often used. It's as if crying and having upset and vulnerable feelings are signs of weakness rather than expressions of our humanness. The breaking down might in fact be a healthy sign that he is no longer "putting up a good front" and "trying to be strong for the others."

In my own personal growth I know how one can be reinforced by family dynamics, peers, and societal gender-role expectations for not revealing true and hurting feelings, no less actually expressing them through a public display of tears. From the time I was about ten years old to about twenty-five I remember only crying once. I had learned to keep it all inside. As a result of my own work on myself, I have come to terms with my own internalized enabler. I am now able to allow the tears to come when I feel them. I, like many recovering from emotional enabling, now welcome the tears as evidence that my system is running smoothly. It also results in a wonderful feeling of release. This more gross form of emotional repression is more commonly perpetrated on males in our culture; however, in enabling families this applies to all the members.

Another way that emotions are distorted through the dynamics of an enabling family is by what I call the all-or-nothing style of communication. Feelings, especially angry or negative ones, are repressed and not expressed unless they are very powerful. It's as if there were a circuit breaker hooked up to the anger that can be flicked on only after there has been a sufficient buildup, a critical mass of emotion. At that point the negative feelings usually come pouring out, flooding everybody in their path. This kind of expression offers little opportunity for negotiation and constructive resolution, only destruction. Blame is often thrown around in the process through the violation of emotional and sometimes physical boundaries. A much more healthy and constructive expression of feelings would be to exchange a dimmer switch for the on/off switch. This would allow for a gradual recognition of angry feelings and an opportunity for expression before they get out of hand. But this is often not the way in enabling families.

Control of Self and Others

Enablers are often obsessed with controlling themselves as well as others. They learn to exert control in their families of origin because one of the basic myths perpetuated in the enabling family is that "I must be in maximum control of myself." This type of control is very restrictive. While some sense of being in control is necessary in order to feel stable, the control mechanism in an enabling family goes far beyond the legitimate need for homeostasis. The inner dialogue suggests:

> People never come through. Because of their inadequacy they can't be relied on to fulfill their obligations. Because I am a compassionate person, I will take it upon myself to keep a constant vigil to make sure things run smoothly. I have to keep him or her upright and also make sure the relationship doesn't sink. It is my duty. It's all up to me.

If there is one central theme that is the common denominator of all enabling relationships, it is the felt need to control, to be hypervigilant in all situations. This "need" is not just a mere feeling, it is a full-blown obsession that is acted out compulsively. In the most extreme of cases—as reported to me by my ACOA clients—people feel responsible for keeping themselves and their siblings alive. If they were to let their guards down just once, the alcoholic parent might wreak such destruction that there would be nothing left. Imagine an eight- or nine-year-old child, especially an eldest child, who must confront that assumption on a daily basis. Such a person might actually come to believe that he or she truly controls the universe. One lapse, one moment of fun, one instant of irresponsibility and the whole fabric of creation might come crashing down. The worst part about this nightmare is that it is actually happening each day in thousands of families across the United States.

When out of our perceived need to control we repeatedly fill in for the other, cushion the areas of contact around his or her dysfunction so the friction doesn't disturb the equilibrium, heal the wounds in others that the dysfunction causes, and ultimately allow him or her to abdicate all responsibility, we are committing ourselves to a form of perpetual servitude until we decide to call a halt. We do more than empower the other person to have control over our lives, we provide the measure of that control and, indirectly, exert a greater control over the addict's life. We say, in effect: Your dysfunction has become my dysfunction because it keeps us together in a certain way. My assumption that you can't deal with the full responsibility of adulthood quickly becomes a self-fulfilling prophecy. You won't come through because you and I have come to an unspoken agreement: We don't even expect you to. Like water, the enabled individual will seek the lowest level. It would be a different story if there was a true physical impairment or medical handicap in the other. But truly handicapped individuals are the least likely to let themselves be enabled. They won't play the game because they know they have to survive on their own abilities in the world if they are to survive at all. If, for instance, your twenty-year-old son had Down's syndrome you would have to be the one in control. But even in that circumstance you could make him accountable for certain appropriate tasks. In this way you would be conveying the expectation that he is capable up to his level of ability.

Guilt and Shame

Feelings of guilt and shame usually fuel the training of enablers in families and accompany them the rest of their lives. Guilt and shame in themselves are not necessarily negative feelings. Having a sense of what makes us feel guilty usually reflects an internalized sense of right and wrong. And feeling shame about having committed wrongful acts is also natural and appropriate. Most families teach children the meaning of these feelings, but some go overboard. In a dysfunctional family guilt and shame are used as mechanisms to control its members. If I want you to do something and you don't want to go along with my desire, then perhaps I could get you to behave the way I want you to by imposing a sense of guilt on you. For example, a mother wants her son to turn on a light so she can see better. At least that's what she tells herself. However, what's important is not that the light be turned on, but that the son turn it on. Rather than directly ask her son to turn it on, the mother conspicuously sits in the dark while talking to her son. Finally, more out of the obviousness of the situation than out of any desire to turn on the light, the son may ask, "Do you want the light on?" "No, it's alright," the mother may say. "I can sit here in the dark." At first, the guilt is expressed verbally. But later on, when it has become internalized, all that may be needed to press the guilt button is a look or gesture. Sometimes after the guilt mechanism has been installed it operates automatically without any external prompting. You see your mother sitting in the dark, you turn the light on.

The tragedy about guilt is that it too often serves as the only measure of what is right and alters the source of decision making from an internal process to an external paradigm of imposed values. This is one of the differences between a healthy and a guilt-burdened child. If you wanted to raise a healthy child, you would instill in that child a sense of values and a respect for the self. In this way, the healthy child would use his or her own value system as a measure of right and wrong. It's nice to be that healthy, and a lot easier than you might think. However, burdening a growing child with layers of guilt about his or her family situation is the perfect way to lead that child along the path to becoming an enabler. In an enabling family the children and its other members learn not to rely on their own internal judgments, but on the reactions and expectations of others. Whatever someone else wants, the enabler is taught to give.

In enabling families there is very little room for individual variation. For instance, when a family member tries—even tentatively—to break the pattern of enabling by stepping back and saying, "That's your responsibility. I'm no longer going to live your life for you," the person being enabled merely has to press the right guilt buttons to bring him or her back into line. There isn't really one specific pattern to the guilt assault either. It may be subtle and passive-aggressive or an out-and-out attack. The range is quite broad. In some families all a parent need do is whisper, "I can't believe you could hurt me like this, I'm very disappointed" in order to bring the enabler to heel. In other families there is the threat of actual physical violence. In either event the guilt that is imposed is an attack on the enabler's ego, upon his or her very essense of self. And I have found that guilt is usually one of the most powerful reinforcements of enabling behavior.

Guilt is especially damaging to children who need to know that their autonomy is truly valued. If, because of the guilt imposed upon them by their parents, their still-fragile egos are intruded upon, then they learn to become outer-directed. In other words, they learn that the way to define their sense of self-worth is by keeping busy taking care of others. As a client of mine recently told me, "That way I at least can't be accused of not trying. I may not have made things work out for my mother, but in trying to protect her from feeling hurt, I don't feel as guilty." Adult children who haven't yet come to grips with their tendency to enable are often depressed and exhausted. It's a very demanding job.

Fear

Finally, the most basic and painful of the enabling fuels is fear: a pervasive and all-encompassing fear of the world, fear of being abandoned by a parent or partner, fear of being fired from a job or ostracized at school, fear that neighbors will find out about a child's drug problem, or fear that one will be seen as selfish and unworthy of love. Fear is at the heart of the enabling family. Fear is the mind killer that closes down all rational thought. At its worst, fear replaces one's perspectives of reality with one's deepest nightmares of childhood—being swallowed up or abandoned. In either case the child and the self are disintegrated.

Regardless of whether the home was dysfunctional with alcoholism or with a rampant protestant work ethic, one of the main tools of manipulation and emotional control that parents wielded was fear. In very violent families the fear was the reality of actual physical abuse that could occur at any moment. The child heard, saw, and sometimes felt the wrath of the out-of-control parent. The terrorizing that takes place in an abusive family need not be physical violence; it can also be emotional. Sometimes the damage done by a parent who exclusively uses emotional coercion and guilt is all that is needed to plant the seed of fear in the child that stays throughout his or her life. The result of these kinds of indirect assaults is sometimes a more pervasive and insidious damage.

"My mother never touched me," Linda explained to the rest of the group.

Maybe she hit me only a couple of times in my life. But I didn't need to be hit in order for her to control me. She did it with her words and sometimes just her eyes. Even to this day, before I go anywhere or wear anything, I first stop and think of what my mother would think about it. If I'm going somewhere or wearing something that I know she wouldn't approve of, I'll feel guilty. It doesn't matter what I want. And to think I'm the one who grew up always protecting her from feeling hurt.

Linda never experienced physical violence, yet in her young adult life she is dogged by the scars imposed upon her by her mother's guilt. This type of fear is in some ways more difficult to overcome than if it were physical. While I are not minimizing the trauma of physical child abuse, I am suggesting that at least the physical can be recalled as sets of specific tangible events. The fear of disappointing a mother may be more difficult to recognize because it was more ephemeral even though it permeated the very air in the household, turning what should have been a sweet relationship with a parent into a bitter one. In Linda's case she was told by her mother that she was her favorite child. Linda knew this meant she had high expectations to satisfy. She was scared to death that she wouldn't.

Childhood fear can be so painful that it can all but destroy the lives of its victims. The evidence in support of this is overwhelming enough to be beyond question. In my practice I have worked with clients whose entire professional careers, albeit objectively successful, have been flights away from the fears and tortures that robbed them of their childhood bliss. In some of my cases, prosperous middle-aged business executives at the top of their professions have revealed that their quiet addictions to alcohol or serial sexual relationships, to an endless quest for success itself, or to a fascination with child pornography, were driven by their childhood fears. And yet, once revealed in therapy, once exposed in a nonjudgmental and supportive environment, the fear shrinks and becomes manageable. It can then be dealt with. This leads me to believe that what most people hide from is the fear itself, or, worse, the fear of being afraid. Perhaps Franklin Roosevelt was right. At least within the context of my own clinical practice, his admonition that "The only thing we have to fear is fear itself" makes a world of sense.

Facing and Overcoming the Need to Enable

In coming to terms with your own tendency to enable you must understand what it is that you as the enabler get out of this dance. Most people would quickly say that they get nothing out of it, that if only she would do the housework and raise the kids, or if he could only keep a job, or if only he would own his insecure feelings then everything would be all right. It is obvious, at least on the surface, that were the addict or dysfunctional person responsible for him- or herself, things would be better. But beneath the surface it might be a very different story. The relationship between the enabler and addict is usually so intricate that it often appears as if the enabler needs the addict to be dysfunctional in order for the enabler to have a sense of purpose. Accordingly, once the addict is in a recovery program, some enablers may work very hard to undermine the therapeutic process. Because of this, more and more treatment programs are moving toward bringing the rest of the family in for their own treatment as a part of the chemically dependent family member's rehabilitation.

Most of the time, the enabler is unaware of what he or she is doing. The enabler only knows that he or she feels threatened by the recovery and cannot understand why. Sometimes it's as simple as: "We've lived our entire lives with Bob's gambling, how can you expect me to change now?" Many times I've worked with families in which the addiction itself was only part of the dysfunction. In those families the enabler brought a "need" to enable into the relationships and used his or her radar to seek out the type of dysfunctional personality that required the enabling skills. You've heard plenty of these stories yourself: woman marries abusive alcoholic after abusive alcoholic in a perpetual downward spiral of misery. These problems occur because, to put it bluntly, the enabler is looking for love in all the wrong places. In other words, rather than seeking to establish a relationship on the strength of personality, most enablers rely on their and others' weaknesses. Therefore, unless you understand the payoff you receive for enabling, then the cycle will continue and you, much to your ultimate dismay, will be facilitating the process.

I see this crop up over and over again in my psychotherapy practice. For example, a recovering alcoholic client of mine who has been attending AA meetings and completing his moral inventory with the courage to implement fundamental changes in his life wonders out loud why his wife and children seem resistant to that change. It seems like a contradiction, but it forces him back into old habits. Mostly, though, I hear it from compulsive overeaters who complain that despite their spouses' demands that they lose weight, the spouses perpetuate the same conditions that encouraged them to eat in the first place. Could it be that a fat person who is enslaved by an eating addiction is easier to control than a thinner, healthier, more self-directed person? Why would an enabler undermine his or her partner's attempts to change? What's in it for the enabler? Once you answer that question you'll be in a position to change the direction of your life.

Here is the answer that I suggest to most of my clients. See if it works for you:

In most enabling families there is substantial resentment for the dysfunctional member. Usually that resentment takes the form of a silent hostility that gradually builds over a period of years until it is like a smouldering volcano. The enabler often feels overburdened by the other's dysfunction, even though that dysfunction helps to fuel the relationship. And whether they're aware of it or not, they're also usually quite angry. The enabler, however, is also dysfunctional because he or she is ultimately a destructive force. But what kind of reward does the enabler get by being destructive? Unless there is something concrete that the enabler achieves, the entire enabling situation would be too perverse to be so prevalent. What I've found is that the characteristic payoff is a very clear and measurable sense of worth. "If it were not for me," the enabler says, "you would lose your job, fail school, or have no place to live. Therefore I must be awfully important. I am needed, valuable, and essential to your and the family's well-being. Because I am in control we survive." The exertion of control perpetuates the myth that you are incompetent and I am very much needed.

In the enabling family self-esteem is often doled out according to how much one does for the other. This type of giving, however, is not really giving; rather, it is a form of theft. I take from you the dignity derived from being in charge of your life and use it

to fuel my inadequate sense of self. Oftentimes in enabling households when the family member who had been labeled as dysfunctional gets better, the entire family dynamic begins to change.
Ironically, it is usually the enabler who unconsciously resists the
change. It's as if the enabler is saying, "Don't change! Without
having to take care of you I don't know what I'll do with myself.
Without doing for others and being in control my life has little
meaning." It stands to reason, therefore, that in enabling households there often is an unstated, but nevertheless common truth
among family members that the enabler requires the alcoholic,
addict, gambler, inadequate emotional respondent, or otherwise
dysfunctional partner to continue in order to feel needed and
worthwhile. In enabling households all the members tend to
share the dysfunction.

Thus, when we take the long view, we can see that enabling
doesn't simply come into existence in a vacuum. It grows out of
a basic family structure in which one person surrenders responsibility and in which the other person assumes that responsibility.
Therefore, the most basic and direct way to undo the damage is
to pull away the wreckage of the years, get to the behavioral
engine, and—deliberately but carefully—reforge the emotional
connections so as to relieve the pressures. First we have to recognize the symptoms and the contexts within which enabling most
typically occurs. Then we have to run our Five Step program.
This what the ensuing chapters will show us how to do.

3

The Making of a Codependent

As explained earlier in this book, enabling is the broad term for describing a consistent pattern of perpetuating irresponsible or dysfunctional behavior in another person, while codependency is a narrow term for describing an enabling behavior that perpetuates an addiction to alcohol, drugs, food, or other compulsive and potentially destructive behaviors. Because it is a subset of enabling, codependency, too, has its roots in the dynamics of the dysfunctional family, which in this case is either chemically dependent, substance abusing, or alcoholic. In order to see how codependencies are created, we have to look at the ways that enabling behavior is displayed in chemically dependent families. We have to ask: Who in the family contributes to this behavior? Are friends and family members unwitting accomplices to the alcoholism or other drug abuse, eating disorder, compulsive gambling or various other irresponsible actions of a friend, relative, or loved one? In looking for these patterns we are not trying to lay blame on the victims by suggesting that they are not only responsible for their own victimization but that they're the dark forces behind most forms of addictions. Laying blame is not the point. We want to find out what the roles in a dysfunctional family are, where codependency begins, how can it be remedied, and how victims of these families can escape the destructive burdens of being a codependent.

In this chapter we'll address these questions by examining the architecture of the prototypical pattern of codependency that is usually manifested in families in which at least one member is seriously involved with alcohol. Keep in mind, though, that "alcoholic" is a generic term. Any other addictive chemical may be substituted with equal potency in destroying the health of the individual and disrupting the life of the family. In fact, most contemporary case studies show that there are few "pure" alcoholics entering treatment programs, most are polydrug abusers who are supplementing their addiction to alcohol with cocaine, marijuana, crack, or some other combination. Therefore, as you read this book, realize that I use the term *alcoholic* to mean anyone who abuses himself or herself with any chemical substance and as a consequence suffers impairment in his or her life's work, relationship with loved ones, and/or physical health. And we'll be able to apply much of what we describe here to families where there are dependencies on food, gambling, and even on sexual or physical abuse.

It is the unique circumstance of alcohol and other drug abuse in the family that has given rise to the concept of codependency. Accordingly, we all can learn a great deal about enabling in the broader sense of the term by first understanding in the narrow sense how all the players perpetuate the codependency drama and then watching how that drama unfolds in the substance abuse or alcoholic family. Then we can examine enabling in other types of dysfunctional families.

The Cast of Characters

A positive result of all the current books and articles written about chemical dependency as a family disease and the roles played out in childhood by adult children of alcoholics, among others, as the victims of that disease, is that the cast in the enabling drama is recognizable. By now many of us are familiar with the "scapegoat," the "hero," the "lost child": the roles acted out by children who grow up in dysfunctional alcoholic households. The very act of taking on these roles helps to preserve the status quo of the family. It keeps the family in a form of equilibrium. In their own ways, the children of alcoholic families enable the alcoholic parent to continue to drink by playing out their roles. The children of alcoholics are blameless. They rarely have any choices. They're just trying to get along in families they didn't elect to enter. As would any child in their situation, they're the ones who quietly suffer the most at the hands of the alcoholism as well as the result of parental neglect. It is the adults in families who, through their códependency, perpetuate the addiction on a daily basis. But they couldn't perpetuate it without the participation of the central character who brings the house down night after night and especially on holidays: the alcoholic. This is the pivot around whom the drama unfolds.

In order for the alcoholic to do his dance, the cast must accompany him. They must dip when he dips, turn when he turns, and if he spins out of control, they must always spread themselves out as a safety net to catch the alcoholic before he or she hits bottom. These supporting players are the enablers in the broadest sense of the word. More specifically, they are codependent on the alcoholic's use of alcohol and can be referred to as co-alcoholics.

It is not up to us to lay blame on the codependents' doorsteps; they do enough of that all by themselves. Often they see themselves as "bad seeds" because they shoulder the guilt and the shame of the entire family. Our purpose is to understand how enabling plays itself out as codependency in chemically dependent families and, in so doing, understand the dynamics of codependency in action. In this way, you'll quickly realize the remarkable similarity between dysfunctional alcoholic families and supposedly "normal" families in which other types of dysfunction are played out. This will help you demystify one of the major myths that all of us believe about our childhoods: normal families are perfect; normal families have no problems. Intellectually we may reject this myth, but if you grew up in a dysfunctional family, you have emotionally accepted this belief and probably act on it every day of your life.

In a traditional alcoholic codependency we always find a significant individual in the life of the alcoholic who acts in ways that perpetuate the alcoholism. Typically this person is the alcoholic's spouse or parent. However, it's not at all uncommon for other relatives, friends, employers, family physicians, in addition to mental health professionals, to also act as the alcoholic's codependents. A few or all of them may form a constellation around the alcoholic to protect him or her from causing damage to him- or herself or to others or attempt to nudge him or her into recovery. It is a rare occurence when this codependent safety net actually gets the addict into treatment. The reality is that the alcoholic entering treatment and thus beginning the recovery process is often contingent upon these significant others beginning to recover from their own codependency.

As this human safety net develops, different codependents may take on different roles. In my experience working with chemically dependent families, I have come to understand three prototypical roles played out in codependent relationships: the victim, rescuer, and the adjuster. Exploring the obvious differences among these three areas of codependency will help you to grasp the subtle and always insidious nature of this family disease. The victim, rescuer, and adjuster also appear in enabling families in which there is no chemical dependency or substance abuse, only there, the three roles are far more insidious and camouflaged than they are in addicted or alcoholic families.

The Victim

There are many people in the alcoholic's world who are victimized by his or her irresponsible behavior. The most obvious ones are the children. Younger children really cannot be considered to be enablers because of their genuine state of dependence on parents. Children may become enablers later on as they grow older and adopt more of a surrogate parent role, but until that first time the responsibility for decision making falls upon their shoulders, they remain on the roster of legitimate dependents whose needs are not being met by the alcoholic. In traditional marital relationships, the codependent who tends to most frequently remain attached to the alcoholic by virtue of disappointment and suffering is the spouse. Regardless of whether the "victim" is the husband or the wife the pattern of codependent behavior remains fairly constant.

The victim may not actually be a victim of physical abuse, although physical abuse in some form is certainly a part of many alcoholic relationships, but he or she is clearly a victim of emotional abuse. At the very least, the victim must endure the experience of being repeatedly disappointed and frustrated by the alcoholic. As a spouse, this often takes the form of abandoned dreams, shattered hopes, and broken promises. All plans for an ideal life together eventually unravel before the stark reality of alcoholism. Building a home, raising children, or establishing a life in a community and staking out a hopeful future together are often quietly set aside and only rarely brought up. Denial sets in and the plans are never discussed again except as a form of "family propaganda." The alcoholic may assure his or her codependent that recovery is just around the bend, at which point the family will have the better life they had once planned together. But the codependent knows this will never happen and quietly accepts that as his or her lot in life—and becomes part of the common denial.

The common characteristics of victims are that they suffer a great deal and keep coming back for more. It is likely that you see yourself in exactly this role if you are the spouse of an alcoholic. If you are, then you are as much in need of treatment as your alcoholic spouse because you are indirectly addicted to the same substance that has already trapped your spouse. The codependent's addiction usually takes the form of an unhealthy attachment to the other or the relationship as an entity. The familiarity of the structure, as painful as it is, becomes a way of defining the codependent's framework of reality and thus it provides a sense of self. It forms reality and is more substantial than the emptiness the codependent believes he or she will have in the absence of the structure. This is why the codependent feels attached to the relationship for reasons that often go beyond the codependent's love for the addict. In fact, in most long-term codependent relationships, love has long since fled, the children are grown, and all that remains is the attachment to the petrified skeleton of the relationship. Even the codependent's once compelling urge to hide within the framework of the relationship may have dissipated, but the codependent keeps clinging out of habit to what he or she believes must still be there. Just as the alcoholic "knows," as only an addict can know, that the feel of the first gin of the day along the back of the tongue feels right—often directly in the face of an awareness that it's the wrong thing to do—so the codependent spouse may intellectually know that bailing out the alcoholic either literally or figuratively will ultimately not be helpful at all. But the codependent compulsively acts in ways to enable the drinking and other unsober behavior.

An outside observer might ask why on earth a seemingly capable person would put up with repeated abuse from an alcoholic spouse. If this is a question you've asked of yourself, then you know that the answer lies in yourself as victim and not with your alcoholic spouse. What unacknowledged emptiness silently directs the actions of the victim? If a person repeatedly allows him- or herself to be walked on, how valuable or worthwhile can that person really feel? The answer to this lies in the greater context of how people are conditioned in their families of origin.

The overwhelming majority of codependents who tend to be victims in relationships with alcoholics come from alcoholic or other dysfunctional families. The unfortunate legacy of these families is that they set the stage for the dysfunction to be passed on into the next generation. It is no surprise for professionals in the addiction field to see a very competent and successful adult child of an alcoholic marry a partner whose degree of dysfunction mirrors the pattern experienced as a child in the family of origin. The ACOA is simply repeating a pattern of learned behavior. While this may seem quite hopeless at first glance, ultimately there should be no reason for despair. Quite the contrary, there is plenty of reason for hope because once individuals from a dysfunctional past or present begin the process of honestly acknowledging their vulnerabilities and weaknesses, this awareness can be used as fuel for the journey along the road to sobriety and health. This begins when one works the Twelve Steps of Alcoholics Anonymous, the First and Fourth Steps in particular. Specifically, one must first admit that his or her life has become unmanageable and that he or she feels powerless to keep from acting as a codependent. Then one must become introspective and in doing so have the courage to take an honest and fearless inventory of his or her strengths and weaknesses of character. Through this process many individuals such as yourself have acted to free themselves from the burdens of their personal, learned, and sometimes, genetic history. The challenge is for the victim to do the same.

The alcoholic's spouse is not always the only victim. If the alcoholic is employed, the scenario often plays out in some form in the workplace as well. The victim may be the secretary or a subordinate who forever carries the ball when the alcoholic fumbles. Usually these codependents are in key positions wherein without the alcoholic's adequate performance on the job their lives become much more burdened. We are all too familiar with the caring and concerned secretary who has learned to become adept at covering for the alcoholic boss, especially after his three-martini lunch at his favorite watering hole. "He's not in right now," "They're in a meeting," or "The final draft's still stuck in word processing," she'll say in an impassive voice that brooks no challenge. All these excuses wear pinstripes, they pass muster, and in the world of normalcy are legitimate corporate responses to delays or postponements. In our culture we tend to reward loyalty, and unfortunately that is precisely what has served to perpetuate the dysfunctional pattern of alcoholism in the workplace.

The secretary is not the only one at work who is willing to cover for the chief. There are often other key employees who are rewarded for metaphorically taking the bullet meant for the alcoholic boss. In fact sometimes the victim is not a subordinate at all but rather the supervisor or foreman. These victims take it upon themselves to get the work done when the alcoholic falls down on the job. Like most codependents, these workplace victims, although well-intentioned and sincerely seeking to protect and help the alcoholic, are also acting out of an enlightened self-interest to protect their own jobs. In reality, however, they do not help the alcoholic. Their tendency to overprotect merely speeds the alcoholic along the progression of dysfunction. It increases the likelihood of the alcoholic's inevitable disaster and in the end makes their own lives much more difficult. But for the victims, the ends are the means.

The Rescuer

This person is typically not a family member but becomes so close and intimately involved with the activities and failings of the alcoholic that he or she might as well be a spouse or parent. The alcoholic's "rescuer" goes about waging a personal campaign to save the alcoholic from him- or herself. Almost always the rescuer is a person who evidences all of the stereotypical behaviors of the enabler and is working on the rescues of all sorts of people simultaneously. The rescuer expends a good deal of energy taking care of people who are having difficulty making their lives work out. Regardless of the nature of the problem, the rescuer charges in to solve it: a kind of white knight tilting at the phantom dragon who threatens the rescuer's friends. However, the rescuer is as paradoxical as anything else in this life. On the surface it may well appear that the efforts of the rescuer are purely altruistic, but the rescuer is not as straightforward as he or she seems. The sad fact is that most of the people who assume this role are actually trying to save themselves more than they are others. That is, of course, all well and good. Most healthy people can take care of themselves by looking out for their own best interests while they help others. However, people who are inclined to volunteer for emotional rescue missions on a routine basis rarely own up to the self-serving side of the rescue business. As a consequence, many times they do more harm than good, because when the problems of the alcoholic threaten to overwhelm the rescuer's self-interest, the rescuer pulls out. This is only inevitable. Then it is up to the victim to come to the alcoholic's aid as the alcoholic continues to fall ever lower toward bottom.

Many people who seek training and eventually work in the helping or human care professions are initially drawn to this work as a venue for helping themselves. Some are curious about their own emotional makeup, having come from dysfunctional families themselves, and often wish to work out the emotional residue in their personal lives. Most all "helping professionals" are motivated by a fascination with human dynamics and relationships and possess a desire to understand more about themselves and the human condition. This, however, is not to say that all service members of the human care industry are enablers, even though these helping professions can and often do encourage enabling tendencies in many members. For those who are already enablers, the professional field offers a legitimate and "normal" way to vent these tendencies while allowing the enabler a certain level of righteousness. Enablers can perpetuate their denial by claiming that they are only doing their jobs.

The phenomenon of helpers who primarily help themselves is not at all restricted to those who make a profession out of it. A great many individuals recovering from alcoholism or other drug addictions act out this part as well. It has been my experience that once a recovering person has spent at least a year or so in continuous sobriety and is no longer afraid of the imminent possibility of a slip every day, that person begins an advanced phase of recovery that often involves rescuing. This phase is usually characterized by an impassioned zeal to tell the world about this wonderful universe that sobriety has opened up. Sometimes they feel compelled to push chemical dependency literature on people who aren't yet ready to hear the word. Sometimes they go around diagnosing alcoholism where there is none. This is not unlike the unique quirk of human nature to treat everything as if it's a nail, just because you learned to use a hammer.

A client of mine, for whom I have the utmost respect, found himself taking on the role of the Super Alcoholics Anonymous Sponsor. By the time he decided to contact me for counseling in an effort to understand why he found his life to be dissatisfying despite his seven-plus years of sobriety, he was sponsoring well over twenty "pigeons" in Alcoholics Anonymous. He was generally known around Princeton as "Mr. AA." Even with all of his genuine efforts and good work in helping many young people into sobriety, he found himself harboring the quiet pain of loneliness. He finally realized his need to look deeper into his feelings about his past. While his rescuing activity initially helped him along in his sobriety, Dave T. was able to recognize that to continue to live his life in this way served only to cover up his inner struggle. But now that he was secure enough in his sobriety, he could dare to muster the courage to face his own inner conflict. Dave is both a recovering alcoholic and a recovering enabler, and because of the courage he displayed in facing his problem he is a much healthier and more satisfied individual.

Dave T. illustrates how enablers are well-intentioned people who act from their own pain as much as from a genuine compassion for the afflicted individual "needing" to be rescued. That need is often only a mirage perceived by the rescuer who, although he or she may feel truly sorry for the alcoholic, probably feels sorrier about the need he or she thinks is there. This circumstance is especially evident when there is little knowledge of the disease concept of addiction and the alcoholic is understood to be a hapless soul with no willpower who simply drinks him- or herself into oblivion. For people who drink but who do not have the disease of alcoholism this misunderstanding is quite common. For instance, a social drinker who parties heavily but otherwise seems to be a relatively healthy individual usually turns out to be a classic rescuer. Rescuing alcoholics fills a need to address the problem of drinking, but that is his or her need, not the alcoholic's.

Rescuers are almost always sincere and are often quite unaware of the fact that they are attempting to work out some of their own issues by orchestrating their missions of mercy. But their individual rescue operations nevertheless keep the unfortunate objects of the rescues from ever confronting their own problems. They don't have to. The rescuer will confront them for the alcoholic and in doing so inadvertently push recovery that much further off.

Perhaps you might see yourself taking on some of the characteristics of the rescuer in some of your relationships. If you do, try to allow yourself this insight without quickly running to defend yourself or rationalize why the person in your life needs you to perform the rescue. If you can, try to observe yourself objectively as you interact with the significant others in your life to see if you fit the bill as a rescuer. If the shoe fits, wear it, but realize also that you are in a good position to use this realization in building part of the foundation of an honest and healthy relationship with yourself and others. Although the truth may sometimes be upsetting, facing it will help to free up your life energies. After all, what's true is still true whether we expend our energy trying to deny it or not. The same is true for the chemically dependent individual. Facing the problem—Step One of AA—is the pivotal realization to make. Once accepted, the alcoholic has taken the first step on the road to recovery.

The Adjuster

The person who is at the absolute center of the codependency problem is the "adjuster." He or she is the enabler who most perpetuates addiction of a spouse, lover, parent, child, or friend by consciously smoothing over all of the bumps in the alcoholic's path. This person is usually, but not always, a member of the alcoholic's immediate family. For instance if a husband is the alcoholic, the adjuster would typically be his long-suffering, martyred wife. The adjuster is the hub of the wheel, connecting all the spokes. Her activities serve to enable the entire family to revolve around the alcoholic, protecting him, and keeping him functioning at his low level of productivity. The deeper he slides, the more the adjuster must fix and hold, becoming the glue that holds the family together despite the trauma the alcoholic may inflict upon it. Without the adjuster the show could not go on; the family could not operate as normal, and the alcoholic could not continue the drinking and other acts of irresponsible behavior without facing the consequences of these actions.

Along with feeling the stress, upset, disappointment, and burden of carrying the extra responsibilities of the alcoholic, the adjuster feels very special. Regardless of the pain of martyrdom experienced by adjusters, they oftentimes use their role with the alcoholic to compensate for feelings of inadequacy or emptiness that have usually been carried inside for years. It is therefore no surprise to find many adult children of alcoholics and other members of dysfunctional households falling into the role of adjuster in their adult relationships.

Adjusters employ a variety of tools in fulfilling their roles in the alcoholic family. They tend to be very persistent people who hang on in the most difficult of times by hanging their heads, denying the obvious reality, and focusing on the most mundane of problems. You can compare them to the dogged individuals you see on the evening news who, in the face of a tropical storm lashing their beachfront homes, will busy themselves in the kitchen making egg salad as their way of facing the fear. In so doing, they may actually give themselves the illusion of protection, but by denying the danger they make the entire family more vulnerable to the real consequences of a common threat. It follows then that in their singularity of action adjusters often possess a very controlling nature. While this is true for codependents and other enablers in general, the perceived need of adjusters to be in charge of the show is paramount. The controlling attitude often plays itself out beyond merely an attempt to fix the outcome of a destructive alcoholic outburst. It becomes a series of repeated attempts to influence and control the feelings and thoughts of others. Linda, a client of mine, often recalled her mother's attempts to cover up and compensate for the angry drunken behavior of her father at yet another family gathering when she expressed her disappointment with her father: "Don't say that. Don't even think that! Your father is a good man who means well." Denial and control go hand in hand with the behavior of adjusters.

Adjusters like to exercise control by using guilt to keep the rest of the family in line. Just as an alcoholic sometimes attempts to make a spouse who is confronting him on his actions feel guilty as a means to take the focus off his drinking, the adjuster uses guilt to keep the children from raising challenges or asking too many disturbing questions. The unfortunate consequence of this imposition of guilt is the immediate confusion it creates for the children in alcoholic households when their legitimate feelings of anger and disappointment are contradicted by the proclamations of the adjuster who is concerned only with keeping the family together. This conditioning of the children to deny their true feelings is the greatest damage done by the adjuster in the alcoholic household, and his or her use of guilt is the most common method of accomplishing this.

Deep down inside adjusters generally harbor a good deal of resentment, although they usually don't know it. This is sometimes expressed by their rather cynical attitude toward people and events. Since adjusters have to absorb a lot of personal pain, they tend to feel intolerant toward the pain of other people and although they may behave and "act" to the contrary, the adjuster finds it truly difficult to empathize with others. In particular, the adjuster is resentful of the addicted person in the family. For instance, while she might compensate and cover up for an alcoholic husband, the adjuster holds on to a bitter anger that oftentimes resists healing even after the alcoholic begins to recover. There is every reason in the world for the spouse of an alcoholic to feel disappointed and angry, but the adjuster doesn't use these feelings to confront the alcoholic in an effort to bring about change. Rather, because change is feared, these feelings are held in. The repression of these feelings often makes the adjuster an unpleasant person to be in contact with and also gives rise to feelings of depression in the adjuster herself.

The bottom line with adjusters is that they desperately want the family to remain intact at all cost. To that end, they will not risk the dissolution of the family by taking a stand against or confront the alcoholic in any way. The basic behavioral axiom is that adjusters never expect the alcoholic to change. This message is conveyed to the alcoholic overtly and covertly with every adjustment, every compensation, and every rewrite of the family's history. In the face of this assumption, the adjuster continues to bond the family together into a pattern of dysfunction. Accordingly, adjusters are always there for the alcoholic because they are willing to compensate and realign themselves in reaction to whatever crisis is evoked by the alcoholic. Regardless of whether it be a potential or actual loss of job, a legal problem such as an arrest for drunken driving, the abrogation of household responsibilities, or a lack of emotional commitment and honesty with family members, the adjuster, more than any other codependent, is the one whose enabling totally insulates the alcoholic from any consequences. Adjusters live at one end of a seesaw and continually change position to allow for the inconsistency of the alcoholic. Adjusters know if they remain in one place, the seesaw game will end. So they compensate to strike a new equilibrium and allow the game to continue. However, because the adjuster is always there for the alcoholic the corollary must also be true: the alcoholic must never change so that he or she may always be there for the adjuster.

The consequences for the adjuster require that he or she live a less than satisfying life. But what are the consequences for the alcoholic? There is the inexorable downward spiral of dependence. The actions of the adjuster allow the alcoholic to lower the floor of addiction so that he or she may never hit bottom and be offered the chance of recovery until it is too late. The bottom may drop so low that the addiction may very well result in death or at least a severe physical impairment. As a result, the lives of any who are significantly connected to the alcoholic are also affected. All will suffer as this drama is allowed to go forward, mired in hopelessness and with no end in sight. Because of the well-intentioned but ultimately destructive work of the adjuster, the original strategy to keep the family together becomes more and more of a means without ends. It is both ironic and tragic that the adjuster's acting as the glue for the family unit ensures that the legacy of addiction is passed on to the next generation.

You may recognize some of these characteristics of codependency as applicable to your own life. In fact, it is only reasonable that if your personal life and family history led you to read this and other self-help material, you may well find some of yourself in here. If you have a tendency to feel guilty, I suggest you stop yourself right now. Before you go any deeper into self-recrimination, be assured: there is no need to blame yourself. There should be no pronouncement of judgment, only an acknowledgment of the past. That you are thinking about codependency issues is reason alone for forgiveness and hope that you will not be consigned to perpetuate addiction and other emotional dysfunction in your life. I urge you to appreciate that understanding your past and realizing where we are right now in the present is the key to change. If you identify with the victim, rescuer, or adjuster, that's great. Change first begins with awareness. By honestly looking at yourself, you are opening the door to a new, satisfying, and free existence. Regardless of which of the codependent roles you find yourself playing out, consider the following questions:

1. Which role do you generally find yourself playing?
2. What do you get out of being a victim, rescuer, or adjuster?
3. Which of your personal needs are you trying to meet?
4. What do you fear most about confronting the addicted and otherwise dysfunctional individual in your life? What's the worst thing that could happen?
5. What is the most vulnerable area in your life?

There are no standard answers to any of these questions. If you are a codependent, answering these questions will help you identify the role you play in your family. This will establish your direction, and help you decide on the course to recovery. By determining your role, you are in a better position to short-circuit your enabling reaction. Remember, it is entirely all right to have needs, weaknesses, and vulnerabilities. These are the logical and reasonable results of your personal and family history and are what makes you truly human. You can face yourself and grow. That is what *Strong Enough for Two* is all about.

4

Overcoming Enabling

I've met a great many people who take great offense at the suggestion that they may be enablers. If I point out that they are giving off all the enabling signals, some of them take it as criticism and feel downright offended. Their reaction isn't at all surprising considering the basic myth in our society about having to be perfect, strong, and never inadequate or vulnerable. It is my hope that you might sidestep this kind of defensive reaction as you examine your own Enabling Potential score based on the self-assessment questionnaire you answered in the first chapter. After all, if Babe Ruth had focused exclusively on the fact that he held the major league record for strikeouts, he might have never allowed himself to hit 714 home runs. You don't really need to pretend to be anything more than human because there's something beautiful about our imperfections, especially when we're honest about them.

Ask yourself: Am I an enabler? Have I acted like a codependent with an addict or alcoholic in my life? Have I, through my "take-charge" actions, allowed someone important to me to become irresponsible? What if I am an enabler, but I don't know it? If I am, is there any hope for me? What if I feel ashamed and guilty for all the times I've practiced at enabling? All of these questions will begin to sort themselves out as you honestly examine your EP.

In order to help you understand and discover the roots of your enabling I'm going to suggest that you use your Enabling Potential score as one measuring stick in examining several aspects of your life: actual enabling situations; your propensity for denial of the truth; dreams; and memories of your past. In my psychotherapy practice, I urge clients to look at their situations both with their intellect and with their feelings. In a similar fashion I urge you to tune into your thoughts and feelings and in doing so attempt as best as you can to suspend judgment.

Situations

One of our early steps to overcoming enabling is to determine whether your enabling behaviors might be situational. That is to say, might your enabling be a coping mechanism designed to ease you through certain difficult situations? If so, it helps to evaluate those situations and relate them to other aspects of your life. Ask yourself: In what contexts do I generally find myself playing out my enabling tendencies? Do I usually reserve it for very intimate relationships while functioning with fairly healthy boundaries in other areas, such as work and casual interactions? Or do I see myself like most "active" enablers who tend to color all their relationships with some shade of enabling?

It has been my clinical experience that most enablers feel most out of control in their primary relationship but are able to apply a veneer of self-assuredness in how they present themselves to the outside world. Regardless of the façade employed, the feelings held inside are still those of an enabler. What are these feelings? Do they differ somewhat from when you deal with your boss at work or when you encounter your spouse at home? Is there a familiarity to these feelings? Do you have a vague sense that you are visiting familiar territory? If you have this awareness, can you connect how you feel in the present with how you remember feeling with your parents or other significant family members? Is there something you feel they expected of you? Was it fair or realistic? Do you feel uncomfortable with these expectations now? Do you find yourself quietly concerned that you won't be able to measure up in either your family or work situation? Do you feel that unfair demands are placed upon you or do you feel put down and saddled with the responsibility to pull off what seems to be the impossible?

Denial

Many people find it hard to relate negative feelings they have about people and events in the present with the feelings they've had in the past about similar people and events. People tend to reject these feelings. They don't like to listen to the little Jimminey Cricket voice inside that tells them they've played this script out before and always walked away hurt. Why is this? How is it people will voluntarily block out events in the past in which they've been hurt or victimized, and they'll do it over and over again in a seemingly endless loop of pain? Do you willingly forget that stoves can be so hot they can burn the skin off your fingers or that the edges of razor blades are sharp? You may not forget, but you may willfully deny the existence of the pain you will feel if you violate the rules. This all-too-familiar and sometimes quite normal activity is actually a mental trick we play on ourselves called denial.

Denial is part of our human heritage. Instances of denial are found in the culture of almost every social group on this planet. It's part of history, part of myth, and part of our popular culture. Denial can be positive: the pie-in-the-sky hope in the face of impossible situations. Like Dumbo's feather it keep us up or gets us through on faith alone because we simply deny the impossibility and keep on pushing. It ranges from the normal human optimism that tells us that a glass is half full instead of half empty to the blind faith in our own abilities that make individuals into overachievers that seem larger than life. In these respects denial is good.

Denial can also be very negative. It is the term most of us are familiar with from the field of addiction, and we are alerted to acknowledge it in ourselves and others. Recovering alcoholics, adult children of alcoholics and other dysfunctional families, and individuals who have learned the language of twelve-step programs understand full well the danger of perpetuating the delusion that there is no cause for concern while sitting in the center of a cyclone. Rampant denial is moral blindness in the face of the inevitable truth, and it eventually leads to ruin. However, as destructive as denial is, like enabling it has its roots in a genuine attempt to cope with a difficult situation. And it is as that all-important transient coping mechanism that the positive and negative aspects of denial intersect each other.

Assumptions

Negative assumptions about ourselves and our pasts can beget most forms of denial and result in enabling behaviors. Where do these emotional assumptions come from? I believe that people are intrinsically good and that the natural tendency of people is to move toward wholeness and the fulfillment of self. That tendency toward fulfillment is sometimes blocked or thwarted by external events that can arise at any time during a person's life. The horrors of war, for example, can inflict deep, emotional scars on a person that remain painful for many years. Spend a Sunday afternoon at the Vietnam War Memorial in Washington, D.C., and you'll see what I mean. Victims of child abuse and incest sometimes never recover fully and may never achieve the level of fulfillment they might once have been able to. And victims of violent crimes such as rapes or attempted murder have revealed to me in therapy that those events have forever changed their lives and have dampened the sense of optimism about life they once felt. All of these traumas can create sets of negative assumptions about oneself and the external world.

When a person's basic perceptions of self or others are altered by some tragedy or trauma, the person is literally split between what he or she once was and now is; between the capacity the person once had for fulfillment and now has, or between what a person once thought about the world and now thinks. This is called, logically, "splitting," and it's something that most therapists encounter in their practices when counseling victims of tragedy or trauma.

Almost always, emotional splitting and division is the usual cause of and also the result of psychological distress. It's part of a vicious cycle. Therefore, before I work with a person who seeks counseling and psychotherapy with me I present my philosophical and psychological beliefs about wholeness, fulfillment, and splitting in a written format. My point is simply that all people want to do well, but oftentimes are prevented from doing so because of the set of assumptions they have developed about themselves and the world around them. Often, these assumptions take the following form or something similar:

> From the way my parents dealt with me I learned to feel a sense of shame and inadequacy. I have learned that I am essentially unworthy and therefore I am worried about losing whatever I have. My world seems beyond my control. I just can't seem to do enough to change the things that are wrong. I don't feel loved or worthy of love. When I do receive love there seem to be too many conditions placed on it. It seems I have to perform to stand any chance of getting love and there are still no guarantees. The problem is that I can't allow myself to know this because I don't really have enough emotional resources to hold myself together in the light of this knowledge. If I allow myself to acknowledge the truth, I might not survive. So I have learned not to speak the truth to them and not to speak it with me.

Most of the time we learn unhealthy patterns of communication and behavior because we were conditioned to do so in childhood. As this inner dialogue reveals, we can see the roots of denial as a means to preserve the sense of self. We can also see the germinating seeds of the external reward system that operates in most enablers and codependents. There is no blame attached to these developing patterns, especially for the child. This is important to keep in mind as you explore the origins of your own enabling tendencies because it is also quite common to judge ourselves unfairly, bear the guilt and shame from those unfair assessments, and do penance for them the rest of our lives. This is part of the burden of codependence and will get you nowhere.

The difficulty in remembering our past is almost always linked to the reasons that one develops enabling and denial in the first place. It usually has to do with having to deal with a situation for which the child is not equipped. As children, we do the best we can to cope with our tragedies and emotionally overwhelming experiences. In so doing, we develop attitudes and assumptions about ourselves and the world that help us get through. We enable ourselves to survive the trauma. While these coping mechanisms are survival oriented, they eventually lose their usefulness as we reach adulthood but have given rise to those areas of denial and sets of enabling behaviors. As adults, these are still very active, even when the trauma has long since passed. In the cases of incest or other physical abuse the sense of being overwhelmed is even more intensified. If you took an emotional inventory of your own life, what would be the overwhelming incidents that you might cite?

Dreams

Can you remember what you dreamed last night? Can you remember the specific details of your dreams when you awaken or when they awaken you? These are important questions that we work on in therapy. A great deal of psychological research has been conducted that demonstrates that the dream state is a vital part of our brain's internal gyroscope. Dreaming in fact is one of the most important ways we automatically repair ourselves so that we can keep on functioning. Through the process of dreaming, people often work out the issues and emotional experiences they struggle with in their conscious lives. They bring conflicts to a head, identify threats, isolate sources of discomfort, and they resolve disputes that might otherwise remain buried for years.

Often, feelings or thoughts are revealed in dreams that lie just below the surface in people's conscious waking lives. Accordingly, we have to come to recognize that dreaming is a fail-safe screening system that gets us ready to face ourselves. We all dream, whether we know it or not. Just as we automatically use dreams to screen our emotional "calls," we are also able to screen our knowledge of having had a dream at all. In other words, our brains, because they might not be ready to overcome a state of denial, simply forget the content of the dream. The emotional backwash may remain, and that's why you may feel uncomfortable or even frightened after a dream that you simply cannot recall. This is not to say that dream recall is beyond your power. It's not. You have the absolute capacity right now not only to remember your dreams but to contend with the content of your dreams no matter how painful that content might be. All it takes is a bit of training, and that's one of the processes we work on in the early stages of therapy. I suggest to my clients that before you can grant yourself permission to dream, you must first acknowledge the fears you may experience when dreaming. If you can then acknowledge your fear of dreaming, you can contend with what your dreams have to tell you. You will never reveal something in your dream that is beyond your capacity to cope with.

To many ACOAs, alcoholics, and their codependents, dreams represent what cannot be controlled and, accordingly, are things to be feared. Dreams can be a frightening medium, the bad news about our past that intrudes into our present. These are reasonable assumptions for adult children of dysfunctional families to make because in those families we learn as best as we can to keep a lid on things. Dreams represent the opening of a Pandora's box of repressed fears and the ensuing torrent of volatile feelings, painful memories, and forbidden fantasies. We try to avoid these nightmares, denying their existence and suppressing the feelings associated with them, as quickly as we can. The problem with this is we also cut off a valuable and creative part of ourselves in the process. As odd as that sounds, fear can be creative if it is used to explore parts of ourselves that we try to keep behind locked doors. The most creative and potentially the strongest parts of an individual are those things he or she fears the most, those things that invade complacency in the form of dreams.

We must explore our dreams, especially those of us from dysfunctional families, if we are ever to understand what it is we deny so strongly during our waking hours. The suppression of our dream memories out of fear may be likened to the decision not to enter a love relationship for fear of eventually losing that love. While this may minimize the risk of getting hurt, it also eliminates the possibility of loving and being loved. If you understand yourself to be an enabler who is apprehensive at the idea of dreaming, consider yourself normal. However, it is vital that you accept that it is your fear of not being in control that is the true force behind your enabling tendencies. Only then will you not be plagued by your demons that visit you at night.

If you can't remember what your dreams are when you awaken each morning, consider tricking yourself by empowering yourself to dream. This is the same thing as giving yourself permission and may be accomplished by saying to yourself:

I intend to remember my dreams. While I usually don't think I dream, I know that the chances are that I have been dreaming. It is OK for me to dream. I can face the feelings in my dreams and survive. It's OK for me to experience being afraid and out of control in my dreams. It's only a dream and I can remind myself of that if I become fearful while dreaming.

Interpreting, Recording, and Using Your Dreams

Allow yourself to recognize your dreams as a medium to explore the forces that play out in the subterranean regions of your consciousness when your senses have shut down for the night. All of them represent one thing or another of great importance to your sense of yourself. Your dreams are written, produced, directed, and choreographed exclusively by you. Understand that you're the star of your dreams and the only actor. You play all of the roles, including the setting: the monster chasing you in slow motion, your mother complaining about your terrible behavior or most humiliating weaknesses, your partner in a moment of sexual passion, or a thunderhead gathering strength over a valley. There are no external forces, no real monsters, only internal parts of what you perceive yourself to be. All of these are aspects of yourself fragmented in the dream state so that they won't be fragmented in your waking state. This is what is supposed to happen. Healthy psyches use this procedure as a way of confronting forces that are too painful for them to deal with logically, so they do what I like to call a "fantasy purge." They dump fears into fantasy situations and actually fragment the personality so that the different figures in the personality—parent, child, courageous persona, fearful persona, sexual persona, repressed persona—each has an opportunity to express itself. Again, all of this is perfectly routine. This is the way dreams allow you to counterbalance the opposing ideas and feelings that are always at war in the healthy psyche of normal people. If you were not able to do this, your personality would have to seek the same outlets in other ways. This is one of the explanations for many psychotic disorders such a paranoia and dissociated personality disorders. And, as you might expect, dream therapy is one way that psychologists treat psychotic disorders in the latter stages.

The only methods I have found consistently successful for recording dreams are a "dream journal," which you keep by your bedside and in which you write down everything you can remember from your dream as soon as you awaken, and a tape recorder that provides the same function. Your entries in this journal, whether written or verbal, should be completely unstructured, or stream of consciousness. You should make no attempt to impose any structure on your journal entries, nor to conform consciously to the rules of grammar, style, or even spelling. Just write down or dictate what you felt, saw, and experienced in your dream. Immediately upon awakening from a dream or the following morning, before you let the thoughts of the new day wash across your brain, close your eyes, let your dream images play against the darkness behind your eyelids, and begin writing or speaking. Be nonjudgmental. Censor nothing. Allow the feelings associated with the images to come to the surface and flow out through your pen. If, as you try to write, you sense you are blocking yourself, immediately switch to your other hand. You will write slower and with greater effort, but you will be surprised to see how uncensored your writing becomes. If you are trying to dictate your dream memories and run into trouble, pick up a pencil and begin writing. Sometimes, clients have told me, they are able to write more easily than they are able to dictate.

You can mentally key yourself to rouse out of bed after a vivid dream. Don't let yourself slip back to sleep. Turn the bedside light on and begin writing at once even before you think about what you're writing. If you are as descriptive as you can be about the images in the dream and as honest about your feelings, even within two weeks you will be surprised at how much you are able to retain from your dreams. You will find that you need not be a dream interpreter to work with your dreams as source material. Standard interpretations of dreams rarely work and since dreams are self-referential anyway, it usually makes no difference how you interpret the significance of a house, river, or a steep cliff. The appearances of dead relatives or close friends in dreams only serve to establish feelings you had in your relationship with the other parties or feelings that those people aroused in you. What's most important are the feelings or emotions you remember about your dreams. Therefore, focus on those emotions because your own feelings associated with the images in your dreams are the specifics you need to get your honest memories flowing.

For your purposes, once you come to see dreams as your built-in way to tune into yourself, the frightening quality of the dreams will pass. Some dreams may still be upsetting, but with the knowledge that it is your own production, you will probably allow yourself to take the point of view of an observer. Look and feel what your dream is all about as if you had the perspective of a hidden camera. Your dream is a way you are trying to work something out. It is a message to yourself about how to uncover healthier ways of dealing with yourself and those in your world. As a recovering enabler, your dreams may well provide you with a key to set yourself free.

Memories

Perhaps it is too painful for you right now to engage in any serious analysis of your dreams. The feelings that come to the surface might keep you from functioning productively during the day. If so, postpone your dream work until you've worked with some of your active memories. This might pave the way for you to deal with your dreams later. Actively exploring your memories of past events is an excellent means of understanding the roots of your enabling. I am always touched with sadness when a client in a counseling session tells me that he or she does not remember any dreams and doesn't remember his or her childhood. There is of course a psycho-*logically* sound reason for this "loss" of memory.

The act of knowing also implies responsibility for what you know. And once you've acknowledged responsibility, you've lost the ability to say that ignorance is bliss and you must do something about what you know. In the abstract, this makes perfectly logical sense. However, it presents a dilemma if you acknowledge responsibility at a time when you are powerless to take action and effect a change. This is what it felt like to be a child growing up in a dysfunctional family and that's why you learned to practice denial. Denial means that you don't know, even when you do, and you can therefore shirk the responsibility of confronting the need to change.

It is completely natural that the child learns to defend against any force that would threaten to destroy him or her. Running to the aid of your mother who is beaten or assaulted by your father; admitting the awful truth about your alcoholic parent to yourself, outsiders, or to your parent; acknowledging your emotional fragility and the dependence of your parent upon your abilities to keep the family together and hide the truth: these are just some of the risks you faced in your own day-to-day survival and your sense of security in the home. The consequences you faced by taking action may have ranged from being seriously emotionally rebuked to risking actual physical harm. Children learn very early in life the meaning of the ancient practice of killing the messenger who brings bad tidings. Children of dysfunctional families who become adult enablers have learned to hide the truth. They learn this in families that make the truth hurt. No wonder you may not recall your past. Denial probably kept you alive, but you don't need it anymore. Now is the time to trust yourself and trust in the present.

If you feel ready to remember some of the events that set the stage for your codependent and other overcontrolling behaviors, consider the following:

1.   As in the recall of your dreams, *first acknowledge your apprehension* about what you might find out. It's OK to be afraid, but remember that you're strong enough to face the truth. If you get upset, you have the resources to seek assistance. You can talk things over with an understanding friend, participate in an ACOA, codependents, Alanon, incest survivors, or other self-help group, or you may wish to consider contacting a mental-health professional who specializes in helping victims of dysfunctional families. Try as best as you can to allow yourself to feel afraid if that's what comes up for you. It just means you're normal and human. These are normal feelings. They won't last forever.

2.   Some people find it helpful to get through the rough edges of the fear by asking themselves: *What's the worst thing that could happen?* As you begin to answer this question try to keep in mind that memories are past events. The ghosts from your past are still back there and can't harm you now. The memories will come back to you as seen through the eyes of the child you once were. The colors may be vivid and the sounds perhaps ghastly,

but remember you are now an adult reading the records of a world long ago as experienced by the child within. Remember, too, that you will never let yourself have access to information that you are not able to handle. This is another type of fail-safe mechanism. Through an internal self-regulation process, you will only remember events that you are ready for emotionally. Allow yourself to take comfort in the knowledge that you have this safety switch.

3. Once you are honest with yourself about your fears, then *give yourself permission to remember.* By the honest intent to remember you can help to speed the process along. You cannot force yourself to see more than you are ready for, but you can consciously open yourself to the process of self-discovery. Your sincere intent and will are the components necessary to begin to retrieve your memories. All you have to do is be open to the process. This is one of the simplest and at the same time more difficult things you may ever attempt. The process of self-discovery is one of life's paradoxes. Because of the difficulty in sometimes not seeing the forest for the trees, you may wish to consider entering counseling. That way you don't have to be as concerned about remaining objective as you subjectively experience your past and integrate it into your adult world.

4. My clients often ask me how they can tell for sure if a memory or a fragment of recollection is real or fantasy. These individuals are understandably concerned that the events they are recalling did, in fact, occur. "Was I really sexually abused by my father?" "Did my mother really demand that I hide my insecure feelings?" and "Were they really going to disown me if I wasn't perfect at everything?" These are some of the types of questions that arise in reaction to the emergence of past images. Because you didn't videotape it, you can't tell for certain what went on in your past. But the fact is that part of your brain is just like a tape machine and images of these events were recorded in your memory at the time and in some form. Even if you can't picture the exact details, you do have an accurate sense of the experiences.

It is very important, therefore, that you allow yourself to *respect your experience.* This memory is how it felt to be living as a child in your family. Whether it is an exact copy of reality or not, the fact is that something had to happen to give rise to these memories. You wouldn't have remembered it this way just for fun. Furthermore, the assumptions and perceptions of the world reflected in these thoughts are what gave rise to the development of your enabling tendencies. In any event the chances are that what you remembered really did happen. Try not to discount your past memories. Experience them!

5. If you have difficulty recalling past experiences you might try what I term *recall by association*. Many of my clients have found it helpful in jarring their memories loose. Like all true self-help techniques it is simple and common sense. On a piece of paper make a list of as many things as you can that you associate with your past. The list may include people, places, events, and objects. For some people the list will be comprised exclusively of childhood objects, such as teddy bears, dolls, and baseball bats. Others may include a high-school sweetheart, the bedroom you used as a sanctuary as a teenager, the long driveway leading up to your house, or a familiar bottle of beer. If you can, include significant events such as report-card day, birthdays, holidays, the loss of a parent or sibling, as well as the birth of a sibling.

Once you have compiled your list, on a separate piece of paper begin to write as much as you can recall about each object or event. Try to remember what it felt like, smelled like, and sounded like. Discern, if you can, whether you were feeling tense or at ease. Most people find it helpful to keep the list and adjoining commentary for each object and event in a personal journal or notebook. This way they are able to return to it and read through it, in addition to adding bits and pieces as they are recalled throughout the day.

The task you are taking on is not unlike the mystery cases of Sherlock Holmes. Your mission is to uncover the truth. And like Holmes you can set about your task of discovery with the calm assuredness that comes from knowing that the truth about events always comes to light. Becoming more and more aware of your personal history will help you enormously in understanding the roots of your own enabling behavior. It is through this understanding that you will increase your ability to change your behavior.

The Five Steps

This is our five-step program for overcoming enabling. I have premised it on your having acknowledged your personal history in a dysfunctional family and your honest attempts to look at your present enabling scripts as objectively as possible. The first step reaffirms your need to get beyond the denial and embrace the truth.

1. Stop the Denial and Acknowledge the Dissatisfaction in Your Relationships with Yourself and Loved Ones.

This first step to overcoming your enabling behavior is really another way of letting you trust yourself to face the reality of the relationships you are in and the life scripts you continue to play out. Just as the veil of denial keeps us from coming to know and understand our capacity to make significant changes in our lives, it also serves to obscure that there is any problem in the first place. This is a part of the very nature of all forms of enabling: I enable because I want to deny a truth.

People deny for all sorts of particular reasons, but at the heart of the issue is the fact that to not deny is to have to face a truth. To an outsider that may sound just dandy, but to adult children of a dysfunctional family who have learned to use enabling as a means of coping in an emotionally unsafe world, the truth may represent a shaking of the very foundation of their sense of personal stability. The inner self-talk of a male enabler of his lover who is emotionally and physically unfaithful might be:

> If I allow myself to acknowledge that she really isn't being faithful to me I'll feel very hurt. At the core of my being I don't know if I can survive such pain. The emotional devastation feels so familiar to me, I don't think I can face the memories of past hurts that it may rekindle. So I'll do whatever I can not to feel it.
>
> Over the years I've learned to insulate myself from these type of feelings. So I always come up with excuses. I always rationalize to myself, "It's the booze that's making her this way. I can change her. She really doesn't mean to hurt me. I've got to stand by her!"

I know that even if I survive these feelings of hurt and betrayal I must do something about the relationship. I have to ask that she change and I fear that she won't. I fear also that I might have to leave her or, worse yet, she might leave me. If that happens I risk facing the devastation all over again. And so I continue to stand by her and the hurt continues. Somewhere inside there is a scream, but no one ever hears it, sometimes not even me.

As is evident here, enablers use denial in order to maintain the status quo. Keeping things stable would be fine if we are getting enough of our needs met, but when it only serves to keep us in the red we continue to lose more than we gain. Any accountant would tell you that's the road to bankruptcy. In the case of an enabler, this is emotional bankruptcy.

In order to stop the denial and acknowledge your dissatisfaction in your relationships it is important that you understand *how* and *why* you tend to perpetuate your enabling behavior from relationship to relationship. Ask yourself:

1. What am I afraid to face in this relationship?
2. What am I afraid to face about myself?
3. What would be the worst possible thing that could happen?
4. What feelings would probably be there?
5. What actions might I have to take?

Chances are you might very well not like to face some things about yourself or a significant relationship. Chances are also that you could deal with it. What usually serves as the glue that keeps enablers as slaves to this negative cycle of attitudes and behavior is an ancient personal mind-set of the self and world. This is what we are trying to suggest in questions one and two. It is what enablers don't like to acknowledge about themselves and their relationships. Nonetheless, this worldview was probably the result of a dysfunctional relationship earlier in your life. You were a child and so were not responsible and deserve no blame for the way the relationship developed. Chances are that you chose enabling as one of the means to attempt to control your world.

If you are like many enablers, you may also be prone to using guilt on yourself and others as a means of control. Guilt, as we suggest in question three, is a means to prevent us from facing our worst fear: that we really want to break free from the ties that bind us to our addicted or dysfunctional family member or spouse. Obsessional thinking and compulsive behavior are also used as a means of control. Why all the fuss about control? Because enablers are people who feel very out of control. This is what is at the heart of the denial. Enablers deny in order to not face the fact that they feel unable to make their world OK. The way to get honest is simply to stop lying to yourself. If you feel that you can't trust your capacity to be honest with yourself you might want to attend some Twelve Step meetings and/or avail yourself of the services of a mental health professional who is trained in dealing with codependency, addictions, and general forms of enabling.

When we are willing to face denial we automatically get in touch with our fears. The fears usually are a series of "what if's" that sometimes end up scaring the hell out of you. The fact is that when we stop denying we have to take some kind of action. It's important to remember two things:

1. The action you take will be of your own choosing.
2. There is no urgent need to act today.

The felt need to take action or make some kind of change is coming from the inside, not from the outside. You are not a little child who is being told what to do, feel, or say. As long as you keep clear in your mind that your decision to convey a need or demand or to take action is coming out of your being honest with yourself, any resistance to implement these changes must be attributable to your own anxiety and not to a reaction to someone's pushing you into something. It's perfectly all right to feel anxious. It may not be particularly pleasant, but it's a way of telling yourself that what you are about to do is important and therefore you should pay attention. The reality is that these are your feelings of dissatisfaction based on your needs. Because these decisions are inner directed you can rest assured that they are evidence of the healthy part of your self. By stopping the denial you are allowing this more balanced, healthy self to emerge.

Many people who are just beginning the process of overcoming their enabling attitudes and behavior oftentimes feel the impulse to act immediately, if not sooner. Once the walls of denial come down, there is often a felt sense that "I better get while the getting's good." It is important to not be fooled by this impulse to act quickly. Doing this is really the other side of the denial coin. The one side is: "My God, I can't let myself face the pain of the truth." The other side is "I might never, ever get another chance, so I must hurl myself out with all my might."

Just because you finally allow yourself to see the ways in which you are dissatisfied in a relationship doesn't mean you must take drastic steps right away. To feel the impulse to leap is what we would naturally expect of someone who has felt bound-up for so long. It is also natural for someone who does not yet have faith in his or her inner strength to impulsively try to sneak out as if a participant in a jailbreak. There is no urgency. The changes that will last will come slowly, with hard, honest work and personal courage. There is no quick fix for enabling, but the genuine changes that you can make for yourself can help empower you to live a rewarding and satisfying life.

Facing the ways in which you deny, what you're denying, and why you're denying is the first step to overcoming your tendency to enable. The first step taken in overcoming enabling behavior, as in any twelve-step program, is to acknowledge your own powerlessness over your tendency to enable and to recognize that because of it your life became unmanageable. The paradox is that in the process of admitting our powerlessness we gain humility. From humility springs the ability to change our enabling behavior. Because this change comes not out of sheer will, but out of an inner wisdom that through this process begins to be tapped, we can be more sure of its durability.

2. Recognize the Ways in Which You Enable.

What are the particular ways in which you display enabling behavior? Do they change based on different settings or different people? Is there a particular kind of dysfunctional behavior in another person that triggers your enabling response? Would you call yourself a universal enabler? Do you do it in all your relationships or do you mostly limit it to your spouse or children? Do you tend to enable one particular person in your family? Does that person really need you to do so? What do you tell yourself would happen to them if you stopped? What would happen to *you* if you stopped? Are these concerns real or imagined?

Once we are honest with ourselves and begin to acknowledge both the ways our needs are not being met in a significant relationship and our fear of the pain and loss that might result if we stopped enabling, we can begin to truly see ourselves in action as enablers. What would have been impossible to do while under the influence of denial is the next step in getting a handle on a coping mechanism gone out of control.

Answering the questions at the beginning of this section will help you to focus on your behavior. There is of course no single way that you enable; it varies according to context, relationships, the stakes at risk, and the unique qualities of your individual personality. Therefore it is important that you understand the particular pattern you have developed over the years. Remember, as you begin to see yourself in action as an enabler, there is no need to judge yourself or to take immediate action. The task at hand is only to observe and record as if you were a silent camera. By suspending your self-judgment you should be short-circuiting any tendency you may have to distort, deny, or to otherwise misrepresent your actions. You are going to practice "detachment," in which you observe your enabling as if you are scouting next week's opponent. Scouts don't judge or plan strategy, they merely observe the game playing on the field in front of them. They only write reports for coaches to discuss later. This self-observational quality is enormously helpful in seeing the real you in action. Therefore I encourage you to see yourself as a nonjudgmental camera would when you next interact with your spouse, child, boss, parent, or lover. Take note of your impulse to criticize yourself, but try not to give into it. Try instead to "see" yourself as a complete and integrated person: your actions, inner thoughts, feelings, and attitudes as you interact. By seeing the truth, you have nothing to lose but the burden that enabling always brings.

3. Understand What You Feel When You Enable.

Now you will learn how to understand and observe your enabling from the inside. In this way, you will understand the internal mechanism that drives your tendency to enable. The key to getting an accurate reading of the enabling drive is to tune in to the way you feel when you enable. Specifically, it will be helpful if you can get a sense of what and how you feel *before, during,* and *after* you enable. Although you may feel driven to understand *why* you feel what you feel, becoming aware of *what* and *how* you feel is much more helpful in empowering yourself to change your enabling behavior.

Remember, developing personal clarity is a process and a skill. If you practice tuning into yourself one encounter at a time, one day at a time, you will increase your effectiveness in seeing yourself through your mind's eye. Try to be patient. Try to forgive yourself when you find you've slipped into becoming judgmental, angry, or overly demanding. Don't hurry this, either. It's a gradual process of awareness and personal growth that deserves your honor and respect. Your attitudes and behavior took a lifetime to develop. Although they may be counterproductive now, you originally constructed them as a means of coping with a difficult situation. Accordingly, there is a logic to these coping mechanisms that requires your understanding and even acceptance. As you gradually begin to accept them, you will find it much easier to transfer this sense of self-acceptance into all areas of your life. Once you begin to develop faith in your inner capacity to make changes, you'll find it easier to tolerate yourself when you aren't changing fast enough or when you occasionally slip up.

BEFORE.   Let yourself recall a recent time when you acted as an enabler. Close your eyes and image that you're back in that situation. Remember the room you were in, its atmosphere, and where you were positioned. You might have been with your lover, child, friend, boss, or employee. Try to remember your thoughts and feelings about this person. Now answer the questions on the following checklist:

A. Can you distinguish your feelings and thoughts?

B. What assumptions do you carry about this person?

C. Do you see this person generally in a positive light (check as many as apply):
    smart
    responsible
    capable
    trustworthy
    secure
    talented
    loving
    supportive

D. *Or,* do you see this person in generally negative terms (check as many as apply):
    hostile
    stupid
    irresponsible
    immature
    unreliable
    threatening
    demanding

E. Relate individual emotions you associate with this person. When considering encounters with different people, many enablers report feeling responsible for one, the need to control the other, a fear of the other, and even a fear for another.

F. Map your associations for different people on a large grid or continuum. Now ask yourself:
    1. Can you associate your familial or professional responsibilities with specific people?
    2. Can you associate your familial or professional responsibilities with specific feelings?
    3. Do any patterns emerge?
    4. Do you feel one way toward family members, a different way toward co-workers, and a third way toward friends?
    5. Do you identify your feelings about your children with feelings about your parents?
    6. Do you have a "universal" enabling tendency for everyone?

Sometimes there is a mind-set that conveys a felt responsibility to be a "Mr. or Ms. Fix-it" for whoever is encountered. If so, ask:

a. What does it feel like to have to come through for everyone all the time?
b. In what ways does it feel like a burden? In what ways do you feel gratified by it?

Sometimes enablers attempt to fill a feeling of emptiness inside themselves with the special feelings that come from being recognized as being so dependable and so competent. Sometimes enablers perpetuate their perceptions of themselves as martyrs as a means to feel special and sometimes even to maintain a distance from the dysfunctional member of the relationship. In this case the self-talk might sound like:

> God forbid if he really stopped drinking and became more responsible in this relationship, then I might actually have to encounter him. As long as I enable him to be dysfunctional I am relieved of the risk of opening myself up and showing who I really am. Because I am frightened of being vulnerable to anyone, I will choose to have the miserable, but safe life of a victim.

EXERCISE: Keep a daily personal journal in which you explore what you feel and think in reaction to encounters with others. Spend between five and ten minutes every day focusing on your inner experience.

Describe in the journal which of these patterns of feelings arise in you before you leap in to save someone from themselves. Many people find journal writing an invaluable tool in increasing their awareness of thoughts and feelings. Remember, the key to overcoming your enabling behavior is your awareness of the inner experience from which your actions spring.

DURING.   In order for enabling to take place, there must have been some action that in some way did not live up to a prior implicit or explicit agreement between the two people involved. Examples are an employee failing to perform up to a reasonable standard, a spouse becoming emotionally irresponsible and withholding by not sharing thoughts or feelings, a child displaying a pattern of irresponsibility at school and home, a friend consistently late for dates or not following through as planned, or a lover or close friend shirking from responsibilities to the relationship by making a drug of choice a higher priority.

Whenever someone of importance in our lives fails to meet a reasonable expectation there are a variety of feelings that result. The feelings could range from disappointment and hurt all the way to betrayal and rage. If these feelings are allowed to be experienced without emotional censorship, most people would recognize that their very presence necessitates some sort of action in response. On some level enablers know this and are prone to do whatever needs to be done in order to avoid a confrontation with either themselves or the significant other.

Enablers usually take these feelings and quickly shift them out of their immediate consciousness into the recesses of their minds. This attempt to cover up the normal reaction to the dysfunctional or irresponsible actions of the other would fail without the enabler's active suppression of these feelings. Consequently, the enabler assumes emotional responsibility for the other by: doing without, acting as if he or she is indispensable, acting as a martyr, acting as if he or she doesn't really mind feeling hurt or angry or disappointed, and/or substituting compassion and pity for righteous indignation by denying the truth about the other person.

By refusing to see the other as a competent person who is on some level choosing not to come through, you devalue that person and yourself at the same time. The other is not good enough, so you must take care of him or her emotionally. You are not worthy enough to have a relationship with an equal, so you must make excuses for all people who want to have relationships with you. In order to come to terms with your enabling behavior, it is imperative that you become aware of how you feel when the dysfunction occurs. This is another form of observation that you will practice and then use only sparingly once you've begun to master the art of self-assessment and adjustment.

AFTER. As you did when you explored the antecedent feelings of your enabling behavior, it will be helpful if you can either imagine or remember what went through you when the other failed to live up to your hope or expectation. Carry this self-awareness with you on your next encounter with the dysfunctional other in your life. Take note of your feelings as you find yourself falling into your old enabling patterns. It might be helpful to imagine that your experience with the other is on videotape. Try to see if you can slow down the VCR so that you can see what you felt with every succeeding frame. You'll notice that there are several points at which you chose to act one way or another. Freeze-frame on those points. At each one you'll find yourself deciding how to act and what to say. When observed with objective hindsight you'll be able to see what feelings and assumptions motivated you. Take note and become aware of as much of this information as possible. Remember, you're on a mission to understand a pattern. And as you increase your awareness you'll link together enough clues to solve the mystery and in doing so overcome your pattern of enabling.

4. Gain Insight of How You First Developed Your Pattern of Enabling.

Coming to terms with the enabler within us requires more than just simply acting differently. Along with an alteration of attitudes, it is often helpful to gain insight into the origins of the behavior. This involves looking back into our previous relationships, and almost always at least some examination of the relationship fostered between parents and siblings in your family of origin. It is not necessary to undergo in-depth psychoanalysis in order to make changes. That is not only unnecessary, it's impractical. What is needed is a pragmatic understanding of how the present continues to be influenced or out-and-out determined by the past.

As I mentioned earlier, a very helpful tool to see the connection between past and present is a genogram. Genograms are most useful when information on at least three generations is included. You might be very surprised by the pattern of information about your own family if you draw one.

Below is a rather cursory example of a genogram using a client's family history, we'll call her Lori.

LORI'S GENOGRAM

Paternal		Maternal	
GRANDFATHER	GRANDMOTHER	GRANDFATHER	GRANDMOTHER
alcoholic	nice lady	died in war	mean
spirited	supportive	not much known	hard to please
abusive			
	FATHER	MOTHER	
	alcoholic	enabler	
	distant	overinvolved	
	unavailable	dependent	
	independent	needy	

LORI *(30 yrs.)*	divorced after husband left	HUSBAND *(29 yrs.)*	SISTER *(24 yrs.)*	BROTHER *(20 yrs.)*
needy		irresponsible	oblivious	selfish
enabler		selfish	distant	spoiled
nice person		withholding		
trusting		skeptical		
warm		cynical		
disappointed		cold		
		unfeeling		

SON
(6 yrs.)
bright
manipulative
demanding
spoiled

Lori is a bright and caring young woman, a classic enabler who was given on-the-job training all throughout her childhood by one of the best in the business: her mother. Not only was her mother a model enabler of her father's alcoholic and otherwise distant behavior, but because she was also needy, her mother implicitly demanded that Lori support her emotionally. This of course is a role reversal. Mothers are supposed to comfort and guide their daughters.

Lori grew up believing that her role in life was to take care of others. Therefore, it came as no surprise to those who knew her when she entered one of the helping professions. She also grew up with a sense that people just don't ever get what they want out of relationships, especially women. She believed you had to settle for what someone else could give you. She never saw herself as a winner in life because for her there was no victory, only compromise. Lori became an accommodator who made herself happy with her portion, no matter how small it was. Men were a different matter. Try as she might, men just never seemed to be able to come through for her. No sense worrying about what can never be, she told herself time and again. And sure enough the family cycle played itself out when her husband left her. Although they shared the same bed for three years, he was never really present in the relationship. His unwillingness to relate to her and her willingness to perpetuate that behavior illustrates a pattern of dysfunction and enabling that's been passed on from generation to generation in Lori's family. Can you find a similar pattern in your family?

> **EXERCISE:** Sketch out a genogram of your family. Try to make it as detailed as you can. It might also be helpful to interview aunts, uncles, parents, and any other family members who could provide additional information.

Many people find that going to twelve-step groups such as an Alanon, families anonymous, or an adult children of alcoholics support group is helpful in hearing about other families. These meetings are safe places where old feelings and memories about your own family are likely to surface.

The most surefire way to explore the family dynamics that gave rise to your enabling behavior is in counseling and psychotherapy with a trusted and competent professional. If you choose to explore counseling, here are a few suggestions to make the entire experience easier on you and your family:

1. Consider a mental health professional who has a speciality in working with codependency, chemical dependency (given

the historical connection of enabling to alcoholic families
they are very familiar with these problems), and/or family
therapy.
2. Interview the therapist before you make a commitment to
treatment. Remember, as a consumer of mental health services you have a right to know their philosophy and methods
of treatment.
3. Do not stay in counseling with someone with whom you are
not comfortable.
4. Do not stay in counseling with someone who refuses to provide guidance when you make a request.
5. When in counseling or psychotherapy, don't bail out too
soon. When the going gets tough, share your concern about
the therapy not going well with the counselor. Often this
kind of dialogue leads to a renewed period of productive
therapeutic work.

5. Begin to Practice Using Attitudes and Behavior that Characterize Healthy Relationships.

Observation always increases awareness. And that is exactly what
we need in order to make a change as significant as altering a
longstanding pattern of enabling. When you begin to feel ready,
let yourself experiment with *not* enabling. Observe what it feels
like when you try out this new behavior. Like anything new it
will feel a little strange at first, but remember just because something seems unfamiliar doesn't necessarily mean it can't be helpful.

The last step in overcoming your pattern of enabling is to take
the knowledge you have been gathering about yourself and put
it into practice. Before you do this, forgive yourself in advance for
messing up. I urge you to do so because it is only natural to expect
that mistakes and errors of judgment will be made. In golf, they
call them Mulligans. Give yourself plenty. Remember, your future will not be based on how well you *perform* but that you
begin your experiment in responding in different ways. Therefore, lighten up! If you can let yourself ease up and not take
yourself so seriously, it will help in the long run.

5

Enabling in the Alcoholic and Addicted Family

The codependent is at the very center of the alcoholic or addicted family, the hub of family activities, and catalyst of all that happens. The enabler role he or she plays keeps the family in a tenuous balance by compensating for the shifting and oftentimes dead weight of the addicted family member. The enabler is so important to the ongoing dynamics of the family that his or her vigilance and tireless efforts virtually lock the rest of the family into place. When there is more than one codependent in the family, they establish an implicit and unspoken agreement to enable the alcoholic or addict, guaranteeing that there will be no drastic changes in the patterns of family communication. As a consequence, the behavior and expectations for the addict become even more strongly entrenched. Because change is the codependent's enemy, the preservation of the family's pathological dysfunction is one of the primary focuses of energy for the enabling family system. In the addicted household it is a very much self-perpetuating process.

Differences and Similarities Between Alcoholic and Addicted Families

The internal dynamics of the alcoholic and addicted families are very much alike. There is an abuser whose addiction is like a vortex, sucking in money, energy, and family resources. There are children who are deprived of an active parent and there is a codependent whose enabling behavior prevents the abuser from hitting bottom and makes his or her problem even worse. The more the abuser shifts the equilibrium of the family, the more the codependent shifts in the other direction to compensate. Both abuser and codependent deny the truth of what is happening and communicate the urgency of that denial to the children. If nothing intervenes to upset the balance, the family may drift in a downward spiral for years. The children may grow up, having adopted elaborate coping behaviors to adjust to their family, and may leave the household. They may, in turn, become enablers and abusers. The addict may eventually become seriously ill as a result of toxic poisoning and may even die. The codependent may be left to carry on alone or may find another addict who requires the support of a codependent. In the absence of recovery, this is a very bleak scenario.

Where the alcoholic and addicted families actually differ is in their ability to obtain the abused substance. Alcohol is a perfectly legal drug and may be purchased by any adult. Narcotics are illegal and their purchase, use, and possession is a crime. Accordingly, alcoholics may perpetuate their addiction under the protection of the law. Drug abusers, however, are outlaws. Where an alcoholic's codependent may appear to be righteous in his or her denial of any problems in the family, a drug addict's codependent is an accessory to a crime. Whereas the alcoholic can walk down to the local liquor store or bar where he can buy a drink or a bottle over the counter, the drug addict must commit a crime in order to procure the drug.

Both alcoholics and addicts deplete the financial resources of their families. However, because of the habitual nature of chemical dependency and the high cost of supporting the habit, drug addiction may cost more. In the absence of the necessary resources, the addict begins to ask for hand-outs from unwitting family members. He may use a variety of excuses, from car repairs to gambling debts to emergency medical expenses. As long as the addict asks rather than takes money, he or she is simply a constant drain on the family. At a certain point, however, the sources of legitimate loans or hand-outs dry up and the addict has to resort to petty theft of money and property from family members. This sort of intrafamily theft creates an additional degree of disruption in substance abusing families. With the habit funded for another day, the addict then heads for his or her supplier.

In contrast, the typical alcoholic family needs no special trappings to camouflage its substance abuse. The trappings of normalcy are camouflage enough. If they have a house in a suburban community, you might see them raking leaves or cutting the grass or doing whatever neighbors do to keep their property up. They work hard at it, almost too hard. Although the dysfunction in some alcoholic families is evident by the physical deterioration of the house itself, most families spend inordinate amounts of time on repairs and fresh coats of exterior paint. It is as if by zealous house maintenance, they expect to maintain the veneer of their normalcy. And in most cases it works. It is at the front door, however, where the similarities between the alcoholic family and the normal family stop short. For a family member entering the house, it is not unlike walking into a kind of twilight zone where the rules and expectations of ordinary reality are left outside. Indeed the world of the alcoholic family is very much a matter of insiders and outsiders. It is a world of definitions and alternate realities. But most of all it is a world of contradictions.

The System

The alcoholic family system is a closed reality. Adult children of alcoholics have also described it as a black hole that absorbs all light from the outside but emanates nothing. The family has one real purpose: preserving itself.

The closed family system that usually accompanies alcoholism is often mistaken by its members as being "close" rather than closed up. While the former connotes warmth, understanding, support, and caring, the reality of the alcoholic household is that it is restrictive, exclusive, and secretive in nature. It is a fortress under siege with walls around it and guard posts that are manned by the ever vigilant enabler. The walls may not be visible, but just try to walk through them. In fact their transparent quality serves to create the illusion that they really aren't there, that the system really is open after all. Deep down, all the members of the family know that a terrible secret is being harbored. And in the minds of the children, where the art of denial is not as sophisticated as it is in adults, the secret is especially difficult to ignore.

The family system of the drug addict serves the same function of preserving the addiction and the accompanying irresponsible behavior of the impaired family member as it does for the alcoholic. However, there is an additional form of denial that drug-addicted families, at least those families in the middle and working classes, typically employ. Because most people stereotype addictions to cocaine, crack, heroin, and marijuana to the lower classes and to welfare families, middle-class families simply tell themselves that because they are not members of the lower class, their families cannot be plagued with the problem of drug addiction. If Junior is "experimenting" with drugs, it is a phase that he will soon grow out of. In reality this couldn't be further from the truth. The abuse of drugs acknowledges no social, racial, or sexual boundaries.

Communication in the Alcoholic Family

Both the content and process of communication in the alcoholic family are dramatically affected by its closed nature. What is said, how it is said, when it is said, and to whom it is said are actively regulated by the family system and censored by the enabler.

Content

Only certain topics are allowed to be discussed within the family, and the codependent monitors the content very carefully to make sure no family members raise taboo subjects. If you tamper with the rules of content, you are punished by the codependent, who marshals the forces of the family against you. You will either be ignored until you return to the party line or attacked by the other members of the family for rocking the boat. Should any child inadvertently alter the content, which children so often do in their alcoholic families of origin, the enabler begins altering the "official" version of the truth about the family to compensate for the changing situation. Accordingly, the actual nature of the dynamics of the relationships within the family is constantly obscured as the family members try to find their own truths. For the members of the family who try to maintain some semblance of emotional health, this can be a very disturbing experience.

The members of the alcoholic family most susceptible to this upset are the children, especially those children who struggle against living in a state of denial. The children in the alcoholic household are quite impressionable; they have no automatic prejudices or preconceived opinions, and simply want to perpetuate a natural state of childhood "bliss," which is common among children in any family. Because of their dependent status, they rely on the adults in their immediate environment, especially their parents, to tell them the truth about what they see and hear. If that truth is distorted to the point where it conflicts with what the children can see for themselves, they reject it despite themselves. Children can smell alcohol on a parent's breath; children can see that a parent is not just napping when he or she falls asleep on the couch at odd hours; children can also perceive that a parent is not acting as competently as the other parents he or she has encountered. A child in elementary school will receive a picture of the world from his teachers, peers, and educational materials. When that picture conflicts with the picture of his or her own homelife, the child will realize that something is wrong. You can't hide it from the kids, just like your parents couldn't hide it from you.

In addition to being able to see the truth, children also react to that truth, no matter what their parents tell them to do. Like Pavlov's dogs, children develop early visceral reactions to the fear of an angry or irrational parent, the sound of parents fighting in the night, and the hostility in the eyes of the enabling parent when he or she takes out frustration on the rest of the family. Children want to please their parents, to earn their love, but in an alcoholic family this is close to impossible. Even the most passive of children who act out the denial of their parents cannot move fast enough to cover all the bases in advance. More often than not, that child will be caught standing on the wrong base and will be summarily punished.

How many times can you remember being caught out in the open by a parent simply because you didn't move fast enough to get out of harm's way? Did you feel resentment, anger, downright rage? Did you feel guilty about these feelings later? How did you bury this guilt? All of these childhood emotions and fears may be still churning within you, preventing you from seeing yourself clearly and connecting with the world around you. Try to acknowledge these fears and emotions. Try to pinpoint the exact situations that call them to the surface. As you begin to become successful at this, you will notice that your wall of denial will start to thin out and become transparent.

Go back to step one of the Five Steps in the previous chapter and acknowledge those residual feelings that you still experience. Bring them to the surface and let the memories play out in your mind. By exposing your rage, fears, and resentments to the light of your present life, you will be able to cope with them as an adult instead of protecting them as the child you used to be. You will naturally take the necessary steps to remedy the pain and heal the wounds of your past as you work through the successive steps in the program.

Do you remember what it was like when you were a child? You seemed to understand without being told, see without being shown, and hear without being spoken to. This is why children are magic, I explain to my clients. Children begin to learn very quickly what's expected of them by picking up sets of cues from their parents. Perhaps a result of having to operate in the world for at least eighteen months without the ability to communicate verbally. Children are quite adept at sensing the unspoken tension between a mother and a father. As a very insightful client of mine once said, "Children know!"

The distortion of content in the alcoholic family begins as early as a child can perceive and experience the other as a separate person. From an infant who's "comforted" by an overanxious and stressful mother, depressed and angry because she's found out that her husband's promise to stop drinking after the baby was born is now one of the many broken promises, to the nine-year-old who's told that his alcoholic mother is just having "women's problems" and that he's got to be more of a "man" around the house and start cooking the dinner before his dad gets home, the results are the same. There is a stark and painful distortion of what everyone in the family knows to be true. The family agrees to lie so that the status quo can be perpetuated for one more day. But the lies don't work.

A pattern of routine interactions with parents in which a child's perceptions are regularly challenged and denied can only lead to the child's developing self-doubts and feeling distrust toward the outside world. The distorted communication within the family also distorts all of the cues the child relies on to test for truth in his or her environment. Accordingly, children in alcoholic and addicted families grow up doubting the truth of their own senses. Is that what happened to you? Is it happening to your children? It's the same script with different players. Don't blame yourself; change the script.

An otherwise rational person may wonder why it is that sympathetic relatives wouldn't want to acknowledge the reality of a problem and get help for the alcoholic in their family. The reason is that the dynamics of the family prevent it. The enabling system that distorts and censors reality eventually forces its new members into just the right mental set. This is not unlike the *Invasion of the Body Snatchers*. The adults in the child's family may look and act like real mothers, fathers, grandparents, uncles, or aunts, but they don't communicate like adults in other families. Children sense this and they can feel the static.

As children grow they eventually learn to find their niches in the family. Once the system is settled, all its members resist any change. The system has become so comfortable that it's more important than the dysfunction it was designed to protect. The effects that change have on a family are similar to the way any crisis impacts. It literally shakes up the family system as it exists. Family therapists often use these crisis situations as opportunities for constructive change. During these critical periods the roles shift from static to a state of flux, at which time it is important to take action while attitudes are still fluid. That's why automatic changes like marriages, divorces, births, and deaths are so important. Each presents a new opportunity for the members of the family to realign themselves and to restructure the reality around the alcoholic. If the unthinkable happens and the alcoholic begins to talk about getting sober, going to Alcoholics Anonymous, or even just cutting back on the booze, the same family members who might ultimately benefit from the change are threatened by the pending shake-up to the family system and become unconsciously motivated to sabotage the alcoholic's efforts to recover. "You can still drink a little!" and "You're not fun to be with any more," are some of the statements uttered by the alcoholic's codependents. This may also be accompanied by a family member's bringing home that favorite brand of gin or scotch and prodding him to "only have a little." All of this can transpire without even the batting of an eye and without any conscious recognition of the double message being given.

Process

Just as the content of communication is altered in the alcoholic family, the process of communication is skewed. In the alcoholic family, the process of communication involves making sure that family messages are routed through the appropriate channels, making certain that specific family members are either in or out of the message loop, and making sure that the codependent acts as the switchboard as well as the translator. If you grew up in an alcoholic family or if you live in one now, you understand how the enabler oversees all communication. If you are an enabler, you might recognize this behavior in yourself. You can understand that the process of communication is the means by which the prevailing order of the family preserves itself.

Most of the time the process of communication is rigid: All dialogue among family members must first be channeled through one central person. In this centralized form of communication the key player is virtually always the primary enabler of the family. While acknowledging the pitfalls of stereotyping, it is reasonably safe to say that if the husband and father is the alcoholic, the wife and mother is the lead enabler. This is a process I've seen repeated in family after family: The codependent wife filters all the communication. Children bring their family business directly to their mother. The alcoholic father usually isn't even spoken to by the other family members, except for greetings or at formal family rituals. "What was the use?" one of my clients said, describing his own childhood situation. "He was usually so drunk or confused that he forgot everything you said within hours. It was like talking to someone who wasn't there." "My mother was like a central planner," another client reported. "You had to clear anything said or done concerning the family with her." The codependent's role in switchboarding the family's communications is so powerful that even as adults, twenty to twenty-five years after they've moved out of the home, children from these families will still route communications through the enabler—even in one another's presence. In more than one family therapy session I've seen an adult child asking the codependent mother something about the other adult child sitting right in the same room. Sometimes the mother is even requested to tell the other child something. Sometimes the central codependent feigns a complaint at having to do all this work for her adult children, but even that remark is more rhetorical than true.

Because no one is supposed to speak directly to anyone else in the alcoholic and addicted family, the process of communication in the home is marked by indirectness. If a child feels something or wants something from a sibling, he or she usually does not make a direct request. Instead, the request is channeled through the mother who translates it—more often than not changing the actual nature of the request as well—and passes ît along to the other sibling. Thus, not only can't you get what you want in this type of family, you can't even ask for it directly. You have to rely on the abilities and benevolence of the enabler to get your request through channels to the proper person, always hoping that the request stays intact, that it conforms to family policy, and that it gets its approval at every level. Given the general atmosphere of emotional distrust and instability that often characterizes the alcoholic family, this is of course not at all surprising. A person who dares to say what he or she really thinks runs the risk of some form of familial condemnation. A person who allows him- or herself to become vulnerable by actually requesting help or a shoulder to lean on runs the risk of being hurt and disappointed. And lest you think this is an extreme situation, you should know that I have met with families in which this structure has prevailed for three or four generations. With the passing of one generation, new players assume the same roles enacted by the parents. The only things that change are the names of the players.

Regardless of which role in the cast of characters a person happens to be playing, the end product is usually the preservation of the unhealthy situation in the family. Whether the child is the hero, lost sheep, or scapegoat, or whether the alcoholic is the mother, father, adolescent child, or Uncle Ned living with the family, the process of communication usually reveals an anger at the powerlessness in not being able to get needs met. This sense of powerlessness and the accompanying anger is so pervasive that it tends to remain with adult children from these families for the rest of their lives.

Therefore, it's the conspiracy of silence that is the first thing we attack in intervention therapy for both alcoholics and substance abusers. That simple process of sharing how an individual's drinking or drugging has negatively impacted on one's life is the central component of intervention because it directly challenges the denial that has built up in the addicted family. Once the intervention has been mounted, the ability of the enabler to prevent the alcoholic or addict from seeing the truth is taken away. Even the enabler must confront the facts of his or her denial and perpetuation of the addiction. It has been my clinical experience that the process of directly and clearly communicating, without anger, how a family has been affected by the drinking of a loved one is the single biggest factor in getting the alcoholic to agree to enter a rehabilitation program.

If the dysfunctional family system is unsuccessful in its preliminary efforts with the family member who dares to speak the truth, then the next gambit is to create a "we versus you" situation in which the healthy family member more often than not capitulates in the end. The risk of losing the family becomes so great that the errant family member forces him- or herself to deny the truth rather than face exile. The efforts of denial by the addicted family are indeed formidable. They go after the "honest" heretical member like human antibodies surround an invading virus. There is a good reason for this. The honest family member is like the messenger of doom who strips away the denial and points to the one truth that can break apart the family by upsetting the status quo. This is what the family is most afraid of. Accordingly, the family bands together to silence the messenger of truth by smothering him or her with rejection and exile. In the special cases of substance abuse, especially in violently dysfunctional families where the drug of addiction is PCP or crack, the tremendous psychological dependence on the drug can motivate people to kill renegade family members who are too vocal and threaten the out-of-control addict with police intervention.

Social Sanctions Against the Alcoholic Family

Nothing more effectively promotes denial then a healthy dose of good, all-American social sanction. It's OK to drink. One more for the road. Open up any upscale magazine and you'll see top people from all walks of life telling you that they're cool and their brand of scotch is Johnny Walker Red, Johnny Walker Black, or Dewar's single malt. Nothing's wrong with any of this as long as you're not an alcoholic. In fact it's easy to deny a dysfunctional cancerlike disease eating away at the core of your family when the rest of the world says it's not a disease. The problem is that all of the social sanctions about alcohol actively encourage people to deny the existence of alcoholism in their own families. The whole world says that your husband is more of a man because he drinks, so who are you to put a stop to it?

To breach a hole in the wall of denial is difficult even under the best of circumstances. To breach that same hole when the world reinforces that denial can be next to impossible unless you're prepared to assume the role of "bad cop" or whistle-blower in front of your family. What's worse, once you've blown the whistle and forced your spouse or parent into recovery, you know that a big part of your identity and sense of purpose will have to be dramatically changed, if not completely discarded. Consider the amount of anger and recrimination that will eventually have to float to the surface before it can be dealt with. Consider that recovery may entail an entire restructuring of your marriage as you explore what elements kept you and your spouse together during the period of his alcoholism. Are you prepared for that? Are you prepared for the alcoholic's transformation from a "mean drunk" or lush into born-again sobriety? Recovery is a process, too, and unless you're there to support it instead of fight it, you'll be working at cross-purposes with the alcoholic. The results might be disastrous for him, for you, and for the rest of the family. Maybe you've seen other codependents whose families worked their way into recovery only to relapse into alcoholism again and don't want to put yourself through it. Remember, your motives are as important if not more important than those of the alcoholic, because you are the one who's in control. You've helped to perpetuate that alcoholism by working out the family ground rules, and now you are going to change the playing field. Are you prepared?

In terms of your family, beginning recovery brings to the surface your history and your spouse's history. The two of you will acknowledge your dependencies, admit to your collective and individual losses of control, and undertake your respective "fearless moral inventories." This process in itself will be difficult and emotionally demanding. Suddenly the social sanctions will change. What was a socially acceptable habit of drinking at parties will become a socially unacceptable disease. Remember, when you could "handle" liquor, you were a member of the club. When you have a disease called alcoholism, that same club may perceive you as damaged goods. It may not be fair, but that's how social sanctions tend to work.

For this reason, it would be helpful, as you begin, to put your problem with alcoholism into perspective. Understand early on that you are neither weak nor guilty of a great sin. You are human and live in a society of human beings that has not only embraced alcohol as an insidious drug, but has raised the consumption of alcohol to a ritual. In order to navigate yourself through the corporate denial surrounding your family, it's important to understand the nature of the social ritual and where you will stand once you help your spouse, parent, or child into recovery.

Special Characteristics of Communication in the Addicted Family

In the addicted family, the form of chemical addiction taking place in one generation is rarely understood by the other. Many parents don't understand the lure of cocaine or crack and are not aware of the telltale signs that their child is an abuser. Moreover, many of the attitudes and behaviors typical of normal adolescence resemble the signs of teenage drug abuse. For example, moodiness or mood swings, chronic lethargy, low-level irritability, and occasional withdrawal from usual family activities may be a superficial indication of drug involvement or the condition of temporary insanity that many parents believe adolescence to be. Parents who've had direct knowledge only of the use of alcohol aren't in a position to determine whether their child is a substance abuser unless they've made a concerted effort to educate themselves. Given the widespread attitude of "not in my family" or "not my kid," many parents glide through their children's adolescence oblivious to an addiction problem taking place right under their own noses. It is little wonder, therefore, that there is a lack of communication.

The "thirtysomething" generation might be different because of their own experimentation with drugs such as marijuana during the sixties and early seventies. However, even these typical yuppies are often stumped by the sometimes habitual use of drugs by their adolescent children. A client, Bob, explains:

> Back in college using drugs was so new. It was associated with love and peace and trying to make the world a better place. Many of my friends who smoked marijuana with me were athletes in high school and college and were at the heads of their classes. We were the sparkling products of the 1950s, the best class that ever marched through our respective schools. We believed in fairness, truth, justice, and in having our own way. We were intent on making a positive difference in the world. We were looking to understand the meaning of life, and we used marijuana as a part of an exploration ritual. We believed we were exploring our inner selves. It sounds corny now I know, but we were quite sincere at the time.
>
> But on the other hand, when I found out that our fourteen-year-old son, Jason, had been using pot and cocaine regularly since he was twelve, Heather and I were beside ourselves. He wasn't trying at school and his grades went to hell. He wasn't interested in sports anymore and refused to participate in any other activities we used to share, like fishing and going to ball games. All he wanted to do was lie around and watch MTV with his friends.
>
> First of all, I never used drugs at such a young age. And sec-

ondly, I never turned into a vegetable like Jason. I can't relate to this at all.

Bob's situation is typical. Despite his own prior experience as an occasional drug user, he wasn't able to spot his son's problems until they progressed to the point of becoming blatantly obvious. In Bob's family, as in all drug-addicted families, the communication between the addict and the rest of the family slowly disintegrates from the bottom up. As the child slowly withdraws from the family, his or her familiar habits begin to change. Old established friendships wither, the child becomes less outgoing and more withdrawn and no longer engages in his or her favorite activities. Somewhere along the continuum of this withdrawal, parents slowly realize that the symptoms of an addiction problem have come to the surface.

You can see how communication slowly breaks down in all addicted and alcoholic families and how the denial serves to increase the distance between addict and family. For the codependent, denial serves a real purpose. It allows him or her to put up with the constant emotional abuse and ultimately condone the addict's behavior. Almost all codependents believe they need the addict. They feel that they can't survive without him or her. As long as they go along everything will be secure and airtight. Each day will be patched up exactly like the day before. But in actuality things turn out quite differently. As the codependent regularly enables the addict to drug him- or herself, to treat the children harshly, and to not share him- or herself emotionally with the family, the family breaks down. In essence, what codependents communicate is permission to not change. As a result the entire family ultimately will require treatment.

Denial in the Addicted Family System

The denial is shared by the members of the substance-abusing family in much the same way it is in the alcoholic family. However, in codependent families of drug addicts, the stakes for denial are much, much higher than they are in codependent families of alcoholics. In the case of drug addiction, not only the addict, but the resources of the entire family are jeopardized by the illegality of the possession, purchase, or sale of drugs. If the drug addict is a parent or income-earner, the loss of that person often means the loss of income. If the addict is also a dealer, that loss may be quite substantial in the short-term, especially in economically deprived neighborhoods where dealing coke may be the only means of instant ready cash. Even if the parent is not a dealer but is the primary source of income, the enabler may perpetuate the addiction simply so as not to upset the family's applecart by blowing the whistle and possibly putting the addict at risk of going to jail.

If a child is the addicted family member, the enabling parent may also feel obligated to protect the child from the legal system while looking for a way to get him or her into recovery. However, where recovery also means exposing the child to possible prosecution for the possession of illegal substances, the parent will face a double pressure. First, the mere fact that a child may face criminal charges is enough to prevent a parent from taking action. Second, if the child has information that may lead to the criminal prosecution of a supplier, the child's life may be in danger. The parent may believe that the child is of value to the local prosecutor only insofar as he or she is able to supply information leading to the arrest of those in the supply network. Beyond that, the prosecutor may just as soon see the child go to jail or be a victim of a drug supplier's retaliation. Thus, the parent may feel that he or she is under no obligation to turn the child in to be sued by the criminal justice system and then abandoned to fate. In neighborhoods where there is constant interaction with the police or county detectives, parents are usually savvy enough to have no illusions about what the police can do to a family. What's worse, the parents are probably right. If some of the less-addictive drugs, like marijuana, were legal, the battle against drug addiction would be easier to fight because the fear of prosecution would be lifted from parents and addicts alike. In these instances, the addiction itself could then be addressed, just as in alcoholic families, rather than the question of criminal possession. As far as police and law enforcement agencies are concerned, the criminal aspects of drug use are more important than the health and life of the addict.

Third, parents may believe that the simple fact of criminal

prosecution may expose them to public condemnation. If one's child is questioned by the police on suspicion of drug possession, the rest of the neighborhood may paint that family with a scarlet letter. Unfortunately, the sin is not that a child may be addicted to narcotics but that the family let him or her get caught. If mom or dad is trying to be a stellar member of the community, junior's drug problem is an embarrassment that can't be talked away. Better, therefore, to try a private home remedy rather than blowing the whistle. I face this problem in therapy all of the time and I don't have any ready answers. Normally, I advise intervention therapy but assure the parents that the confidentiality of the normal doctor-patient relationship prevails as long as the child doesn't reveal that he or she is about to commit a crime.

Above and beyond the threat of prosecution from illegal possession of drugs, there is the typical desire to preserve both the status quo and the external image that there is nothing wrong with the family or its members. As in the alcoholic family, the effort to deny the existence of a problem is shared by both the addict and the codependent family members.

The forces that bond the members of an addicted family together are very powerful because the pressure of the addiction is so great. As a means of coping with the pressure, the members believe that the survival of the family depends on the maintenance of the status quo. Consequently, addicted families are usually masters of the process of controlling the individual members, mainly the children, with the use of disinformation and the threat of ostracism. The codependent at the center believes that lies are imperative because if and when the real truth ever came out, the long-established pattern of family dynamics and noncommunication would break down in the face of it. This, the codependent believes, would ultimately weaken the family because as the breakdown took place, the addicted individual would be forced into some form of recovery program and receive initial help and support from outside the family. However, because the family grounded its sense of purpose on the addict's drug dependency, the enabling and codependent patterns would be forced to change, or at least be critically examined, as a function of the recovery process. As the addict's recovery accelerated, the family environment in which the addiction became progressively worse would change. These changes in the family will challenge the identities that the codependents established during the addict's drug dependency. What the codependents had invested in the addict's substance abuse would become worthless. Consequently, these members tend to resist recovery by seeking a return to the way the family originally functioned. They do this by reaffirming the dysfunctional communication patterns in the face of the addict's recovery as a form of challenge.

Codependency and AIDS

As a codependent enabling your spouse, parent, or child to perpetuate a substance abuse habit, you should be aware that you're also actively placing him or her in a high-risk group for exposure to HIV, the AIDS virus. A recent sample survey of municipally-conducted autopsies that were performed by the New York City Medical Examiner's office revealed a frightening statistic: 53 percent of the corpses tested had been infected by HIV. Public health officials in New York are just now trying to track down the sexual partners of these deceased parties to notify them of the likelihood that they, too, have been infected with HIV and will most likely contract AIDS within the next two to ten years. Many of the deceased in the survey were IV drug users, most probably dependent on heroin. Most people don't talk much about heroin because it is considered a drug of the underprivileged. However, heroin addiction cuts across all classes; it is a drug that many cocaine addicts usually start using when they want to "string out" or lengthen the duration of the drug euphoria, and it is an ingredient in the drug mixes brewed up in home labs. Many users start out by smoking or ingesting heroin but quickly overcome their fears of using the needle. Heroin use is again on the increase among young adult users.

HIV is sexually transmitted, but it is also passed directly from the blood of one person to the blood of another by the sharing of needles. Thus, the spouse, lover, or friend of a IV drug user has to be concerned about getting or even spreading HIV infection (as well as hepatitis B, a serious, though not necessarily fatal, blood disease). The fact is, the needle the addict is using might as well be your needle if you are having sex with that person. This raises the stakes for codependents to critical levels. If you are enabling your partner or parent to indulge in intravenous drug use, you are putting your own life at desperate risk, gambling the lives of your children and unborn children, and becoming a partner to the spread of AIDS in our society. I really come down heavy on this with my clients. I suggest they are not only perpetuating the drug addiction, they are perpetuating the spread of AIDS. No matter what they risk by turning their partners in, the risk to them from AIDS is far greater. And once AIDS symptoms show up, the disease will progress until they die. There is no cure for AIDS.

6

The Parent as Enabler

Despite the fact that Mike hasn't seen his children for the past five years, he has few regrets.

> I know I'm supposed to miss them and bend over backwards to be their father and all, but I just can't help feeling relieved of a terrible burden. Raising those kids was hell even though I loved them. Every minute they were around, I felt like I was wearing prison shackles and dragging a heavy ball and chain. If they burped funny, my blood pressure went up. If they even so much as reached for a glass of milk from the fridge, I was on my feet, making sure they didn't spill something that would make them start crying. And when they cried, my world would come to an end. I felt if I could throw myself in front of a truck to stop their crying so they'd be happy, I'd be a successful dad.

Mike was describing his years working the night shift at a Trenton tile factory when his two children were very small and he was alone with them during the day while his wife was at work. It became so bad he often thought of running away during the day and leaving the kids alone in the house.

> You get tired of throwing a safety net around your kids, especially when you know you can't stop. It's like I'd be normal on my job,

normal with other people, normal everywhere else. But with the
kids, I was a complete failure. I acted just like a compulsive who
had to control the whole world so they wouldn't get hurt or be
unhappy. I was afraid to close my eyes or turn my back on them
for a second.

Finally, out of sheer frustration, Mike started having sexual
relationships with his female co-workers at the factory. His affairs
were public, embarrassing to everyone who knew him, and they
literally blew his marriage apart. It was the only way, he confided
to friends years later, that he could put a stop to his feelings about
abandoning his children.

At first there was hell to pay. I thought she was gonna kill me for
trashing everything we promised to each other since high school.
Then she moved away and took the kids with her. She thought it
was a punishment, but for me it was like being let out of jail. I
never even called the kids. I know they hate my guts now and
probably curse the word "Dad." But it's not their fault and I don't
really care anymore.

Mike didn't realize until years later that his need to be the
overprotective enabler for his children was a direct result of his
being enabled as a child. His parents were the ages of most grandparents. They doted on his every whim. If Mike turned up his
nose at what was on his dinner plate, his mother cooked something else. If he wanted to leave the house for any reason whatsoever, his father wanted a complete itinerary before he let him out
the door. And, Mike complained, both his parents always peered
at him as if he were on a microscope slide. "It was as if I was a
pet gerbil in a cage," he once said. It was only natural, therefore,
that when Mike had kids of his own, his only instincts were to be
an overprotective enabler just like his parents had been. He eventually realized that he was projecting himself onto his children.
The more he hated what he was doing to his children, the more
he hated what had been done to him. He was reliving it every
day. There was no escape. "Somebody was gonna get hurt in that
house," he said in counseling years later. "I knew I was losing it
bad."

It became so painful so quickly that rather than seek therapy or talk about his problems with his wife, Mike simply destroyed his marriage. He perpetuated his own pain by continuing to deny that he had a serious problem until it was too late. By then his fear had overtaken him and clouded his ability to deal with the problem rationally. Had Mike been able to break through the wall of denial that he had built up about his past and his taboo negative feelings toward his children, he might have been able to find a solution. Confronting the truth about his situation would have been his first step. Acknowledging the truth about his past would have been his next step. Then he could have taken positive steps to learn *how* to be a "normal" parent.

Unfortunately, Mike's situation is not as unusual as it seems. Being a parent who enables his or her own children is often a painful experience for the parent and child alike. It can be a daily grind of tension that, despite your best intentions, never goes away. You don't want to enable your children, but until you turn around and face the truth squarely, take the active steps to overcome enabling in your life, you will be tripped up again and again. You must use your tensions, your fears, and active feelings toward your children as measuring rods. Use them to assess how you felt about yourself and your parents when you were a child. Chances are, you'll find experiences there that will help you deal more effectively with the present and your own children.

If you, like Mike, grew up in a codependent or dysfunctional family, you know all too well how parents can enable their children to perpetuate all kinds of dysfunctional behaviors, including drug dependencies, teenage alcoholism, compulsive overeating, shoplifting, and even sexual abuse. We expect that parents should be loving and caring toward their children and on the lookout for their best interests, no matter their ages. But loving and caring require that parents know how to set limits and draw boundaries as children grow older. If they neglect to set limits for their children, parents can find themselves enabling their children to become irresponsible, to remain immature, or to become chemically dependent. If you are a parent, see if you feel defensive at the idea that you might unintentionally be enabling your child in some manner. If you are, don't be surprised. It has been my experience that most parents fall into the enabling trap at some point during the child's early to adolescent years.

Don't parents love their children? Most parents do. Why then would parents compromise their children by preventing them from learning to take responsibility for their actions? If a parent has enabled a child, nine times out of ten it is the inadvertent by-product of an otherwise caring intention. The reasonable person might then ask under what circumstances would parents enable their child in a negative way? Would they have to be consciously aware of the enabling in order for it to have occurred? These are the complex issues that tend to bring parents and their children into therapy.

Parenthood: Tasks and Pressures

Parenting is one of the toughest jobs in existence. Parents, confronted with the various demands and needs of their children, are in an almost constant state of vigilance, forever keeping watch over them, making sure that they know how to stay out of trouble. If there is one task that above all others seems to epitomize the duties of parenthood, it's to provide for the safety of the child. No matter what the age of the child, good parenting requires that this be the most important of all missions. There are, however, many different ways to ensure safety.

Safety and the Development of Trust

There are two levels of trust that parents help develop in their growing child: internal and external. We are all familiar with the latter. This is the result of creating an environment in which the child is free from harm and the threat of harm. This safe external trust also encompasses all the various interactions with the child by which he or she comes to learn that those who are entrusted with his or her care are consistent, responsive, loving, and reliable. If the infant could speak it might say,

> Because you have fed me when I was hungry most of the time, and comforted me when I needed assurance, and tended to my needs for good hygiene in a competent and loving manner, I have come to feel safe. I trust you and in doing so I am learning to trust my world.

The development of trust toward the outer world does not require perfection and absolute vigilance on the part of the parent. Indeed, a hyperrigid approach to parenting tends ultimately to infringe on the development of a child's sense of personal space and separateness and also may inadvertently instill feelings of anxiety, fear, and insecurity. The child might wonder what all the fuss is about, and if you, the reliable caregiver, are uptight, maybe there is indeed reason to worry.

Rather, this sense of outer trust emerges from consistent and loving attention given to the child. As long as the child's cries for food and changing are addressed consistently enough for him or her to establish trust and fulfilled expectation from your routine, the child will adequately develop a trust in the rest of the world. At the same time, you should always be prepared to give your child immediate and undivided attention in the event of an accident or other emergency. That requires your being able to monitor the child's activities, behavior, and cries in order to be able to distinguish a normal call for attention from an emergency situation.

The development of a sense of internal trust—that ability to rely on one's feelings and judgments—gives rise to a child's ability to interact with the environment and form relationships throughout his or her life. You'd be surprised how many people never develop this as children and must consciously practice it as adults. It forms a large segment of my own client population.

If a child is assured of safety by his caregivers, then he can proceed with beginning to develop a trust in himself. How he is touched and handled during interactions with his parents tells him a great deal about himself. If the touch is gentle and loving, he learns that he is lovable. If his needs are attended to promptly, he believes he's valuable and worthwhile. The seed of self-worth, when cultivated by parents, blossoms into a resilient, healthy, and confident personality. Beginning in infancy, the child learns to trust his inner perceptions and feelings. When needs are attended to promptly, his bodily perceptions are confirmed. It is this very validation that eventually leads him to develop trust in his feelings, thoughts, and judgments. These are important and necessary strengths in encountering the world throughout his life.

On the other hand, if a child is left to cry away the hours in misery, he learns that he's not valuable. He develops a low self-esteem or a negative self-worth. If he's not valuable, then no one else is. If he can't have confidence in himself, then he can trust no one else. If he's mishandled or if his caregivers inflict pain, then he withdraws from people, never develops an internal mechanism to trust others, and never establishes appropriate boundaries with the external world. Similarly, if a child's needs are met only inconsistently, he will never be able to establish a belief that expectations can be met. Without a set of expectations about the world, children will have anxieties about venturing into it. They will be hesitant—outsiders may call this shyness—and will resist natural attempts at socialization. At the very least, such a child will develop an awkwardness. At worst, this child will become antisocial. All of these reactions are dependent upon the sense of internal trust that parents instill in their newborn child.

Inner trust is further enhanced by the messages that children are given in relation to their own bodies and bodily functions. Not only is it important how children are touched, but how parents deal with them as they begin to touch and explore their own bodies. One of the tasks of good parenting is to assure children and confirm their finding pleasure in touching and experiencing their own bodies, even if it means exploring their genitals. Negative messages and taboos about sexuality and sensuality may be given very early on by parents who don't feel entirely comfortable with their own sexual selves. Therefore it is the responsibility of parents to keep track of their own issues, whether it be about sex or anything else, and to work them out as best they can. Granted, that while no parent is perfect—and there is no need to be—parents must also be mindful about what indirect messages they may be sending their children at any age.

All of this has a direct relevance to the parent who has a tendency to enable. First, most parents who are enablers will have difficulty in establishing appropriate boundaries with the child. They are plagued by doubts and questions: When do you respond to the child's cries? How do you keep from spoiling the baby? Do you trust your own feelings of anger and frustration at a baby who will not stop crying? Why are the baby's needs more important than yours? Does your spouse love the child more than he or she loves you? How much more do you have to put out to wean your spouse away from the baby? These are all negative questions, to be sure, but they are the questions that trouble most enablers.

The real problem is that most enablers don't confront them: They deny them, bury them, and generally treat them as if they are terrible taboos. Enablers don't understand that for many normal people these questions are a part of the routine adjustment to having a new baby in the home. People who've learned to trust themselves acknowledge these questions, hurt feelings, and bouts of jealousy. Once acknowledged, they can be dealt with and eventually overcome. But by denying them, enablers begin to build up the residual anger and frustration that will burden their relationships with their children. To compensate, enablers may overdo, may overprotect their children, and may prevent the children from ever developing the trust and self-confidence that we described earlier. In this way, enablers who don't confront their problems continue the same dysfunctional script into the next generation.

If you find yourself plagued by these feelings of inadequacy, jealousy, anger, and fear, don't deny them. Go back to our early steps of overcoming enabling behavior. Acknowledge your feelings. Drag them right out into the open. If necessary, confront your spouse in a loving way and say "This may sound like a terrible thing, but I just have to talk about the feelings I'm having. If we talk them through, I can get over them." Since the parenting of your children is an issue that critically affects you and your spouse, it's worth the loving confrontation that we talked about in the earlier chapters.

The Child as a Separate Person

It is a crucial task of parenting to respect the child as a separate individual, beginning in infancy and continuing throughout her life. How else can a child ever come to develop a sense of herself and deal with the world out of confidence? Yet there is often a temptation for parents *not* to see the child as her own person. Infants of most species are so incredibly dependent and vulnerable, and human babies are the most helpless of all, with the longest period of dependence on their parents. Furthermore, society encourages parents to regard their children as property and to use diminutives such as "my baby," "Daddy's little girl," or even

"Mama's boy" well into a child's school years or adolescence.

This sense of possession is real, both in terms of your responsibility as the child's parent and your identification of her as a member of your family, but that's really as far as it goes. Any greater claim on the personhood of the child can interfere with her emergence as her own, separate, adult person.

Parents can act out their respect for the integrity of the child as a separate person by responding positively to her initial curiosity and eventual demands to explore the world. Parents are charged with the responsibility to allow the child adequate freedom in which to experience her environment while they watch from the wings just in case there is a need to intervene. Parents should routinely take measurements and reappraise their child and her situation so as to determine what adjustments in the relationship need to be made. This task of attempting to strike a balance between under- and overprotection is required regardless of the child's age, and you will have to determine what the nature of acceptable parental behavior should be. You can do this by taking a step back and acknowledging the physical, intellectual, and social development of your child. In other words, you would not be as physically vigilant of a first grader as you would a toddler playing in the kitchen. You wouldn't follow your child's schoolbus to school each morning to make sure she got off unless you had a compelling reason to suspect danger. Remember, your level of trust is transmitted to your child. Invariably when parents truly understand and come to respect their child as a separate individual, the parent is freed up from having to control the child and the child usually responds by acting responsibly and reasonably. When parents truly *see* their child as her own person with her own wants, thoughts, and feelings, these adjustments in parenting occur more as a matter of course rather than the outcome of a battle of wills.

However, there are real instances where a parent's vigilance is required. Suppose you are afraid of drug dealers in the neighborhood. You can see them take over your street at night, you hear rumors of crack peddlers in the schoolyard, or your child suddenly seems to have cash that you didn't give her. You have cause to be concerned. If you live in a city and fear—not irrationally—that your child may be in danger, you should not be paranoid about making sure he or she gets to school every day. You may have to walk the child to the bus stop and wait there until the bus arrives. These are not overvigilant behaviors if the environment warrants them. You, however, must make the decision rationally and should take the time to tell your child exactly why you are doing what you are doing. Remember, you are not enabling your child by protecting him or her from what you perceive to be real dangers.

How Parents Enable

I don't think parents intend to enable their children. After all, enabling behaviors are as painful to the enabler as they are to the person being enabled. I believe that deep down the most basic and natural impulse of a parent is to act like a strong, competent, and confident adult who raises his or her child with love and honesty. The problem arises when the parent feels incomplete and sees the child as the vehicle for becoming whole. This process is usually unconscious in that it stems from a set of internally held assumptions in which the parent may feel inadequate, unlovable and unloved, insecure, afraid, or a combination of all of these. The parent may even be vaguely aware of loosely perceived feelings of inadequacy, but because this knowledge may produce anxiety, the parent doesn't pursue the emotion to get to a deeper level of understanding.

We all carry within us a mind-set about how we fit into the world. That mind-set addresses such vital questions as:

- "Is the world a safe place?"
- "Do I have the internal resources to manage in the world?"
- "Am I a worthwhile and valuable human being or should I just shut up and be grateful for whatever I get because I am unlovable and really don't deserve anything?"

How we answer these questions determines the personal constructs and assumptions that we will carry inside us as we each make our way in the world. It's like a map always showing us where we are so that regardless of the task or relationship encountered, we have a reference point to guide us. Based on the nature of these assumptions, our lives will either be positive and expansive or negative, fearful, and withdrawn. There is always real concern about the parent-child relationship whenever there is a predominance of the latter.

Parents risk becoming enablers when the set of personal constructs they developed as children is repeatedly confirmed through life experience, namely that, first, the world is generally an unsafe place, and, second, they are inadequate to deal with it effectively. The usual result is inadvertent use of our children as tools to work out our own personal issues or as unwitting victims of our attempts to deny the existence of these issues.

Boundaries

Parents who enable tend to systematically violate their children's boundaries. Because, as children themselves, enablers never developed a sense of their own personal boundaries, they have very little sense of what boundaries would be appropriate for their children. As a result, parents may intrude into their children's personal space physically and/or psychologically. Physical intrusion may range from forever hovering over the child, peering and scrutinizing the child's every move, tending to the child's every possible need even before that need arises, to being either physically abusive and/or sexually exploitive. While hovering and doting convey the message that:

You are very fragile and I must monitor your every breath;

physical and emotional abuse tell the child that:

Everything about you is mine, including your body. You are in this world solely to meet my every need. You have no right for anything else.

Parents who intrude upon their child's space psychologically communicate that their child shouldn't learn to rely on his or her own inner perceptions and common sense. Rather, what their child feels, thinks, or wants, including the child's internal sense of right and wrong, should be determined by the parents. In other words, the child must deny his or her own instincts and rely on the instincts of the parents. This ultimately becomes a basic building block of denial that the adult child eventually communicates to his or her own child.

Parents can overcome their intrusive enabling by recognizing the uncomfortable feelings they experience whenever they assume the burdens of thinking, feeling, and living for and through their children. By acknowledging these feelings, they empower themselves to take the first tiny steps toward letting their children make independent decisions. There is no standard blueprint for when or when not to intervene that can be applied to all specific situations. The basic guideline that I suggest to my clients is to listen to your own internal voice. If you feel burdened by an action you are taking, stand back and don't take it. If you hear your own parent's voice criticizing you or blaming you for something, don't repeat those statements to your child.

In parenting, sometimes a laissez-faire attitude is more than sufficient to provide the necessary guidance and supervision. This doesn't mean you should disregard the obvious presence of danger or let your toddler hurt him- or herself. But it does mean that you should try to create a safe environment for your child and, once created, let the child experiment with that environment without your constant intervention. Practice in small ways that don't create too much anxiety. If you and your child respond positively, lighten up a little more. Gradually, you will find that you don't have to intrude upon your child to show that you are a caring and competent parent.

Working Out Issues

Both physical and psychological intrusions are often the results of the parents' working out or denying their own senses of inadequacy. When parents attempt to work out their personal issues through their relationships with their children, they are reacting to problems that have been dogging them throughout their lives. They intrude their own private battles into the lives of their children. For example, I have been working with a client on her tendency to act out with her daughter her fear of being out of control. What we found was that she carried the burden of being dominated by her family, including her other brothers and sisters, throughout her life. Even in her adult life, my client feels she has to answer to her seventy-year-old sisters and brothers. Jill was never allowed to grow up and feel competent in herself, and as a result she found herself attempting to work it out through her daughter. To her credit, however, Jill is able to acknowledge her tendency to compensate for these feelings and acknowledges that she presents herself as an immovable object to her child, never compromising or willing to hear what her daughter has to say. Through the creation of this rigidly controlling parental style, Jill acts out the part played by her parents and siblings, and unfortunately passes on to her daughter the legacy of being out of control. Parents don't have to be perfect. They only have to acknowledge their vulnerable areas and take steps to adjust for them. Jill, for example, by increasing her awareness of her tendency to control is able to correct for her enabling behaviors so they no longer interfere with her daughter's needs.

Denial

Many enablers consistently perpetuate a denial system when it comes to dealing with their children. In other words, the parent simply pretends that his or her mind-set of the world being an unsafe place and of feeling inadequate to deal with it doesn't exist: "If I say everything is OK, everything is OK and don't tell me otherwise!" In order for this illusion to work, the child is required to buy into it completely and assume that the parent's reality is the child's reality, despite what he or she may see in the outside world. Anybody who challenges that reality is perceived as a threat and summarily silenced just like the little child in *The Emperor's New Clothes.*

Denial is the most destructive root of all parental enabling. The more entrenched the pattern of denial, the greater the resistance to acknowledging its existence in finding a remedy. The enabling continues to build momentum and perpetuates itself over and over. This is much like a person who tells one lie and then another to cover up the first and ultimately becomes entangled in an increasingly intricate labyrinth of self-deception. There is a continual attempt to delude and misconstrue what the parent is really feeling and what is actually occurring in interactions with the child. The denial that occurs in parental enabling is just as insidious as it is with alcoholism.

Denial is very dangerous because of its potential for damaging the fragile and formative ego of the child. Because children constantly seek affirmation from their parents to confirm their perceptions of the world and their worth as people, the reception of a warped view of reality skews the child's perception and serves as a direct challenge to his or her own internal frame of reference. Your child is taught not to trust him- or herself.

It's not easy to counteract a pervasive denial of reality. If you are enabling your spouse to perpetuate denial, you are contributing to it by investing in the denial system. This is especially true if your spouse is tied up by his or her fear that reality is perceived as a serious threat. Your role, as the enabling partner, should be to confront your spouse with reality. Seek help from a licensed psychologist or family therapist if you need it, or from your spouse's employee assistance program (EAP) if the service is available from his or her employer, but don't neglect the problem. You will be asked to engage in a loving confrontation with your spouse in which you should be prepared to describe the reality you perceive and challenge your spouse's denial of it.

At the very least, your spouse's attempt to work out and compensate for feelings of insecurity and inadequacy in the relationship will provide a level of awareness that there is something wrong. This opens the possibility of self-awareness, intervention, and change.

Insecurity

Enablers are typically very insecure individuals. It stands to reason, therefore, that as parents they tend to instill a chilling and excessive fear of the world in their children. Initially, very young children need to develop skills to deal with the outside world. This process is completely instinctive. They begin their socialization by developing trust and a feeling of being safe and secure, at first in the family and next in the immediate environment outside the family.

The parent's role is to ensure that this development takes place first, by letting the child know that he or she is a loved and worthwhile human being, second, by encouraging the child to experiment with his or her newly emerging personality, third, by stimulating the child to place trust in his or her surroundings, and fourth, by not interfering with the child's natural course toward becoming a socialized human being. If the parent impedes the child's ability to develop trust, the child ends up with a very weak foundation on which to build social relationships. From this shaky base all encounters with challenging situations will probably be met with a pervading sense of inadequacy and hesitation.

Children who grow up feeling insecure tend to manifest various forms of avoidance behavior and attempt to sneak through life by avoiding failure rather than aiming at success. Insecurity is instilled in children either through the effects of inadequate parenting during infancy and early childhood or, as mentioned earlier, by the parent attempting to work out his or her unresolved personal issues through the child. These parents are directed by a set of internal and unperceived programming instructions that are almost always proven out by their child's negative actions and tentative behaviors. It becomes a self-fulfilling prophecy, the result of which can be a frightening reflection of the parent's own fears in the behavior of the child.

This is what happened to Jeff who was bright, personable, and even charming, but who rarely allowed himself to experience any positive feelings about his life because of his problems with inadequacy and low self-esteem.

JEFF

How many people do you know who can honestly say they hate themselves? I can honestly say I do. I can't think of one thing good about me. So I can write some rock-and-roll tunes. Big deal! Anybody can do a thing well. When it really counts I'm just not good enough. On the inside I don't feel like I count.

My mother always told me the way things should be, whether it was what I should wear to school, what activities I could get involved in and that I should take piano lessons, and even the friends I should keep! Not only did she tell me I had to go to college, she even told me where I should go to school.

My mother told me that my thinking was wrong all the time. She told me that I had the wrong attitude and that I should change my feelings. She was the one who had the only one correct point of view. Everyone else was wrong.

And Dad just stood there, always watching it all happen. He never once tried to intervene. He rarely stood up for me, even the times that I know he agreed with me! I think he was afraid of taking her on too.

What bothers me most of all is that throughout it all I actually listened. Even though I knew what I really wanted, I always went right along with the program, like I didn't have a right to what I wanted.

Now look at me. I never go out on dates. I'd like to, but I'm afraid of women. I do well if they're married; they like me and I feel at ease. But the minute a good looking girl comes along who's available, I turn into the mess I know myself to be. I'm just afraid of women and I don't think I have anything to offer them.

I had the opportunity to meet Jeff's parents when after eighteen months of individual psychotherapy he finally agreed to have them come in for some family therapy sessions. Though his mother was bright and attractive and presented a confident can-do attitude to the world, deep down she harbored a fear of the world and of being victimized. It took her seeing her adult child in the throes of emotional pain before she finally began to let down her guard and show herself.

His father, on the other hand, initially appeared to be timid, but that turned out to be a cover for a sudden, violent temper. It came out in therapy that the course of Jeff's childhood was frequently rocked by the severe, emotionally violent rage of his father. It would come out of nowhere, completely unpredictable like a summer cloudburst, rocking the family. Both Jeff and his sister grew up with the constant fear of saying or doing the one thing that would trigger his temper. This contributed to Jeff's feeling insecure about himself and his world. Because both his father and mother had skewed perceptions of the world and were basically insecure as well, Jeff's emotional foundation was very fragile. It could not sustain any stress whatsoever.

Through her attempt to shore herself up emotionally, Jeff's mother inadvertently set the stage to enable Jeff. She distorted his perception of the world and challenged the validity of his thoughts and feelings. Although she didn't set out to do so, she helped to enable Jeff to see himself as insecure, dependent, and fragile. At the same time, Jeff's father, through his own silence, enabled his wife to avoid facing her private insecurity and control issues and allowed the damage to be done.

Despite Jeff's appearance and confident demeanor, he is deeply fearful of confrontations and protects his vulnerability. Because these are two of the components on which intimacy is based, Jeff is almost completely handicapped socially and unable to form relationships with women he's attracted to. After years of not feeling validated, Jeff quickly gives up on himself. He avoids challenges, especially interpersonal challenges, and backs down from confrontations even when he knows he's right. Although he is no longer living in his parents' home, he has internalized the communication and the negative affirmations that he often received there. His situation is not anywhere near hopeless, but because he tends to undermine himself, he will have to continue in his struggle to face himself. With time and courage, he can overcome his feelings of insecurity and self-defeating behavior.

Issues of Chemical Dependency and Parental Codependency

We have already described the general family dynamics of enabling when it takes the form of codependency. Parents, however, are in a special position when dealing with children who are suffering from drug or alcohol dependencies. They have to make a thoroughly honest appraisal of their relationship with their children, both as it applies to the chemical dependencies and their roles in the family in general. This is especially important in light of the epidemic of drug abuse sweeping the nation.

If you are a parent with a score on the Enabling Potential Test high enough to be of concern, here are the issues you should be aware of as you confront the problem of your child's experimentation with drugs and alcohol.

Physical Health

The critical concern that parents should have about their children's use of alcohol and other drugs is the physical damage that will inevitably result. There are children in communities today who start to abuse drugs when they are as young as eight and continue to use them regularly throughout their adolescence. These children can come from upper-middle-class subdivisions on the outskirts of Princeton just as easily as they can come from the housing projects in the center of Trenton or Newark. If we assume that treatment and detox for these drug abusers begins at age twenty-five, it would mean that an artificial and foreign chemical has been poisoning their growing bodies for seventeen years. For certain parts of the neurological system, the kidneys, the liver, and the cardiopulmonary system, the damage is probably irreversible by the time the twenty-five-year-old begins treatment. Though there is a wide range of use patterns in terms of type of substance and frequency of use, as well as the manner of administration, the use of substances during adolescence can impair the extensive physiological growth and development that occurs during that time.

Emotional Health

In addition to the physiological damage that drug abuse causes, there is the retardation of emotional growth. There is a biological basis to the emotional damage from drug abuse because of the effects drugs have on the nervous system. Children whose neurons are dying off because of drugs simply don't have the same emotional capacity and resilience as children who are developing physically at a normal rate. Most of this "mature" growth takes place during adolescence, that unique period of rapid development.

The primary emotional task of children during the teenage years is to develop a sense of who they are and to emerge in the world with clearly defined and separate identities. One of the true measures as to how well a child has met the task of adolescence is his or her ability to make meaningful connections with other people. This encompasses a drive to be involved with other people and to be willing to face the emotional, social, and psychological risks that the development of intimacy entails. The main indicator of the successful resolution of your child's adolescence is his or her ability to establish an emotionally intimate or "courting" relationship.

The main problem with adolescents who use any drugs or alcohol at all is that they tend to arrest their emotional development at the age at which the drug abuse began. In other words, a teenage drug abuser may emotionally remain a fourteen- or fifteen-year-old until he or she enters a recovery program. At that point, the young person's emotional development will have to be restarted from where it left off. Researchers believe this phenomenon occurs because of the extreme emotional malleability of most adolescents who use this emotionally turbulent period to experiment with life in order to find themselves and their niche in society.

When children act like "druggies," they slowly begin to take on the characteristics associated with this new crowd to whom they find themselves drawn. Once inside the cycle of alcohol or drug use, the child's actions are reinforced by both the psychological and physically addictive qualities of the substance, peer pressure, and the social reinforcement provided by the new "friends." What we in the treatment community find time after time is that when adolescents come out of a rehabilitation program and begin their recovery processes, they usually have nothing in common with the group that wooed them into the abuse cycle in the first place. The reality is that the former friends are usually nothing more than drinking and drugging buddies, and in most cases there is no depth to the relationships whatsoever. This underscores how much the social development of children is retarded through the use of addictive substances.

Legal Ramifications

The legal ramifications of an adolescent's use of alcohol and other drugs are so deceptively obvious that most people overlook them. Through the use, possession, and distribution of alcohol and all other drugs an adolescent runs the risk of arrest and prosecution.

In addition to the difficulties that being caught up in the legal process entails, it also may lead an otherwise law-abiding youth to feel alienated from social authorities. If this occurs, not only will it impair the child's relations with his or her parents, but it will negatively affect how he or she deals with everyone who, in the adolescent's mind, carries the symbol of authority. This group may include teachers, ministers, and the leaders of sports and other activities with whom the adolescent previously had a positive connection. This can be one of the most difficult ruptures to mend because the adolescent—once alientated, prosecuted, processed by the criminal or juvenile justice system, and manhandled by that system as if he or she were an adult—is rarely able to step back into childhood naiveté or to shoulder the adolescent mantle of invincibility. The child has been compromised. Drugs wipe away the magic of being young, and that is the greatest tragedy of all.

Breaking the law by "buying and possession" also creates a paranoia at being caught and an increased resistance to anyone who threatens to terminate the addiction. Over time, as the child progresses in the addiction and drifts closer and closer to bottom, his or her continued alliance with a taboo substance makes it harder to accept help when it is offered. Unfortunately, the adolescent's life has to come to the point of being so unmanageable that only then is the young person able to overcome his or her own resistance to the constructive intervention of a treatment professional. Up until that time, increased alienation, on top of the normal dose that comes naturally with adolescence, serves only to keep the adolescent distant from the "straight" and healthy world.

Enabling Behaviors You Should Recognize

The way that parents might enable a child who is abusing him- or herself with alcohol or other substances is entirely similar to the pattern of codependency described earlier. Parents in the role of codependents have both a vested interest in the welfare of their adolescent son or daughter and in preserving the appearance of a well-functioning family and their perceptions of themselves as "good parents." There is nothing wrong with the manifest concern that one's child is healthy and does well. The problem centers around having a vested interest in preserving the appearance of normality at all costs, and it is here that enabling enters in the form of codependency.

When parents serve as their child-addict's codependents, all the dynamics of this type of enabling come to be played out in the relationship. The family system tends to be closed and resists any information that runs counter to the established image of the family. This is reflected by both a conspiracy of silence and an extensive system of familial denial. Shot through the interactions of all the players are the assumptions—unspoken statements of denial—that (1) the adolescent does not really have a problem and (2) the child's use of alcohol and other drugs will never change.

How can you not see what's right in front of you? And when you recognize your teenager has a chemical dependency problem how is it you feel so powerless to do anything about it? These are questions you may be asked by people outside the family. The answers lie in the very nature of codependency.

Parents Can Be Blind

The first problem of parents having a chemically dependent child is that they are blind to it. This is usually a function of a lack of education and/or too much denial. Lack of education is inexcusable but understandable. It is something that any caring, well-intentioned and relatively healthy parent needs and should seek out from the hundreds of free sources available to them. In this era of rampant alcohol and drug use among young people it is crucial for all parents to learn about the nature of drugs, signs of their use, and ways to address these issues with children as a preventive measure.

Parents May Treat Chemical Dependency as Something Else

Well-intentioned parents often treat alcohol and drug use as a disciplinary problem when it is a medical problem. Grounding a child with a chemical dependency will do no more to remedy the problem than grounding a juvenile diabetic. Diseases don't respond to punishment, they respond to medical treatment. Parents who believe their child is exhibiting a pattern of habitual and excessive use of any kind of drug, including alcohol, are well advised to seek the consultation of a mental health professional with a specialization in addiction. Professionals without specialized training, however competent they are in their areas of expertise, may prove to be more of a liability than a help if your child is chemically dependent. You should also use the guidance counselor in your child's school as an ally. The guidance counselor may recommend one of the scores of free or almost-free professional treatment programs in your community or may point you to a private substance-abuse therapist. In our list of resources, you will find several references that can prove to be invaluable resources in both the prevention and intervention of alcohol and drug problems with children and teenagers. Remember, it's almost never too early to start educating yourself and your child about drugs and alcohol.

Two-Stage Denial

Denial in the home has more to do with the thin line that separates healthy parenting and unhealthy parenting than it does with actual education. All of us want the best for our children. We also want to think the best of our children. However, our dreams for our children can also blind us from seeing who they really are and what they're doing. This is part of the problem when parents are codependent. With a heavy investment in an illusion of the future, a parent risks overlooking the wonderful qualities of the child in the present and denying the existence of self-esteem, alcohol, and drug-related problems that are begging to be addressed.

The reason a parent is so overly invested in the child's future is linked with the second half of the denial puzzle: the dreams the parents *want* to impose on the child. The two pieces of the puzzle are linked because most parents have preconceived notions about their children. These are OK as long as we call them dreams. They stop being OK when the dreams are compensation for the parent's own failed aspirations and are imposed on the child to the point where the real child gets lost in the parent's illusion. Arthur might be the perennial hard-working assistant manager or "assistant to." Arthur's daughter will have to sit in the executive's chair in order for Arthur's ambitions to be fulfilled. Freddie has worked on the automobile assembly line for his entire life, watching the managers in pin-striped suits go to their power lunches. He wants his son to be in pinstripes no matter what, and he's willing to buy that dream so he can live out his retirement on his son's career.

Such dreams end by up putting children under tremendous stress. As a consequence of the stress the children sometimes have an emotional or chemical-dependency problem and sometimes manifest real physical ills such as headaches, asthma, low-grade fevers, and stomach problems. We call these "somatic" or "psychosomatic" symptoms. Further complicating the matter is the parents' inability to see the chemical dependency because they are looking at the reflection of *themselves* in the child instead of at the child. Parents lapse into total narcissism instead of looking at the facts. Their overinvestment in shoring themselves up through the accomplishments of their children has made it impossible for them to notice the problems the resulting stress has created in the child.

Bruce, a senior at Princeton, tells of the dilemma he faced in his family.

My father is a banker and my mother is an executive secretary. They have always excelled at their work, but felt they've been pretty much failures as parents. Especially my father. I graduated number two in my high-school class. I wanted to be a concert pianist and applied to two music academies and for my parents' sakes I also applied to five Ivy League universities. I got into both academies and four Ivy League schools. Despite my vehement opposition, my father made me go to Princeton. The worst! I wasn't even allowed to major in music or English and if I didn't choose microbiology at Princeton he wouldn't pay. I was angry, but because of the way things operated in my family I didn't show it.

When I was a freshman I had a near nervous breakdown. Although biology was a love of mine in high school, the idea of *having* to take it was too much. I did very well my first semester, but then decided to stop turning in my assignments. I would still do the work. I just wouldn't turn it in. Needless to say, grades indicated a rapid decline, and I got the attention I had wanted from my father, but still he wouldn't budge. That's when I started with the coke. And it took me getting bounced out of school to get help. I hate that I've had to put myself through all this pain to face up to the fact that I want my parents to see and understand me and to accept me for who I am. Although it's taken me a long time to realize it, I'm not such a bad person at all.

Bruce is finally facing the fact that it is not in his power to heal his father's pain. Although it was never said to him directly, Bruce was asked to excel so that his father could feel better about himself. For most of his life Bruce complied, but finally could no longer continue the façade and became addicted to cocaine. Unfortunately, his parents' denial was so complete that they missed many opportunities to intervene early in his addiction.

Identity Absorption Denial

Sometimes the problem of parental denial results not so much from parents who attempt to compensate themselves through their children but from parents whose senses of identity are too closely aligned to the identity of their child. Therapists call this "identity absorption," and it is one of the more critical and *growing* problems in this generation of single-parent families. Simply stated, the parents may not know where he or she ends and the child begins. The child is only an extension or an appendage of the parent. This makes it all the more difficult for the parent to see the child as the child really is and notice any problems the child might be having. What complicates this even more is that because the child feels so tightly bound to the parent, he or she will more than likely be confused as to who he or she is as a separate person. The child will be unable to establish boundaries or stake out territories, and will be forced into more aggressive forms of behavior in trying to establish a separate identity. Given that the main task for adolescents is to find their own identities, the child may be prone to act out negative behaviors purely in an effort to achieve this goal. Some of these exploratory activities may prove to be dangerous, some will inevitably involve drug and alcohol abuse. In this way, the parent's denial of the adolescent's independent personality creates the situation that results in negative behavior. But because the parent can't see the child for the individual he or she is, the parent denies the clear evidence of substance abuse, and the child sinks deeper into addiction. The parent also realizes that addressing the addiction means that the child will have to go through a form of recovery in which he or she will establish an independent identity. This is like a death sentence to the parent who would rather let the child poison him- or herself rather than become a separate individual.

Maybe you can see how this problem tends to crop up in single-parent families more often than it does in two-parent households. But it occurs more often in families where one parent is a dysfunctional addict and the other is an active codependent. The codependent acts as if he or she is the single parent holding the family together and absorbs the identity of the only child, eldest child, or youngest child. In single-parent households there is a form of bonding between parent and child that can take place in which the parent imposes an "us versus them" reality on the child. In order to reinforce this emotional state of siege, the parent absorbs the child's individual identity to such an extent that there is neither parent nor child: They become one emotional entity. The child begins to suffocate emotionally while the parent works overtime to remain vigilant to encroachment from the outside world. The harder the child tries to resist, the tighter the parent twists the emotional knots.

After her divorce, Karlene, an adult child of an alcoholic, experienced these feelings as she tried to protect her fragile sense of identity against the demands of her ex-husband's family.

All I really had left were two years of undergrad education and my eleven-year-old, Heather. I'd left college to help put Paul through law school after I got pregnant with Heather. So when Paul

walked out, I didn't even have a college degree to fall back on.
Paul's mother was solicitous enough in wanting to help, sending
the kid clothes, even paying for the riding lessons that Heather
needed like another head. I was in no position to turn my back on
the family at first. Eventually, I got my back up. Heather was
beginning to look, act, and even talk like Paul's mother. She would
come home from a weekend with Paul and give me the same
disapproving-eyebrow look that Paul's mother always did. She was
my only child. I left college rather than get an abortion so she
would be born, while Paul went to law school, and she winds up
disapproving of me. That was all I needed. They were turning her
against me.

I packed the kid up, pulled her out of school, and got us on a
plane for Madison. Maybe my mom wasn't much of a parent when
I was younger, but she was on the wagon and could find us a cheap
place to stay until I found a job. I didn't even listen to Heather
when she screamed at me. I just repeated: "It's you and me" and
"I'm all you got." She didn't buy it at first, but she seemed to come
around. And after we found our new place, she even seemed to
like it.

The problems started within six months after we moved to Madison. Heather was always precocious and started hanging around
with a crowd of high-school kids. No matter how much I complained that she was too young for them, it had no effect. She
began dressing in black leather jackets and T-shirts, wearing knee-
length boots and bike chains around her waist, putting blue streaks
in her hair, and wearing little upside-down crosses as earrings. The
values I had taught her, the rules I laid down, seemed to have
made not even a dent.

The night the police called and said they had picked her up for
possession of cocaine was probably the worst night of my life, even
worse than when Paul told me that his "options were foreclosed"
by our marriage. Heather and I had been a team when all the
world turned hostile. She was what I had sacrificed everything to
have. How could she have done this to me?

If any of this sounds familiar enough to be uncomfortable, you
should try to examine your relationship with your child by honestly describing his or her personality in terms of the child, rather
than yourself. If it seems too difficult at first, don't be disheart-
ened. Involve your child in these discussions by opening up the
channels of communication until you can almost see life through

his or her eyes. Encourage children to talk about what they do of a day. Ask them to be as honest as possible in their descriptions of school, their friends, their successes, and their disappointments. Don't be confrontational and, above all, don't be judgmental! You will eventually get the hang of it and be able to see your children as independent entities. Once you do this, the child will automatically step back from the brink in his or her establishment of a separate identity. Your adolescent will still seek to challenge you with forms of outrageous behavior at times, but as long as they don't involve substance abuse or criminally destructive activities, they probably won't backfire. Both of you will be the better for it.

Help for Parents in Denial

Codependent parents have to get help for themselves before they can help their children. Even after parents finally break through their own denial, they will still have tremendous difficulty in intervening in their child's problem. The reason is, the codependency of the parents will present as much, if not more, of a problem to treat as their child's chemical dependency. Accordingly, many parents feel powerless to do anything about their child's pattern of substance abuse. This disarming of themselves is something that codependent parents do quite well. "What am I supposed to do, tie him to a chair in his room? I can't do that!" I have heard that and similar arguments from affluent people who feel that it would simply be uncivilized to confront their child firmly and decisively. I have also heard this from parents of inner-city teenagers who feel overwhelmed by the widespread drug use so endemic to their communities. While I have far more empathy for those parents living in the inner city and without the financial means to change their environment, there is a remarkably similar circumstance to them and their more affluent counterparts. All of these parents are codependents in emotionally challenging and potentially life-threatening predicaments.

Steps You Should Take

Regardless of the environment, our tasks as parents are to address the problems that plague our children. You can set about this task in the following manner.

1. SET LIMITS.   All children need limits and need attention. Rather than abdicating our parental roles, as codependents do, we have a responsibility to set reasonable limits and to confront the chemical dependency problems of our children in constructive ways. Work out reasonable limits of behavior with your children and *stick to them.* Your kids will appreciate your following up on decisions you and they have made together. If there's a problem, confront your child in a loving manner: "I notice you've been having a problem with [school, eating, sleeping, specific friends, appearance, attitude, curfews, chores around the house]. Is there anything I should know about?" That may be all it takes to start a meaningful dialogue with your child. But if it requires more following up, don't shrink away from the task. Use the limits you and your child established together as a means to measure any changes in behavior. A little tension now may save a whole lot of grief later on.

2. ASSUME THE LOVE; WORK ON THE PROBLEM.   Many codependent parents are afraid of losing the love and affection of their children, but as many of us know, the temporary disapproval and anger of teenage children is pretty much standard fare. To live your life in the hope of getting unqualified approval from your child is to give far too much power to that child. Don't be afraid of being on the receiving end of their disapproval if they do something that you don't like. Call them on it! Confront them in a loving way and challenge them to face their own disapproval of you as an adult, while discussing any problems they may have. Be aware that your kids will love you even if they may not like you because of a specific issue. Once you solve the problem, the adversarial nature of your relationship will quickly disappear.

3. ENCOURAGE INDEPENDENCE.   If our kids hang around us too much and ogle us with approving eyes, we should know that

something is very wrong. Kids have to be independent. If you're an enabler, you know you are afraid of this. You can get over it by acknowledging your fear openly. Share your fears with your children, if necessary, that their independence is threatening to you. If you simply allow your fear to force you into binding your children to you with hoops of steel, you're surrendering to the fear. In addition, you're surrendering yourself to the child rather than letting the child grow. Your child has to grow. It's a law of nature. By hanging on, you're stunting that growth and impairing the child's ability to think and live independently. If you understand the stakes, and acknowledge the truth about your own codependency and enabling behavior, you will have an easier time making the right decisions.

4. BE HONEST WITH YOURSELF AND YOUR CHILDREN. "Know the truth," we were taught, "and the truth will set you free." First, acknowledge the truth about your own codependency. Then acknowledge your enabling behaviors in the family. Finally, assess the ways in which you may be enabling your children. By overcoming your codependency and getting on to the business of honestly addressing the upbringing of your teenage children, whatever it brings, you will be able to look in the mirror without remorse. Both you and your child will be better people for it and better able to get in touch with your own feelings for one another.

Eating Disorders

Eating disorders are special kinds of chemical and emotional dependencies that many parents routinely help to perpetuate without even realizing what they're doing. Parents can fall into the enabling trip when it comes to food just because their kid looks too skinny or too fat. In the absence of a medical doctor's opinion about a child's weight or nutritional intake, a parent's dietary decision can be completely subjective. If you have scored high enough on our Enabling Potential Test to be concerned, you should pay special attention to the types of conscious and unconscious "food messages" you may be transmitting to your child. Unfortunately, it's all too easy to enable a child into a serious food addiction or eating disorder.

One of the greatest sources of concern to parents is to find that their child has an eating disorder. Regardless of whether the child has bulimia, anorexia nervosa, a food allergy, or a compulsive overeating condition, this has to be considered as a serious and potentially life-threatening problem. Like chemical dependencies, eating disorders are essentially a family disease whose effects are profoundly magnified by a pattern of enabling in the child's relationship with her parents. In fact, it has been estimated that over 30 percent of those diagnosed with an eating disorder also abuse themselves with alcohol or other drugs.

There are a variety of ways in which eating disorders may manifest themselves: uncontrolled eating, compensatory snacking, single-food addiction, starvation dieting, and binge-purge syndromes. As clinical as these types of disorders sound, they are all insidious and camouflaged by the child's normal habits or daily routine.

Symptoms of anorexia nervosa, for example, can be easily overlooked by parents who dismiss the behavior as yet another silly fad being tried out by a daughter (its frequency is much higher for females than males) and her friends. While this lack of awareness may be innocent, it may also be evidence of the parents' denying that there might be anything wrong. As in the case of chemical dependency, the reasons for parental denial vary greatly, but usually center around the perception that the truth, whether it be about the daughter or the parent, would be too great a burden to face. As a consequence of parental denial and enabling, the eating disorder may be left unchecked and allowed to progress to the point of physical complications coupled with the emotional trauma.

Parents who enable their children to continue their eating disorders sometimes choose inaction out of a sense of futility or powerlessness. These disorders, however, are not in anyway hopeless provided that the problem is identified and proper treatment is provided. The enabling takes place out of problems inherent in the parents, not the child. Unfortunately the effects of the enabling are detrimental to the child.

Those who are anorexic are suffering with an obsession with having to be thin to the point of starving themselves. Although there is an endocrinal aspect to the disorder, there is also an emotional component. Usually the emotional stability of the child is disturbed to the point of having a distorted body image, depression, and sometimes even thoughts of suicide. On the other hand, bulemic children are lost to a pattern of craving for food and binge eating that is followed by extreme or violent measures to purge the food they've consumed. These methods include self-induced vomiting, obsessive fasting, and a compulsive or excessive use of laxatives. Most of this activity has been associated with adolescent women, although adolescent men may display some of the same behaviors.

Other anorexic behaviors that have been associated with adolescents and even older teenagers involve strenuous exercise regimens that are repeated day after day, long after reasonable physical fitness goals have been achieved. While there may be valid reasons for most regimens of this type, such as exercises for team or varsity sports, body-building competitions, or individual weight-lifting goals, these routines may be camouflaging seriously pathological or obsessive behaviors. This is an alternate side of anorexia nervosa.

Symptoms of Eating Disorders Among Adolescents

Be especially attentive to teenagers who may:

- Binge on specific foods or food groups uncontrollably.
- Indulge in alternating periods of binging and starvation dieting.
- Diet until they are excessively thin.
- Overexperiment with whatever food or diet fad is most current.
- Gravitate obsessively from diet to diet, as if dieting were the child's only activity.
- Repeatedly perform extreme exercise routines that go well beyond the point of a normal and reasonable approach to fitness.
- Become unduly fascinated or even fixated with achieving a hyperdeveloped or grotesquely developed musculature.

Underlying Emotional Problems Indicated by Eating Disorders

Let me stress again that there is nothing wrong with strenuous exercise or healthy dieting. Most Americans routinely overeat anyway. However, the obvious obsessive or compulsive attitudes that sometimes accompany anorexic and bulimic behaviors are symptoms the child is having serious problems that call for parental attention. Overeating oftentimes arises out of an interpersonal dynamic that has its roots in family relationships. Regardless of the eating disorder, an attempt to cope with the emotional stress of living is being made through the use of food. This attempt at coping is ultimately nonproductive because it usually gives rise to feelings of guilt, shame, low self-esteem, and depression. Parents who do not address these problems head on are enabling their child to continue down a very dangerous road that not only increases isolation from peers, but may also lead to death through physiological complications or, at worst, suicide.

Parents are in a key position to effect change by addressing these problems early on. Through the use of professional treatment programs and the Twelve Steps of Overeaters Anonymous and O-Anon, a great deal can be done to turn a young life around. What is ultimately required, however, is for parents to be willing to face themselves, their child's feelings, and the interpersonal dynamics that may have contributed to the development of the eating disorders. Without this honesty, we can only expect the enabling to continue.

Underlying Physical Causes of Eating Disorders

Enablers of children who might have compulsive eating disorders should recognize that there are often clear physical and behavioral causes for the problem besides the emotional causes we talked about. These physical causes should be raised with your child's pediatrician or your family medical doctor, as well as with a counselor or psychotherapist. Sometimes the causes are physiological or metabolic disorders that will respond to medical treatment. Among the broad variety of typical physiological causes of eating disorders are:

1. *An often clear misunderstanding of nutritional requirements.*
One of the most paradoxical aspects of compulsive overeaters is that they have never learned the basic facts about food, nutrition, or eating habits. As a result, they overeat certain foods just to catch up with their daily nutritional requirements. However, because their diets don't provide even the minimal requirements, they never manage to eat what they need, and as a result, live in a state of chronic malnutrition. If your children seem to display tendencies toward this behavior, they might literally be starving themselves everyday, even while they gorge themselves on food.

2. *The presence of toxins in packaged foods.*
What seems like a compulsion to overeat might simply be a reaction to certain substances in packaged foods. What are perfectly safe preservatives and additives according to the FDA might be deadly toxins to the systems of some people, especially if they are taking certain prescription drugs or other chemical substances. Cross drug/toxin reactions may cause bloating, overweight, eating binges, periods of self-starvation, rapid and uncontrolled weight loss, respiratory or cardiovascular reactions.

3. *Inadequate childhood diets—the Twinkie Syndrome.*
You don't have to be a professional nutritionist to understand that children need certain food types in their diets that adults don't need at all. For much the same reasons, there are foods adults may eat routinely that should not under any circumstances be a part of your child's diet. In other words, the body's nutritional needs change as one gets older and what children require as their bodies rapidly build new tissue and burn off excess fat, adults simply store away—usually around their midsections and thighs. However, if children don't get the food nutrition their developing bodies require, they could conceivably go through the rest of their lives in a chronic state of malnutrition unless their adult diets compensate for what they didn't have as children. A very high percentage of the population of food addicts fall into this category, and can be helped medically, before they are

treated psychologically, by a change in diet. Obviously, the earlier the medical and nutritional attention they receive, the better. It makes the behavioral change much easier because once their diets are corrected, they are no longer fighting against themselves. If you are an enabler and having a difficult time confronting your child on this issue, you can use the medical indicators of a severe nutritional disorder as a wedge to begin the discussion.

4. *Genetic predisposition to nutritional disorders.*

This might be a tough pill to swallow, but some people are obese simply because their parents are obese and their parents' parents were obese and, bluntly put, that's all there is to it. So if your kid is obese and your spouse is obese and your mother- or father-in-law was obese, the obesity may well be out of your hands. About the best you can do is to control the obesity with a sensible diet and a strict avoidance of the danger foods that trigger binges. If your child eats sensibly and he or she is still obese, just be supportive, recognize the danger signals of food addiction, and encourage a medically supervised exercise program to control your child's blood pressure and cholesterol. I mention this category only because if you are an enabler in this area, you're going to burn yourself up with guilt because the pounds aren't melting off your kid. It's not your fault. Blame the genes, but don't feel guilty about it. And don't fatten yourself up just to keep pace with your kid's genes. Encourage your children to develop positive self-esteem—as difficult as that can sometimes be—and be supportive of them in their travails. Just remember: It's not your fault!

5. *Genetic predisposition to metabolic disorders.*

Whatever was said about genetic predisposition to obesity holds for this category as well. Metabolic disorders can create all sorts of strange behaviors, from binging on specific foods to the inability to lose weight. In many cases, these disorders don't even become apparent until the person has reached middle age or later. Therefore, if you know you have a tendency to be a rescuer, victim, or adjuster, you should try to find out whether a real change in your partner's eating habits is a medical problem. If so, then you can help your partner through the problem without turning yourself into a martyr.

6. *Physiological reactions to substance abuse.*

What you might perceive as your child's simple overweight problem may turn out to be an indicator of substance abuse or alcoholism. Substance abusers and alcoholics rarely go through their addictions without some sign that they are deteriorating physically. More often than not, that sign manifests itself as either a chronic obesity or a gradual loss of weight. The dramatic weight loss or gain is actually a result of the chemical changes taking place in the child's body as he or she becomes physically addicted to whatever substance is being consumed. Drinkers generally tend to gain weight. Not only are the typical alcoholic beverages, especially gin, whiskey, and vodka, high in calories, they encourage drinkers in the early stages to consume large amounts of food. Your child's body shape will begin to change, and the telltale signs of a sagging beer belly will, at some point in the process, become obvious. If you see clear changes in your child's shape and eating behavior, you might be looking at a substance abuse problem, not simply an eating disorder. Don't neglect it. Don't enable your child into thinking he or she is successfully pursuing an addiction or drinking problem right under your nose. The longer you delay the inevitable confrontation, the worse off your child will become.

7. *Allergic reactions to specific foods or chemicals.*

Your children may suffer from allergies to specific foods that cause them to have severe physical reactions. Oddly enough, these food allergies also involve addictions to the same foods. People may be allergic to sodium yet heavily salt their food so that they retain water, blow up like balloons, and spend twenty-four hours writhing with a migraine headache. People can also be addicted to chocolate and binge so heavily on candy that they break out in rashes and experience painful gastrointestinal disorders. I have one such client who revealed to me that his mother gave chocolate candies as a reward for his being good at the end of every day. Even when he didn't particularly want any candy, he had to eat it just to make his mother feel good. I suggest that this is a classic example of cross-enabling between parent and child. The mother used a reward system to enable the child to behave himself so as to please her, and the child, in turn, literally swallowed the rewards to keep on pleasing her when he probably would have behaved himself even without the reward. That's how convoluted parental enabling can become. Now, at age fifty and chronically overweight, he is so addicted to chocolate bars that he stashes them in his attaché case so he never runs out.

Advice for Enablers of Children with Eating Disorders

As an enabler to a child with an eating disorder, you should be aware that your child lives in a state of continual frustration. Compulsive overeaters use food to gratify themselves. In other words, because they can't get happy from the things that should make most people happy, they eat their way to happiness.

Most adult compulsive overeaters are so frustrated that they see their inability to satisfy their immediate appetites as a form of failure. Consequently, they are always grabbing for snacks. If they have a craving for an exotic ice cream, they will drive for miles just to get it. This becomes their success for the day, but it is only momentary. Once they have consumed the ice cream, they are usually so overcome with remorse, they require more food to ease the pain. You can see that food can easily become a form of medication for these individuals, salving the pain and easing the frustration they experience as a rule. Eating becomes a fulfilling act, a completely inappropriate emotional reaction to what confronts them in the outside world. You may be able to prevent your child from becoming an adult compulsive overeater by short-circuiting your passive or active enabling behaviors now, while he or she is young enough to benefit.

Your child's behavior can actually force you to become an enabler. Quite literally, if you provided no food whatsoever, your child would starve. Therefore, within the very context of your parenting, sustaining your child can become easily misconstrued as feeding his or her compulsion. What's worse, it is not only very easy to enable a compulsive overeater, the enabling process and the addiction themselves are contagious, spreading from one person to another in the family. For example, I treat many overweight families for whom meals have become an expression of their loyalty toward the family unit, a form of "us against them."

Eating has become a ceremonial sharing. For one member to step off the treadmill is interpreted by the other as a denial of their emotional bond. In this way the overeater enables the enabler to become an overeater, and the two of them exist in a joint codependency on food that may have nothing to do with food *qua* food and everything to do with their fears of loneliness and emotional frustration. This is a vicious cycle that engulfs all members of a compulsive's family and threatens to turn their other children into food addicts as well. Once addicted, these children will grow up with many of the same frustrations and needs for emotional compensation that their parents have and will transmit these to a new generation of children. This is the insidious cycle of addiction and codependency at work.

Fortunately, there is an entire universe of help and support for enabling parents and their children with eating disorders. People who want to overcome their compulsive eating habits can do so painlessly and inexpensively without having to undergo extensive analysis or therapy of any kind. I have seen startlingly dramatic results in clients who have had their children's nutritional disorders medically evaluated and have established diets, firm limits, and boundaries for the entire family. Often, when there is no underlying medical factor, the eating disorder is the result of a family dynamic, an interaction between parent and child or among siblings. Once addressed, dysfunctional family dynamics tend to clear up rather quickly, if the parents understand their patterns of enabling behaviors and consciously remedy them. Parent-child relationships actually get stronger, families get healthier, and most of the collateral frustrations that accompany the obese life-style seem to vanish even before the target goals are achieved. It seems as though just the act of losing weight or committing to lose weight is a kind of breakthrough.

CONFRONTING YOUR CHILD.   If you have been enabling your child to overeat, you have it within your power to turn your behavior around and help your child overcome his or her eating disorders. The soundest advice is for you to remember that if you are not actively challenging the child with eating disorders to recognize that he or she has a problem, you are actively part of that problem. Don't blame yourself or respond with a guilt trip. Just take a hard look at the ways you encourage—either subtly or directly—your child to eat or starve and take a fearless moral inventory of your motives. If you approach it honestly, you will come to the inescapable conclusion that every day you delay the inevitable intervention is a day you've lost. Ask yourself:

1. How do I subtly or actively encourage my child to overeat or compulsively undereat?
2. Do I use food as part of a reward/punishment system?
3. Did my parents or my spouse's parents use food as part of a reward/punishment system?
4. Do I ask my child to please me by eating?
5. Does my child routinely become frustrated at mealtimes?
6. Does my child express sadness or happiness through eating?
7. Does my child stash food?
8. Does my child binge on specific foods?
9. Does my child seem to have any physical reactions to specific foods?
10. Does my child's behavior change after eating specific foods?

If your answer to any of these questions is yes, then assess your own and your spouse's behavior about food. Acknowledge any enabling behaviors you may have and talk them over with your spouse. Whatever you do, you're going to have to make a mutual decision about your children. Maybe you'll decide to seek help from a licensed, certified family therapist who is qualified as a substance abuse counselor. Maybe you will seek help from one of the many support groups listed in "Support Sources." Or, maybe, you'll decide not to enable one another to enable your children. Refer to our five-step program and to chapter 10 "The Enabler's Toolkit." But whatever you do, make sure that you consult with your child's pediatrician or family doctor. Eating, after all, is a medical issue as well as an emotional one.

Irresponsibility

Remember the kid from your old neighborhood you thought was a spoiled brat? Did you ever wonder how it was that he came to be spoiled in the first place? It's likely that he was the victim of parental enabling. His parents probably were attempting to hold themselves together and at the same time deny their own doubts about themselves by acting particularly indulgent toward their child. Spoiling children is an act of enabling because it allows children to take no responsibility for their actions. It's an act of denial because the parents deny the reality of the children's misbehavior. It's an antisocial act because the parents communicate to children that they need face no consequences from other people for their actions. Spoiling cripples a child by impairing his or her ability to integrate into society as he or she gets older.

Children are natural social beings. If pointed in a positive direction, they act on their own to continue to develop healthy attitudes and become socially responsible. This is why it's so important for parents to create a healthy, supportive, nurturing, and mutually respectful family environment. On the other hand, in the absence of such an environment, children tend to adapt and follow the customs of the household. In some particularly dysfunctional families, for example, children are apt to take on the roles displayed by the parents. If children see that anger, violence, and emotional blackmail are the ways conflicts are resolved, then they will learn to incorporate these behaviors and attitudes into their repertoire of social skills. Similarly if children are taught that the sun rises and sets on their whim, they will come to expect that others treat them as specially as their parents do. The teaching of this kind of self-centeredness has detrimental effects when it is time for a child to build healthy adult relationships.

Why would parents spoil their child and set him or her up with a set of false expectations about the world? Why treat their child so special that he or she has difficulties in making friends as a child and in sustaining meaningful relationships as an adult?

As with the other forms of enabling, the intent is often honest and sincere. The parents who enable their children in this manner are guilty of working some of their own issues out through their children. In my practice I have witnessed these scenarios repeatedly in the families of parents who are angry that "I have been shit on my whole life and my kid is going to show them," or who feel inadequate as people and put their whole life into their child, or who attempt to get the emotional connection that is missing in the marital relationship out of the relationship with the opposite sexed child. In the case of the latter, the child is given the lure of tremendous emotional gratification and singular focus and as a result finds himself carrying too great an emotional burden: to fulfill the emotional emptiness of his mother. The exact opposite can happen with a father and a daughter. This is called emotional incest, and it is a growing problem, especially in single-parent households.

Regardless of the exact form of the irresponsibility that the child is enabled to act out, the fact is that the parent responsible is doing that child a tremendous disservice. It does not matter whether the child may come to see himself or herself as beautiful, handsome, brilliant, or talented, these special characteristics are being used by the parent in a futile attempt to fill an empty void or heal an old wound. The consequence for the child is the development of a narcissistic personality to whom nobody can ever come close.

Unspoiling Your Child

This will take hard work and the road will be bumpy, but it will be a refreshing experience for you, your child, and your spouse.

- First, you will have to learn to listen to your feelings when dealing with your children. If it feels bad, don't do it. No matter how much your children want you do to something— whether it's letting them stay up later when they should go to bed, skipping a nap when you know they're acting tired and grouchy, going outside when you don't want to go outside, or taking the car when you want the car for yourself—do what you think is right.
- Next, you must to learn to act out of love, not out of fear. If you're afraid of your child's disapproval, you are a prisoner in your own home. Once your child realizes that by withholding

approval he or she can control your actions, you're nothing more than a hostage. In reality, what's happening is that your old dysfunctional anxiety feelings from your family of origin are kicking in. One of your parents was able to dictate your actions by the granting or withholding of approval. You were taught to send out a signal: "I'm looking for approval and will do anything for it." And you send that signal out to your child. Your child picks up on it and assumes the role of your disapproving parent. But if you act out of love and not fear of disapproval, you will break the pattern of enabling behavior.

- Learn to say "stop." One of the insidious aspects of enabling behaviors is that they build on each other. A small surrender or sacrifice here leads to a bigger sacrifice somewhere else, and finally a big surrender on another issue. As the enabler, you don't know where to call a halt. You don't want to nitpick over small issues and you know that it's easy to get along by going along. The problem is, however, that you know your child or spouse will take advantage of you on every issue because that's the signal you send out. Since you don't say stop until it's too late, why should they? In effect, you're placing the burden on them not to take advantage of you while you make it easy for them to do it. You have to take the responsibility. If you can say stop before events spin out of control, you will have learned an important lesson, you will not put yourself out inappropriately for someone else, and you will feel better about yourself. Therefore, when you feel that your child is taking advantage of you, just say "Stop."

- Get your children to talk to you. One of the things I've noticed in family therapy is that spoiled children routinely will not communicate with their parents. They may be surly or sullen, but they will rarely give their parents the courtesy of a dialogue. Therefore, I urge my clients to talk to their kids, even it if means turning off the TV by pulling out the plug. If you can get your kids to talk to you, get yourself to listen to them, you and they will be a lot happier. Much of what we call the spoiled child syndrome is the result of parents who throw goodies and privileges at their children as a way to compensate for not really communicating with them. That's just another form of enabling.

- You and your child should mutually set limits on behavior and privileges. We raised the issue of setting limits earlier in the chapter, but it bears mentioning again here in the context of unspoiling your child. Setting limits not only shows your child that you love and nurture him or her, it also shows that you're not about to sit back and allow your child to set his or her own standards of behavior. Setting limits doesn't mean coming down on your kid like a tyrant. It does mean opening up a dialogue with the child about behavior, your expectations, what types of behavior he or she comes in contact with at school or in other social contexts, your child's expectations of you, and his or her own wants and needs.

- Follow through on commitments, promises, and punishments. Children can see right through empty promises and threats. Commitments that are made and quickly forgotten lose all their meaning for children who must rely on the truth of their parents' words. If you can't follow through on a commitment or a promise, at least tell your child why and what you intend to do about it. That lets the child know that he or she is important enough for you to show concern. You would be surprised to know how much your child needs you to keep your word, even if that means following through on punishments. Your punishments should be reasonable, they should be appropriate to whatever you're punishing your child for, and they should be carried out or addressed immediately. To forget about them or overlook that you made them only tells the child that you don't care about your own word and probably care less about the child.

- Avoid resorting to physical or abusive punishment at all costs. Abusive punishment simply tells the child that he or she is worthless. Over the years, abusive comments and punishments reinforce the message of worthlessness and the child actually grows up thinking he or she is a worthless adult. You love your child. At the very least your child is worth being loved. That means the child is not worthless and you shouldn't convey the message that he or she is. Therefore, don't use abusive language, don't attack your child's self-esteem, and don't even hint that your child is not worthwhile. If you must criticize, criticize the behavior not the person. "I'm disappointed in what you just did"; "I know that's not the way you want to act"; "You and I have to talk about how you've been behaving in school before it gets any more serious"; and comments such as these are the appropriate ways to address antisocial or negative behavior.

Paradoxically, attacking children, making them feel worthless, and physically abusing them have a counter affect on their behavior. It enables them to act irresponsibly when they're not being punished or abused. Ask any child who has grown up in an abusive home and he or she will tell you that children who are abused are also spoiled. Children who are abused and live in constant terror tend to test the limits of that terror by committing negative and antisocial acts when they believe they won't be caught or punished. You might be surprised to learn that many spoiled children, even the spoiled brat from your old neighborhood, were emotionally and physically abused at home. At the very least, their parents alternate between overindulgence and extreme punishment so often that the children have no reasonable boundaries or models of behavior.

Being Nice

I have said before that "being nice," or "overniceness," is often used as a cover for codependent and other types of enabling behavior. The concern about niceness as a specific type of enabling is of particular concern when it comes to parenting because the family is almost exclusively the source of its origin. Parents teach us many things. As parents we hope that more of the positive stuff gets through to our child than the negative stuff. However, a special caution is required in looking out for the inadvertent development of being nice. In the sense of it as yet another form of dysfunctional behavior, overniceness generally springs from a felt need to cover, hide, distort, or deny feelings, thoughts, or events. It's a form of camouflage that's especially effective in American society. In Asian societies, it actually becomes a source of personal power and a measure of social status. Overniceness, when practiced effectively or actively used as a tool, serves a real function, making it difficult to condemn outright unless it's obviously being used in a dysfunctional way. It can be a tough call!

Perhaps functional/dysfunctional overniceness is best expressed by the character Elwood P. Dowd in the play *Harvey*. When Dowd, who is a "tippler," is being interviewed by a psychiatrist at a sanitarium his sister wants him committed to, he explains how his mother once told him that in this world you can either be "oh so smart or oh so nice." "I tried being oh so smart," he tells the doctors, "and it didn't work. That's why I'm oh so nice." Being nice worked for Dowd because he used it from personal strength. However, being nice can also be a long-term dysfunctional behavior if the person is constantly frustrated with the world.

A child learns overniceness as a form of enabling from a parent who conveys the subtle message:

I feel very fragile. When I hear people's disapproval and judgment I feel devastated. I am so afraid of being hurt that I want you to protect me from all potential pain. You can do this for me by holding back any feelings and thoughts that may upset me if you share them. I don't even want you to acknowledge them to yourself. I also want you to pretend there is nothing wrong, even when we both really know otherwise. I expect that you will do this for me and I will do it for you.

One of the significant assumptions contained within this message is that because the world is a dangerous place and all people are easily hurt and damaged, the child will be hurt as well. It's a consequence of .dealing in human society. Relationships must therefore be entered into cautiously and their survival is contingent upon the judicious selection of words and feelings expressed to the other. It is further assumed that a certain element of deception and shading of the truth is required in order for relationships to work. This of course is not viewed as lying; it's all done in the spirit of "protecting" the other person and for the "well-being" of the relationship.

One of the ways children get the message to enable parents is through their parents enabling them. This can happen in many ways. For example, a mother makes much more out of a three-year-old's falling off a hobbyhorse than is warranted (the child learns that mom has an investment in his *needing* her care); or a child's weak academic performance is greeted by a father's almost pleading "All I want for you to be is average" (she learns that she should choose to excel only at her own risk, that it may be too threatening to her father); or a son hears from his mother that everything he does is just wonderful whether it really is or not (he learns that his mother doesn't want him to feel bad just as she wishes never to face disappointment because it might be too painful to bear).

In the first example, the child risks developing a pattern of being rewarded not for his independence, but for his neediness, especially with women. The risk in the second is that a daughter learns from her father to short-circuit her pursuit of excellence in order to gain the approval of men. In the last example, the risk is that the child will not trust when something positive is said to him because how can he really know for sure? In all three of these scenarios the children have been enabled by their parents to strive for less than their potential and have learned the counter-productive interpersonal skill of not being forthright, honest, and direct with others. Rather than feeling guilty that they might risk hurting another or face the potential devastation of being hurt themselves, they decide instead to shut it down and simply be nice.

On the basis of all the people and families who have come to me for counseling over the years, I am certain that there are as many different forms of parents' enabling their children as there are different families. Parental enabling is so insidious that I consider the denial that always accompanies it to be at least as powerful in holding all the individuals in the family in check as that of alcoholism. A client once came to me who described how her enabling tendencies overlapped her relationship with her nine-year-old:

> Everything I do and in every relationship I enter, I attempt to get rejected. I learned that's what should be expected from my mother. I always tried to please her and got only her angry disgust. I'm aware now of playing this out with our Joseph. I always second guess what I'm thinking and feeling with him, forever trying to get him to not reject me. And what does he do? He turns ice cold and withdraws. I don't know how I did it, but I taught him to be withholding exactly the way my mother always did.

Unfortunately for Ruth, her fishing expedition to engage her son in friendship turned out for the worse. She acted so nice to him that he saw right through it and rejected her as she has come to expect time and time again. Because Ruth hasn't yet come to terms with both her tendency to enable and the emptiness in her from which it springs, she has deprived Joseph of a mother he can look to for nurturance, guidance, and support. In giving him the power to reject her, Ruth placed an enormous burden on his shoulders. It is a burden that nine-year-olds don't know how to carry without negatively affecting their future relationships.

"Being nice" is used to control what people think and how they behave. If parents know themselves to be either emotionally fragile or inadequate in their abilities to affect change in their environment, the chances are that this very knowledge is disconcerting. It is therefore rather understandable that there would be an effort to protect themselves from the upset that would naturally follow an acknowledgment of this truth. This often takes the form of a request that their children pretend that the fragility or inadequacy does not exist. Children are no fools, and they can certainly hear a request from a parent even when it is not overtly given. Consequently, they quickly and quite unconsciously learn how to comply. Unfortunately this is only the beginning of their problems because as the previous examples indicate, learning to be nice has a profoundly disabling effect on attempts to form satisfying interpersonal relationships.

The Great Truths of Enabling

It is important to remember that regardless of the form of parental enabling, as is true with all forms of enabling, there are at least:

1. An implicit agreement between the parent and the child to not tell the real truth.
2. The development of an alliance to "protect" each other from the pain that might emerge if each were really seen and understood.
3. The perpetuation of a false reality upon which the relationship floats.

As we might expect from such an unhealthy alliance, there is a great deal of anxiety. However, this is usually not consciously experienced; rather it remains a constant, always there, churning immediately below the surface. There is a consistent attempt to avoid pain at any cost. The reality is that in the process of avoiding pain, there is a washing out of the color of the relationship that could lead to gain. Most recovering enablers find that the sense of personal relief and freedom that comes from being real, honest, and direct with a loved one far exceeds the anxiety and other uncomfortable feelings that emerge in the process of facing the fears that had long since held them back.

It is important to remember that enabling is like a dance, it takes two to continue. Parental enabling, as in all enabling, is ultimately a reciprocal interactive process. Once the patterns are established, habit and assumptions take over to keep it going. You have the power to break the cycle, and even if your "dancing" partner is reluctant to learn the new step, you can begin your recovery by changing how you move. It all comes down to being responsible for your part in any dance—you can do it!

7

The Enabler as Partner

Beverly and Randy are playing a game. She stares at him incessantly, her eyes following every move he makes from the television to the magazine table to the espresso machine in their apartment's galley kitchen. When Randy, who is trying his best to remain casual during this, looks up to catch her in the act, Beverly looks down again. Neither says a word. They are accomplished players at the staring game and know eventually that it will lead to a protracted fight. Randy will give in—he always does—and Beverly will tell herself that she has won a small victory. Then things will settle back to normal until the next fight. The residue of unspoken feelings, wants, and needs will build up; Randy will lapse into his guess-why-I'm-unhappy mood, Beverly will assume her I'm-too-busy-to-notice-anything-around-me pose. They never talk to one another except in the backwash of one of their monthly fights. Instead they do a dance: Beverly pursues Randy to get him to talk until she gives up and turns sullen. Then he notices that she has become sullen and he, in turn, becomes very nice. He becomes solicitous, offering coffee after dinner before she asks for it, putting the dishes in the dishwasher before he goes to bed, even making sure that there are fresh flowers in her office downtown. He acts blameless and innocent, like a child in a state of pure grace. And Beverly feels waves of guilt overwhelm her in the midst of her otherwise sullen and hostile thoughts.

Someday either Beverly or Randy may storm out of their relationship in a rage without knowing why. Since they rarely speak to each other, it will all seem a mystery. Or, just as likely, they may come to a mutual understanding of their problem and it will gradually dissolve. But it may also happen that Beverly and Randy will continue in this pattern of noncommunication for more years than either of them care to think about; he avoiding any meaningful dialogue, she enabling him to do so until the pressures become too great, both locked to each other in a kind of cold war.

Beverly and Randy's situation typifies the problems in hundreds of thousands of seemingly normal relationships: one partner enabling the other partner over a very long term. Spousal enabling can go on for entire lifetimes without being overtly dysfunctional. It's a bad habit that compromises the pleasure of otherwise happy relationships. In the same way that parents can fall into the enabling and codependency traps, so can spouses and lovers. The process usually begins with the same naive sincerity that typifies enabling parents. Because we want to do the best for our partners, we can easily assume too much responsibility for their lives. However genuine the intentions are, when one partner enables the other to abdicate his or her personal responsibilities to the relationship, the emotional well-being of the couple is compromised. And when there is a pattern of spousal enabling, communication, the emotional health, and the mutual satisfaction derived from the relationship can suffer. Beverly's situation with her boyfriend serves as a good example.

I don't know what to do with Randy. I've told him that I really need for him to share his feelings with me, but he continues to remain the tight-lipped Englishman he is. In the past four months he's told me he loves me only three times. And two of those times were only after I had just been complaining about it. He tells me that he gives me no reason to doubt his love and sees no need to "constantly" remind me. I'm no wallflower, but I do want to hear him share more of his tender feelings with me.

Sometimes when we're together I ask him what he's feeling and he always says, "I don't know." I know he has these feelings so I find myself pulling them out of him. I just about roll up my sleeves and reach down his throat to get the words. Then I arrange what amounts to a multiple choice of feelings he can choose from and eventually I get to find out how he feels. It's exhausting. I hate having to do that, but I don't know any other way of getting him to talk.

What Beverly didn't realize until she worked her issues through in counseling was that she is enabling Randy and in so doing she is meeting the hidden agenda of all enablers: *protect myself from all of my worst fears.* Beverly was very disappointed by the demise of her first marriage. She married a man who was emotionally distant and rather inadequate as a person. As a consequence she was never able to get the satisfaction of feeling that she was really in a relationship with another fully-functioning human being. Furthermore, because he gave her no emotional feedback and interest, she felt alone and invalidated. Having been physically abused by her mother and emotionally abandoned by her alcoholic father who just watched, Beverly's relationships with both of these men touched the old hurts she carries around with her.

I guess what I'm really afraid of is that if I don't find the words for him to say, he won't say any. And I've therapied myself enough over the years to know that I deserve more out of a relationship. When I get honest with myself I realize that I don't want to have to give him the ultimatum, "Start sharing your feelings with me and come to couples counseling with me or I'm going to have to leave you." What if he doesn't do it? Then I'll have to leave and I'm right back to where I started in my family, feeling alone and abandoned.

In counseling Beverly became more and more aware of the dissonance between what she was putting into the relationship and what she was getting out of it. Through her insight and courage she was willing to face the vulnerabilities and insecurities that gave rise to her tendency to enable. As a result, Beverly's awareness increased and she was no longer able to split herself off from her wants and needs. Eventually she found that she could no longer tolerate Randy's emotional irresponsibility, nor her old tendency to cover up for him. She felt stronger, and as she slowly backed away from enabling Randy, she made her wants known to him more directly and clearly than ever before.

Beverly and Randy presented a united front to the outside world, but inside the home there was a tenuousness to their interaction that always threatened to blow up into a serious argument. Their relationship was really very fragile and had to be handled with care. Relationships require the regular and honest examination of both partners. Enabling only serves to put off a difficult task that would be much more easily taken care of if addressed today. Sometimes, however, the fear of not knowing the outcome of being honest and forthright with each other causes us to shrink back.

All enablers operate with the not so hidden agenda that

> Unless I compensate and cover up for the deficiencies in this relationship, then all my worst fears will come true. If I really tell you what I want, then I'll know for sure that you won't meet my needs, either because you can't or you don't want to. That will pain me deeply and will force me to take a stand to either leave and be alone or stay and feel deprived. I fear that you won't come through for me and that I can't make it alone.

The enabler's agenda is not so secret after all because ultimately we are aware of all of the decisions and the choices we make, even if we aren't quite emotionally ready to admit it. But facing the agenda requires the kind of courage to face ourselves that Beverly ultimately demonstrated. This kind of recovering from enabling requires working the first, fourth, and fifth steps of the Twelve Steps.

FIRST STEP:
Admitted we were powerless over our tendency to enable—that our lives had become unmanageable.

FOURTH STEP:
Made a searching and fearless moral inventory of ourselves.

FIFTH STEP:
Admitted the exact nature of our wrongs, our vulnerabilities, and our needs to ourselves, our significant other, and our higher power, however we understood it.

Being honest with ourselves and our significant others is not an easy business; it is, however, the only way to begin to overcome the pattern of enabling. Working the Twelve Steps is the only sure way to climb out of the pit of emotional deprivation that is both created by and perpetuates enabling.

Breaking Out of the Enabling Agenda

The way to break out of an enabling agenda is to confront your spouse not to abdicate certain responsibilities. Practice following these steps:

1. Own your personal investment in the other's not changing
2. Make your needs, demands, and expectations clear to the other
3. Convey the potential consequences if there are no changes
4. Follow through by either: (a) acknowledging the changes the other has made, along with the good feelings you have as a result; or (b) taking action in response to the lack of progressive effort on the part of the other.

Regardless of the type of enabling or codependent relationship, this process works because it is based on both common sense and the use of honesty as a means of breaking the insidious pattern of enabling.

Perpetuating the Enabling Agenda Through Denial

Unfortunately, most people allow the enabling agenda to continue because they refuse to look at the truth. When it comes to relationships, in order for the enabling to continue it is in the best interest of the enabling partner to not acknowledge that he or she is enabling. Rather, enablers must continually stress the denial both to themselves and to their spouses or partners. It is my clinical experience that people do not become aware of their tendencies to enable until they feel emotionally strong enough to confront the obvious facts that:

1. They are turning themselves around and around in order to compensate for the needs of their partner.
2. Making decisions within the relationship are such stressful events that the enabler tries to avoid them, sometimes at all costs.
3. The enabler is building up a residual anger toward the relationship and to the partner, whom he or she can't or won't confront.
4. The partner is not pulling his or her weight in the relationship and therefore is not meeting the needs of the enabling partner.
5. They are enabling in an attempt to cover up some area of personal vulnerability.

Despite feelings of hostility and stress about his or her own lack of freedom, it is still in the interest of the dysfunctional partner that the enabling continue. If the pattern of enabling is interrupted, the areas of inequality and irresponsibility will come to light. Once all the truth is known about the dynamics of the relationship, the couple will have to decide whether they will stay within the same established patterns or risk the possible dissolution of the relationship by changing the rules of the game. This can be the most threatening aspect of a confrontation between the enabler and his or her partner. It is what has been keeping Randy on the run from Beverly and what had been staying Beverly's hand for the past five years. If you are afraid of expressing your real needs, why would you want to set up a confrontation in which each partner openly shares complaints, wants, needs, and vulnerabilities? This is what most enablers must ultimately face.

Once the discussion is underway, the relationship may then move off center and change for the better. However, once two people, whether married or single, gay or straight, old or young, have established a pattern of enabling, a subtle yet very powerful tendency to resist any alteration of this modus operandi oftentimes rises to the surface. This is not unlike the line from R. D. Laing's poem *Knots,* "They are playing a game. They are playing a game at not playing a game."

The Enabling Arena

There are many arenas in a relationship where a partner's tendency to enable may play itself out. The most common are emotional responsibility, stereotypes and assumptions, decision making, and chemical dependency.

Emotional Responsibility

It is said among people who are recovering from chemical dependency that the first slip that somebody takes usually starts long before that first drink or first line of cocaine. Similarly, the affair that ultimately leads to a divorce usually starts long before the "other" man or woman ever appears on the scene. Sometimes the "other" is not a person at all, but rather is a drug of choice. Regardless, the distancing that occurs as a precursor to these various extramarital affairs is a part of the process of emotional irresponsibility that may play itself out in a love relationship.

It is entirely understandable that you feel hurt and wounded upon learning that your partner is having an affair with somebody else, or is doing cocaine, or perhaps simply isn't worthy of trust at all. Yet these revelations really aren't surprises and you know it. They are usually a long time in coming, and the signs can be seen from a long way off. However, the partner who feels betrayed and victimized by the other tends, at first, to look the other way in the hope that anything bad will just go away. The enabler doesn't want to see the signs and will deny them for as long as possible.

These enablers are the ultimate victims of their own ability to camouflage the truth and hide from it. They are true enablers because they have chosen to not confront their partner on obvious matters of concern. They have given permission for the other to be emotionally irresponsible to the relationship. Here are some examples:

JUDY

When we dated we used to party a lot and have a real good time together. We were good lovers and I guess that served as the first bond between us. Then after we were married and had children I suddenly learned that sex was the only bond.

There I was with newborn twins just home from the hospital and what does he do? He goes fishing for the weekend. John knew my mother couldn't come and help until the next week, but he went anyway. He just said, "See ya later." And what's worse yet is that I told him, "OK." That set the tone for our marriage and over the next eight years that was the way it was. I didn't think I had a right to make any demands and John didn't offer to help me with anything. The only time I knew he really cared was when I eventually went for the divorce. Too little too late!

PHIL

I loved Lori from the moment I first saw her. I would do anything for her and often did. I never minded. Sure, sometimes she was moody and demanding, but I always thought that there's always a little good with the bad. Boy, did my eyes finally open once I really needed her.

The first time was when I was graduating from the Coast Guard Academy. We were not married and I really wanted to share this special occasion with my family and Lori. I was to receive a special commendation and that made it even more important. But Lori didn't come. We had an argument a few days before, but it was nothing big. To my disappointment, Lori had decided to hold a grudge and use not going to my graduation as a way to get to me. She did all right.

I got over it in a few days and forgave her, but when my mother died in the second year of our marriage I just could not believe that she refused to give me support or be there for me in any way. Lori told me she hates men who cry. It was my mother after all. I just couldn't believe how cold she turned out to be. I was so hurt, I just wanted to kill her, but I returned to counseling instead.

Both Phil and Judy have suffered a great deal at the hands of their respective partners. They have been victimized by the insensitivity of the one person to whom they had given their trust.

While it is understandable that we may empathize with Phil and Judy's disappointment and circumstances, it is equally important that we understand how they set themselves up for a fall.

Phil and Judy are enablers and through their actions and inactions, they inadvertently have conveyed the message, "Go ahead and take advantage of me. Even though I don't deserve your consideration, I will always be here for you. You don't have to change."

Judy is an adult child of an alcoholic father who was raised to feel not very valuable. Judy manifested this as a teenager by regularly dating boys who were of lesser intellectual and social status. John was one of these boys. It may be true that John was irresponsible of his own accord, but Judy played a significant part in reinforcing his behavior. Judy chose to continue the courtship and eventually married John although there were plenty of signs that his self-centered and hedonistic ways were something he wasn't interested in changing. In counseling, Judy cited incident after incident in which John disappointed her. He put her down and often showed her little respect as a person. Although Judy would occasionally complain, she almost never followed through in enforcing her demands to be treated with respect. For instance, the night after an argument over John's coming and going at all hours without informing her of his intentions, he stayed out until three without even a phone call. Judy felt unimportant, powerless, and angry.

Phil was raised by his mother for most of his childhood. His father had died in the early days of the war in Vietnam. Perhaps out of their mutual grief, Phil and his mother grew to depend on each other for most of their emotional strength and support. While this might have worked for Phil the child as a transient coping mechanism to heal the grief of his father's loss, ultimately the emotional needs of the woman his mother far exceeded his capacity to give. It's not the job of children to satisfy their parents' adult emotional requirements. But as an unfortunate result of his having to satisfy his mother emotionally, Phil carried his untiring need to please into his romantic relationships with other women. Phil only connected with women who seemed to need exactly what his mother needed. And that's what he found in Lori: an insatiable appetite for emotional gratification and attention. They in fact were a dangerously "perfect" fit. In his efforts to feel valuable and loved, Phil would give and give and in her efforts to feed her emotional emptiness, Lori would continue to take without even an understanding of why or how to give back. Lori was extremely narcissistic and self-centered for a host of reasons stemming from her personal history. This was clear for all to see except Phil, who out of a longing to feel special, continued to extend himself to her until he finally felt the slap across his face she had been giving him all along.

The relationships of Judy and Phil typify the spousal enabler pattern in which the enabler allows the other partner to shirk any responsibility to contribute to the emotional structure of the relationship. The worse the enabling becomes, the more the other partner is allowed to shirk, until the emotional irresponsibility is allowed to turn into financial irresponsibility, sexual irresponsibility, substance abuse, or even physical abuse. It's a syndrome that adjusts to the forces of the relationship but is always on the same continuum. That's why emotional irresponsibility is perhaps one of the most destructive elements that may be present in a relationship, even though it is almost always hidden. Veiled by both a desire to not recognize disappointment and a shared set of assumptions about the assignment of responsibilities and expectations in relationships, emotional infidelity is one of the most prevalent forms of dysfunction in the otherwise normal nuclear family.

Emotional irresponsibility and infidelity are oftentimes not conscious behaviors. Rather, they are often bred into the social fabric of our culture. Woman are taught to accentuate their feeling and nurturing sides, while in men these very aspects are devalued. This is still true despite all the efforts of the women's and human liberation movements to make our society more egalitarian. No doubt social changes on such a grand scale will require generations to take hold firmly. In the meantime, how these social learnings and stereotypes reinforce patterns of enabling is of very real concern.

Stereotypes and Assumptions

SANDY

I'd like to think it all started at the fire company's annual July 4th picnic last year, but it had been going on for years before that. Alan came from a huge family that had been raised on the same farm in south Jersey just outside the Pine Barrens for many generations. His whole family was either in the fire company, the rescue squad, the police auxiliary, or all three. All the women were in the "ladies' auxiliaries." When I met Alan in college in the early '70s, he seemed to have no prejudices or preconceived ideas about anything. He kind of lived for the moment, just like many of us did then. But after we got married and moved to Philly, the pressures began building. First his brothers began calling him. They needed him at the dairy farm; they needed him to work at the local grain elevator; the fire company was short on day crew. That kind of stuff. When that didn't work, his father called. "Alan we're short-handed down here. Your brothers are taking on about as much as they can handle." Nothing worked. Alan was happy teaching school in Philadelphia and I had a good job in town with an insurance company. Then his mother called. It was like turning on a switch. Alan became a different person overnight. He quit his job, gave our landlord notice, and then gave me notice. At first I threw a minor shit-fit, but it had no effect. "You can just as easily drive into Philly or take the train," he said. I went along. But it seemed as if he expected me to go along. He not only wasn't worried about my reactions, he didn't think they'd amount to anything. And he was right.

Once we'd moved to the farm, it was as if he didn't even exist anymore. The person I married and lived with in Philadelphia just seemed to vanish. He was replaced by someone else who looked like Alan, but walked from chore to chore, from meal to meal, like a robot. He stopped laughing at my jokes, stopped holding my hand at movies, and stopped talking to me. He had his job and I had mine. I was shunted into one of the ladies auxiliaries, rolling bandages and baking chocolate cake from scratch. If I had take-home work from the insurance company to complete over the weekend, it was tough luck for me. That fire siren went off for a barn fire, and I had to staff the stupid canteen truck. Coffee and doughnuts all night long while the boys ran around the burning hay like a bunch of wild Indians playing with their equipment. I didn't mind what they were doing—I'm sure it actually saved some property—I only minded my having to play their game. But I didn't speak up. The weight of ten generations of "Men fight fires, women make coffee" had me buried. I would go to work in Philly where I was somebody, attractive to men, crucial to my clients, treated like a human being by the lawyers who called me for my opinions, and I would go home where I was treated like an indentured servant. And Alan, he didn't exist either. After dinner, he'd disappear with his father and brothers for a washdown at the firehouse or a drill or a training session with the local police department. Or maybe he'd just sit on the back porch, where women weren't allowed, until he decided to come in. And if I wasn't wearing a smile on my face, all ready to serve his every wish, hey, that was my problem. I was a problem wife. Why couldn't I be like his sister-in-law or his mother.

I blew my top at the fire company's picnic. The local newspaper had some photographer down covering the picnic and asking inane questions about what it was like to live on the land. She asked me what I did for a living and my mother-in-law piped up "She's a farm wife," like that was all they allowed at the picnic. That was it. I didn't think, I just started screaming at her, her husband, Alan's brothers, and Alan himself. What was most galling were their reactions. Instead of the stony silence they usually treated me with, when the first shock wore off, his father fell on the ground laughing. Then his brothers started laughing. Then his stupid mother started laughing. She pipes up again "We know what you ain't been doin'." "Need help?" his oldest brother asked.

I thought Alan was going to die. He turned red. I turned red. I got in the car, drove back to the house, packed a suitcase and left. I let the lawyers settle everything that had to be settled. But I loved him once. When we were in college and living away from his farm, we were people. Once we got to the farm, I was a "farm wife," whatever that was and he was one of "the boys." That's all we were to each other. I'd like to say it was my fault for not refusing to move when I knew it was the wrong thing to do, but I never even challenged him. I never even set up a way to get him alone and tell him exactly what I thought. Sometimes, when I think back on it, I feel I'm as much to blame as he was.

Sandy and Alan were both victims of sexual stereotyping. Once they moved back to Alan's family's homestead, their personalities were blotted out by the weight of generations of stereotyping in the family and their marriage simply crumbled. This happens very easily when social stereotypes are reinforced by family habits that have remained the same for generation after generation. From the moment his mother's voice threw a switch in Alan and he stopped being Sandy's partner and became a full-time son, their marriage was in trouble. Sandy's reluctance to force the issue and bring it to an immediate head when she understood what was happening was one of the contributing factors to the demise of their relationship. Although many people refuse to recognize the impact of stereotypes in situations like Sandy's, stereotyping plays a major role in how people treat each other in a marriage. Stereotypes also reinforce enabling patterns of behavior to such an extent that they can often make the difference between a marriage that survives and one that fails.

Stereotypes are not always accurate, but they are often based on some element of truth. Over the years in my psychotherapy practice a great many women have come in saying in essence, "My husband won't tell me what he's feeling. When I ask him he says he doesn't know. I feel like we speak a different language." These are marriages that oftentimes seem reasonably healthy. A genogram reveals no pattern of addiction or major dysfunction in this or other generations and overall the family system seems to be operating smoothly, as is evidenced by what appear to be well-adjusted children. The source of dysfunction is just below the surface, in the same subtle patterns of communication that tell boys how to act like boys and girls how to act like girls.

If there is an assumption that I as a man am not responsible for sharing my feelings, then I also assume that such matters are deferred to my wife. I place an unreasonable (but unfortunately not atypical) burden on her and also teach my son and daughter how adult relationships operate. To the extent that my wife goes along with this, she is enabling me to continue. To the extent that she confronts me on my emotional withholding then she is attempting to be productive and healthy; however, I might experience her as being unreasonable or simply nagging.

It sometimes isn't easy to discuss these issues with a partner who to some degree is emotionally unavailable. A wife, for instance, is absolutely powerless to "get" him to change. Only her husband can do that for himself. The question is how can one spouse—typically the wife—create the optimal situation that may allow the other spouse to feel at ease enough to reveal not only what he thinks, but how he feels? Sometimes when a husband shares feelings after having not done so, he is likely to come out with broad and oftentimes inflexible proclamations and judgments that are more than either partner is ready to handle. A similar angry and disturbed response is likely if a wife tries to force a husband to share feelings by threats, demands, and emotional intimidation. At this point it too often turns into a power struggle with neither partner willing to give in because neither partner wants to lose face and/or control.

It must be noted that while the male in the relationship is more often the emotionally distant partner, they do not have an exclusive claim to this province. As was evidenced by Phil's experience with his wife and as may be the case in a variety of relationships, women may also be emotionally unavailable. In addition, the woman's demand that she wants her husband or lover to open up might only be a pose because she knows that he won't. If he actually turned on her with the truth and voiced his complaints while she was voicing hers, she might either run away and become emotionally unavailable herself or she might fly into a rage at being challenged. If the man believes this to be true, he may just "sit and take it," because it's easier to be a punching bag once a month than face the unbearable truth about his partner.

The question is what to do when you're a partner in this situation. Certainly, enabling the other to maintain the distance and unavailability is the last thing in the world you say you would want to do. But the reality might be that the path of least resistance is what you choose each day because when you're tired and beaten up from a day at work or with the kids, anything's better than another fight. The problem is not that you sidestep the issue on a Tuesday or a Thursday, but that you sidestep it for ten to twenty years or more. Then, at the end of it, when it falls apart anyway, what do you have left? You should realize that whether you confront your spouse on a Tuesday or Wednesday isn't really the question. It's a matter of awareness, mutual respect, and procedure. You'd be surprised to find out how the right procedures— as bureaucratic as that sounds—can make the entire confrontation not only constructive but downright easier.

Decision Making

How are decisions made in a relationship? To what extent is each partner consulted in regard to the matter at hand? Do the partners express their feelings and thoughts, needs, and wants, as well as their wishes to each other? Do the partners risk being disappointed by directly revealing what they think and want to the other or is there a tendency to be indirect and evasive?

There is no area of a love relationship that reveals most accurately the dynamics of how the partners communicate than in how they come to address decisions of mutual importance. Regardless of the issue being discussed, it is the *process* of how they process the information that is used in eventually making the decision that is of utmost importance. You might find it to be a helpful exercise to take a few days and casually observe how you and your partner interact in the making of decisions. The issues might range from where to go to dinner, what car to buy, to what to do about John not doing his homework. Ask yourself if both partners are included in the process and whether each partner has shared areas of responsibility or if the decision making is carved up into exclusive spheres of influence. Ask yourself if you feel comfortable and satisfied with the decision-making process or if it seems out of balance, wherein one partner has too much or too little influence and responsibility.

There are many ways to operate in a relationship. The issue ultimately comes down to whether the partners are getting their needs met in a fair and responsible manner. It is a sure bet, however, that when there is enabling in a relationship, the balance in the satisfaction of each partner's needs is skewed toward one, at the expense of the other. Take the case of Nancy and Doug.

They met during World War II. She was an army nurse and he was a GI. Nancy is still a nurse and Doug has risen to the rank of major. Although the war is long over, they have become accustomed to operating in their relationship as if it had never ended. There are curfews, martial law, and no tolerance for vocal opposition. All this has been implemented for the "good" of the relationship and in parenting their children. Forty-five years and several children later and Nancy is still treated like a second-class citizen.

I've never really said anything to Doug about his bossiness and I don't think that I was even aware that it bothered me until he started doing it to the kids. Ever since then I've been fed up with his "holier than thou" attitude. I guess it's been OK for him to treat me bad, but mess with my kids and you'll have to answer for it.

It simply came down to him not treating me with respect. He would talk down to me in front of friends. He would go out and buy a new car without even discussing it with me. And when it came to the kids, he would declare an edict and ground them and take away privileges for them just being teenagers. If I voiced opposition he would talk to me with intolerance, as if I too was a child.

Nancy and Doug operate in a closed one-way system of decision making: the only data and thoughts that count are the ones that Doug considers worthwhile. It is one-way: The decisions are virtually unilaterally decreed by Doug and handed down to Nancy. While Nancy has at the most only minimal access to an appeal process, Doug has absolute veto power. Whether we're talking about a government or a relationship, one that does not allow for representation in decision making is repressive. To sit back and idly watch it happen only enables the oppression to continue. When this occurs, self-depreciating messages are reconfirmed to the enabling spouse, the self-centeredness of the oppressive spouse is reinforced and the children are taught by example the nature of communication and gender roles in relationships.

How decisions are made goes very far in setting the tone for the entire relationship. The ideal form of communication approaches an open and sharing dialogue quite in contrast to the closed system as is the case with Doug and Nancy. Adult relationships are capable of directly communicating what each partner thinks and feels. This only works where there exists a mutual respect that is actively and clearly demonstrated throughout all aspects of the relationship.

FAMILY DYNAMICS. One of the clear benchmarks of how a relationship is progressing centers around the ways the couple handles issues of child rearing and the extended family. In all parental relationships, certain jobs, duties, and responsibilities are divided up between the two partners. Sometimes this is done quite consciously, while sometimes it is done without much thought at all. A father, for example, may simply fall into the role of disciplinarian because he assumes that fathers must be the ones to set limits and mothers are the ones who are supposed to nurture. Our society reinforces that notion. Oftentimes, enabling enters into the dynamics of the two parents' roles when assumptions are unconsciously acted out and then consciously acknowledged after the fact.

All children need attention and all the best research in child development has consistently demonstrated that the optimal situation is for both parents to become actively involved in providing that attention by nurturing their children and setting limits on behavior. Without the administration of a careful and healthy balance of the two, the emotional well-being and the social adjustment of a child may be negatively affected. When one spouse enables another to not have to perform his or her share of either the disciplining or nurturing of the children, the entire family suffers. First of all, the children learn negative gender-role stereotyping and come to see one parent as the "easy" mark and one as the "heavy." This polarity of parental functioning inhibits the children from developing a free and honest style of expression. Further, the either/or view of the world so often experienced by adult children of alcoholics and other dysfunctional families is initially formed through the experience of these dynamics in the family.

Children need to know they are valuable people who are capable of trusting themselves and their parents. When one parent consistently carries out the duties of judge and executioner, it inhibits the formation of a bond of trust between the parent and the child. This type of interaction also serves to set the tone for how the child comes to view authorities in general. Given a world full of teachers, policemen, and bosses, a healthy attitude on the part of the child is imperative in order to successfully negotiate through school, employment, and other social institutions. Consequently, a parent who enables the other to carry the bulk of the limit setting does his child a disservice that will affect him his entire life.

Why would one parent choose to serve as the designated source of nurturing for the children? Wouldn't she ever want to share this role that at times may be a pleasure and at others a burden?

These are just some of the questions to be asked of the enabler. The reality with enablers, as we have already discussed, is that there is always a payoff. It may differ from individual to individual, but an incentive is ever present.

Spouses sometimes are prone to enable the other to not be a complete parent because of a vicarious attempt to gain a sense of emotional well-being that seems to be missing. Usually there is only a dim awareness of the feeling of being "less than." However subtle it may be, these feelings of low self-esteem can oftentimes prove a powerful source of motivation for taking certain actions. For example, the wife who allows her husband to take an emotionally distant stance toward their children may be setting herself up to feel loved and valued by her children and absolutely vital to the health of the family because "If I didn't do it nobody else would." This is the typical battle cry of all enablers. This is what helps to make the process of enabling so circular: If one partner is not expected to make the necessary contributions to the relationship, whether it be nurturing the children, setting appropriate limits on the children's behavior, or being emotionally honest, there is little incentive from him or her to do so. For a person being enabled not to contribute, making a contribution means challenging the enabler, asking why only one person is carrying the burden. If the person refuses to confront the enabler, he or she, in turn, becomes part of the dance, and an equilibrium is established for the relationship that may take years to upset. Partners who don't convey the reasonable demand that some changes be made can only be assured of their partner continuing in more of the same ways.

SEXUALITY. A dimension of family dynamics that serves as the ultimate emotional barometer of the relationship is how the couple relates to each other sexually. Furthermore, *how* the couple makes the decisions about how frequently, where, and what kinds of sexual behavior and activities are "allowed" within the confines of the relationship reveals a great deal about the communication and trust between the two partners. The very process of making decisions about these very sensitive matters offers an opportunity for the couple to grow stronger by honest and direct communication. However, the same process allows a couple to grow more isolated and alienated from each other. Partners may hide their true thoughts and feelings for fear of hurting the other partner or because of an apprehension about being so vulnerable about personal needs and wants.

Whenever a couple engages in a conspiracy of silence about sexuality, they are engaging in yet another manifestation of enabling behavior. In some relationships only one partner may engage in this behavior. The classic stereotype of a woman faking an orgasm so as to bring a quick end to what she might perceive as getting her partner to "feel manly," was best illustrated recently in the movie *When Harry Met Sally*. Wives who do this as a rule not only deceive their spouses, but remain alienated from their own sexuality. In some religious families, this type of sexual enabling may be reinforced because the partners aren't supposed to get involved with their own sexuality. They are only supposed to procreate and multiply. Enjoyment is out of the question.

In other relationships both partners may pretend that everything is fine in lieu of expressing a personal want or desire to the other. In either case, both partners lose out on what could be a physically and emotionally satisfying experience. Without the willingness to ask what each wants from the other, and offer feedback as to whether the touch in question feels OK, the couple may be doomed to a lonely physical act that may offer little more than what can be derived from the solitary experience of masturbation. When enabling is played out in the area of human sexuality, the couple forgoes an opportunity at intimacy.

Whether enabling is used by one or by both partners, it only serves to insulate the couple from the vulnerability that intimacy brings. One needn't be naked to feel exposed. Many couples engage in sexual contact without ever really opening up to the other. Enablers play the part of contentment while perpetuating this distance. Regardless of the frequency or intensity of the sexual encounter, without risking emotional intimacy the couple remains apart just as if they were two lonely individuals. How the couple comes to decide what the parameters of the sexuality of the relationship will be reflects the extent to which the relationship is an open and direct system of communication or a closed and dysfunctional system.

STEPS TO OVERCOME SEXUAL ENABLING. Sexuality is a very sensitive issue that has much to do with upbringing, deep-seated fears about the other sex, fears about the sexuality and vulnerability of one's parents, and fears about intimacy in general. American society is historically quite puritanical and generally shies away from exposing questions of sex and sexuality to public scrutiny. American society also has a tradition of respect for the privacy of the bedroom and shies away from exposing sexual habits and proclivities to public scrutiny. This makes the discussion of sex and sexuality all the more taboo, even in the 1990s. Nonetheless, partners who talk about sex and the extent to which their needs are or are not met are, in general, happier with each other than partners who shy away from the issue.

Here are some general steps you can follow to help you overcome your enabling pattern of sexual behavior.

1. Accept the fact that it's no one's fault. Assessing blame or assigning guilt in matters of sex will solve no problems. They will only make the problems you have more difficult to solve and create new ones.

2. Don't be afraid to tell your partner the truth about how you feel. Faking orgasms and lying to your partner about how stimulated you are will only rebound on you. Assume, for argument's sake, that your partner is as unsatisfied as you are. Your telling him or her that everything is more than OK, it's wonderful, will only make your partner feel like damaged goods. Denying reality never helped anyone.

3. Try asking your partner what gives him or her pleasure. In surveys about intimacy and sexual misconceptions, researchers have found that most couples don't have the faintest idea what stimulates their partners. A little honesty and frankness may go a long way to putting real spice into any relationship.

4. Consider a break from the routine. If you and your partner have fallen into a rut, fantasize for an evening or a weekend about what the most conducive setting would be for a rejuvenation of your relationship. Take that vacation in the Berkshires or at the shore if it will get you away from the old routines. Don't be afraid to make a reservation and just take off. A little excitement may be just what you need.

5. Don't be afraid to seek marriage counseling or family therapy. Sometimes sexual problems are only symptoms of much

deeper misunderstandings or stresses in a marriage. If so, it's better to begin by talking about the symptoms. If you are an enabler and can't get your partner to agree to therapy, start out by going yourself. Eventually, with the help of a licensed and certified practitioner, you will either get your partner into therapy or realize that you are strong enough to give him or her the ultimatum: "Either you work on this relationship with me or you won't have one anymore." It takes two people to have a relationship and they both have to work on it and be committed to it.

MONEY.   It has been said of organizations that whoever controls the financial resources has all the power. This is also true in marital and other love relationships. Money is oftentimes central to any decision-making process, and the partner who controls the purse strings is in a position to hold the relationship hostage.

You might find it helpful to ask yourself the following questions about your relationship: Who controls the finances in your significant relationship? How was it decided that you or the other would do so? Was there equal input? How are requests made for funding various family projects (school, clothes, new car, tools, or groceries)? Or was money not a problem in your relationship only because while the two of you were married, you didn't have any? Do you think that divorcing your monies represents an expression of emotional distancing?

However you look at it, money is used as a symbol. Just as it used to represent a value of gold, money symbolizes values in relationships as well. Couples in healthy relationships use money as the means for enriching the quality of life. In these relationships each partner brings whatever material and emotional investments he or she has to offer back to the family. There it is shared freely and equally with no resentments. The healthier a relationship is, the less concern there is when one partner goes through a period of "needing" more than usual. In these families there is a clear sense that there is plenty of love, support, and material possessions to go around. Regardless of the financial circumstance, the couple, as well as their children, feel reasonably complete. There is no sense of deprivation.

The family life of couples who enable around the control of money oftentimes stands in stark contrast to that of the healthier family. In enabling relationships, the value of money usually gets back to self-worth. The giving of money or material objects may be used as a means of demonstrating to one spouse "all that I have done for you, therefore you owe me." However, there is often a feeling in such a relationship that getting from the other carries with it too high an emotional price. Consequently there tends to be a push and a pull between wanting from the other and reluctance to accept what may be offered for fear of strings being attached.

However, while the day-to-day issues seem to revolve around money and the concerns over who gets more and who doesn't get enough, at their core these matters have nothing at all to do with money. They really have to do with love and having needs met, with each partner attempting to address his or her need to feel loved and valued by the indirect use of money. It never works, of course, and both partners tend to get caught in a never ending dance around mutual feelings of deprivation through the use of money and material goods. It fails in securing for the "provider" the esteem and appreciation that are sought because the gratification that comes from giving material goods is always short-lived. However generous the gift, when it is not accompanied by a direct and genuine communication of affection a gaping void remains.

On the other hand, the spouse who enables the other to be the one to dole out the money and make the decisions in this area is on an even shorter end of the stick. On top of a sense of being victimized and powerless, are the feelings of low self-worth that usually accompany such a position. What is gotten is carefully measured and never enough. Further, the enabler knows all along that the love and caring that is really wanted can never be gotten by a demonstration of material giving, however grand.

Enablers sometimes may whine and feign neediness in a futile attempt to make meaningful contact with the other. The cruel reality is that no attempt at making the other feel guilty can ever get what is really wanted. Again, the mistake that the enabler and the false provider make is that money is the real issue. It never is and never was. The couple has merely been using it to avoid asking for the more intimate things that both may fear the other will never give and perhaps feel could never be deserved.

Chemical Dependency

By now you are more than just casually aware of the intricate role that enablers play in the chemical dependency of a loved one. Without these codependents in the life of the addicted, it is much more difficult to continue taking the abusive drugs and alcohol without encountering negative consequences. Oftentimes it is the facing of these consequences that ultimately leads to the alcoholic's hitting bottom and beginning the process of recovery. It is a simple reality that without having to face the music the addict has no tangible reason to change his or her behavior. My own research on the incidents that trigger the chemically dependent into treatment indicates that the causes include financial or legal problems, medical complications, and a feeling of being "sick and tired of being sick and tired." However, the most powerful triggering incident is the impact of a spouse or lover making demands that threaten the continuance of the relationship.

The treatment community is well aware of the importance of helping the alcoholic's significant others overcome their enabling and codependent behavior and attitudes. In fact, addiction specialists preparing family and friends to conduct an intervention on an addicted loved one will not allow the actual intervention to occur until codependency issues are adequately addressed. Only then may there be a reasonably high probability of getting the alcoholic into treatment and the recovery process. As crucial as the role of spouse and partner may be, a great many times their "love" and need for the other takes the form of a codependency that quickly dooms any attempt at a successful intervention. This is the case of Harold and Eric.

Harold is the proprietor of a gallery in a progressive community outside Philadelphia. Eric is Harold's live-in lover. At fifty-two, Harold is fifteen years Eric's elder. Even beyond the differences in age, they are a study in contrasts. While Harold is the product of a stable family and the son of a well-known surgeon, Eric is the son of alcoholic parents who beat him repeatedly throughout his first ten years. Furthermore, Harold is a teetotaler who only has a drink on holidays and special occasions, while Eric has a long history of sedating and stimulating himself with a variety of substances. His current drug of choice seems to be cocaine. Although they genuinely care for each other, Eric's addiction and Harold's codependency stand in the way of the relationship's deepening and growing healthy. Harold is frustrated about this.

I've been trying to get him back into treatment again. Brought him to the program to talk with the admissions staff. Since we came back he seems to have disappeared. I haven't seen him in three days.

So this morning I broke into his room. I had to take the frame off the door since he put the padlock on. I was astonished at what I found. Liquor bottles, ashtrays full of roaches and matches, spoons, little bottles full of god only knows what kind of liquid, a mirror laying on his bed and syringes. It was a nightmare. I'm so afraid for him that I even thought of calling the police. But I couldn't. I just worry about him.

I know I'm an enabler. The counselor two treatment programs ago told me so. What can I say. I keep on getting him dried out and back he goes again. Sooner or later he goes back to his old ways.

The problem is that while Harold knows that he is Eric's codependent, his knowledge of enabling and codependency is limited only to an intellectual understanding. He knows that his difficulty in setting appropriate limits and following through on them is diminishing Eric's chances for recovery, but at this point he is without a clue as to what his investment is in acting as Eric's codependent. Harold is in denial about his fear that if he really did lay down the law Eric would probably violate an agreement to remain sober, get a job, pay rent, and otherwise act responsibly. Harold does not want to be in the position to enforce these rules by making Eric leave. He knows that because he never enforced any of the many other agreements as to what will happen if . . . he has given Eric a very clear signal that says, "It is OK for you to break the rules. You are so special to me and I feel so sorry for you because of your miserable childhood and I know you can't help yourself, therefore, I'll never shut the door on you. You always get another chance."

Harold is codependent on Eric's drug abuse. Until he gets treatment and faces himself, he is in absolutely no position to set any limits with Eric. This scenario plays itself out in virtually the exact same pattern regardless of whether the relationship is straight or gay. As codependents, we must muster the courage to look into the mirror. Our reluctance to follow through and enforce the rules we know to be best has to do with ourselves, not the other. We act out our codependency because of a felt defect and weakness in ourselves. When we enter love relationships we tend to choose partners who allow us to continue to play out our pattern of enabling and codependency. As codependents we often don't feel good enough about ourselves to justify being in a relationship with a healthy and responsible partner. Many of the codependents I have encountered in my psychotherapy practice have literally turned down proposals of marriage from "wonderful" suitors, because they felt so uncomfortable dealing with someone who seemed so "together." When codependents and other enablers say no to potentially healthy relationships, they are simultaneously saying yes to continuing the cycle of dysfunction.

Tools for Enabling Partners

Here are some of the basic premises of all enabling situations. Try applying them to your own.

- If it feels bad, it probably is bad, so don't do it. You're better off doing nothing than doing something you know will hurt you.
- When you approach a decision that you know is wrong, don't make it. It's better to confront your partner than to acquiesce "just this one time" because you know and your partner knows it won't be the last time at all.
- Don't run from the truth. The truth may be slow, but it will always catch up. If you turn around to face it, at least you will be ready for it. If you try to run away, it will sneak up behind you when you least want it to.
- When you're run over by a train, it's not the caboose that kills you, it's the engine. In other words, you began to enable your partner a long time ago. You knew what was coming when you began this pattern of behavior and you've been enabling ever since. There are no excuses you can make. Your strongest reaction is to 'fess up, acknowledge that you've been

perpetuating your partner's addiction or irresponsibility, and take the necessary steps to remedy the situation.

· Always, always acknowledge the truth. You can lie to others, but you can't lie to yourself. Once you admit that, you will find it easier to confront situations that are painful and compromising.

8

The Enabler and the Abuser

Among the greatest tragedies in our society today is family abuse. No one would ever want to acknowledge or admit that a relative or family member is a child abuser. Most of us would find it inconceivable to hold such a thought, especially about a particular trusted individual. But the reality of statistics reveal that most acts of child abuse are committed by these very persons. Fathers and mothers, uncles and aunts, step-parents, siblings, and other family members are known to have abused the family's children from infancy through adolescence. The degrees and types of abuse may vary, but ultimately abuse is abuse, and the victim always suffers as a result.

There are similarly appalling statistics for spousal abuse. Because of encouragement from the many victims' rights organizations that have become more vocal about domestic crime in the past ten years, more and more women are coming forward with stories of terror and violence. We now know that spousal abuse is not restricted to specific economic levels or social backgrounds. Like drug abuse, spousal abuse and family violence occur across the entire economic and social spectrum. Our purpose, however, is to shine a light on the family scenario in which abuse—and by that we mean physical and emotional child abuse, physical and emotional spousal abuse, and physical and emotional abuse of parents and older relatives—is allowed to continue.

Recognizing and Overcoming Enabling Behaviors

There are no quick fixes for domestic abuse, violence, and other family crimes. If you are living in an abusive family situation, you have to face the reality of the issue first; understand what is happening to you and your child, sibling, parent, spouse, or other relative; and set realistic goals to protect the family, remedy the situation, or get out. Answer these questions for yourself:

- Are you or family members in your household victims of a violent abuser, victims of emotional abuse, or under the constant threat of physical violence?
- Have you or a member of your family been threatened with physical violence by the abuser in your home?
- Is the abuser an addict or alcoholic who, from time to time, is out of control?
- Are you more afraid of the abuser or of becoming an object of derision in the community?
- If your spouse is an abuser who is prone to violence, did you grow up in a household with a violent parent who was an alcoholic or an addict?
- Have you or a member of your family been forced to seek medical attention or emergency medical treatment as a result of abuse in the household?
- Have you even once considered or thought about calling the police or the district attorney's office to report an assault or the threat of an assault?

If you've answered yes to even one of these questions, then you are at high risk for becoming a victim of domestic violence. You may or may not be enabling the abuser, but your fears, as expressed by your answers above, are realistic and grounded in the immediacy of your situation.

Perhaps a prototypical enabler would dismiss these fears, at least consciously, and employ a variety of controlling behaviors to keep the abuser at bay and under control. At all costs, the enabler would not want one of the children to blow the whistle on the abuser because that would threaten the structural integrity of the family. Accordingly, all the children would have to keep quiet about what they were witnessing and, above all, silent about their fears. The implicit agreement between the enabler and his or her children is that "If you keep quiet, I'll protect you as best as I can. If one of you has to be the victim, it's for the good of all of us. If you cause any trouble, all hell will break loose and they'll take you away." These are powerful threats to hold over children's heads.

Many abused and battered wives hold similar threats over their own heads, especially if there are children in the family who are not yet the victims of abuse. "If I just keep quiet and try to control the situation, it will be better than what will happen if I try to run away or go to the police. The police won't believe me anyway." Many battered wives are also plagued by the fear of loneliness, although loneliness becomes less of an issue as the abuse in the home becomes increasingly violent. There also is a hostage syndrome at work in many abusive families. People under the immediate threat of violence or loss of life tend to form bonds with the individuals responsible for their lives. Released hostages have been known to express feelings of friendship and admiration for their captors, even though the captors had abused them, threatened them, or even killed members of the hostage party. The same situation may also apply in abused households where the abuser is in the position of captor.

Guilt

Whatever your situation, you must take whatever steps you can to protect yourself and your family. Because you are an enabler, you should try to stop the flow of guilt. In most cases, it's the guilt that's preventing you from acting. You may feel responsible for bringing the abuser into the family, for providing the abuser with children to be victims, for providing yourself as a victim, or for not being worthwhile enough to receive human respect and dignity from your spouse. You may simply feel guilty because you were brought up to feel guilty. It may be an instinctive reaction for you.

You must overcome this guilt by recognizing that there are lives at stake: yours and your children's. In this situation, guilt can quickly become a luxury that nobody can afford. One of your first steps, therefore, is to repeat to yourself the following affirmation:

It's not my fault!

Say it again and again until you completely accept it. You didn't create the abuse. You didn't start the violence. You don't want to hurt yourself or your children. It was your fear that kept you from acting at first, and that is nothing to feel guilty about. You may still be afraid, but you are no longer guilty. You accept that this is not your fault and that you must put a stop to the abuse at once. Do not hesitate to seek counseling if you cannot get over the guilt on your own.

Shame

Perhaps you are ashamed of your situation. "Look at me," you may say to yourself, "I am ashamed of what I've become. What will people say? I'm not worth rescuing." It is humiliating to be a victim in our society. You may think that people believe the myths that: victims are weak, victims are helpless, victims are fragile, victims deserve what they get. None of this is true. It is all in your mind. People don't think that victims are weak or helpless or deserve what they get. People understand that many victims are also victims of circumstances. The victim who understands that circumstances can change, however, is the one who most often gets help. Therefore, repeat this affirmation to yourself over and over again until you accept it and understand it.

There is no shame.

Once you accept the fact that there is no shame in being a victim or in being so afraid that you remain a victim, you can overcome another stumbling block in your path. Perhaps shame is keeping you from seeking help, from going to a counselor or a county agency, or from going to the police. Perhaps it is shame that prevents you from talking about the problem with family members or friends. You can overcome shame by recognizing that there is no shame. Accept your innocence and dignity and you will be free to talk about the problems in your household.

Ignorance

You would be astounded to learn that most victims of abuse who are enablers believe that they are the only people in the world who are victims. Most enablers think their particular dysfunction is unique to themselves. That's why I encourage enablers who attend support groups and discuss their problems openly. After the first session, after they have met ten or twelve other people just like them, the blinders fall from their eyes. Therefore, if you find yourself the victim of threats or abuse and you believe you might be enabling the abuser, accept the fact that you are not alone. There are hundreds of thousands of others in very similar circumstances. But it's one thing for me to say there are others; it's another for you to accept it. Therefore, repeat this affirmation to yourself. Repeat it over and over again until it is part of your belief system:

I am not alone!

Denial

In every chapter I've stressed the critical importance of your facing the truth about yourself, your past, your behavior, your family, and your circumstances. Telling yourself that what you know to be true cannot be true is only perpetuating denial. If you can practice "truth flashes," an exercise I suggest to my clients, you may be able to break through the denial. Here's how truth flashes work: Close your eyes as tight as you can and pretend that you are completely alone, adrift in your own universe, totally unconnected to anything, anyplace, or anyone. Deny all reality: Close off all sound, all light, and as much feeling as possible. Then, when you feel alone and at peace, snap your eyes open and let your mind fill with uncensored reality. You may find that the first thoughts that flood in are nondenial thoughts. In other words, because denial is a form of censorship and cover-up, the reality must be in place before you can begin to deny it. Thus, what comes in first is usually the truth; what follows is usually the denial.

Keep practicing this game until you can see the difference between the truth and the truth you've created. The bigger the difference between the two, the bigger the denial you're practicing. Once you've determined the size of the denial, you should list on paper the reasons that you're practicing the denial. You'll come up with the usual suspects: "This is only temporary." "He'll change, I just have to hold on until he does." "What will I do without my family?" "What will the neighbors say?" "They'll take away my kids." "I have to keep my family together." Now look at your reasons for exactly what they are: lies you tell yourself to keep you from facing the truth. Like the child in the fable, once you see that the emperor has no clothes, you won't be able to keep silent. Believe the truth, and it will set you free. Accordingly, you must tell yourself to believe the truth. Tell yourself that you will not be trapped any longer by your denial. Repeat the following affirmation to yourself until you can act on it:

I believe the truth!

Fear

A mantra in a famous science-fiction novel began, "Fear is the mindkiller!" Nothing could be closer to the truth. Fear, the cold, icy panic that holds you in its grip, closes down all rational thought. It makes you blind to reality. It forces you to do things you would never do if you only had time to think. Fear can be all-consuming.

If you're an enabler to a violent individual—your spouse, your parent, a sibling, or even a child—you live with fear every day of your life. You live with fear that is real and fear that you create. Fear stalks your footsteps and makes you second-guess everything you do. Even if someone else in your family is the victim, if you are silenced by fear, you enable that victim to be terrorized day after day.

Now it's time to stop. Now it's time to face that fear. Now it's time to say to yourself: "I have faced the truth, I am not at fault, I am not alone, and I will face my fears head on." When you stare into the face of fear directly, you will see that what you are most afraid of is not there. You created your own monsters that are worse than any monsters anybody else can create.

When you confront fear, you, of necessity, muster the strongest parts of your own personality. Now you must confront your fear. Repeat to yourself the following affirmation from the 23rd Psalm until you can face your fears in the darkness of the night:

I will fear no evil!

Seeking Help for Physical Abuse

Shelters

Physical abuse, domestic violence, incest, and rape are all crimes. Although you can tell yourself that there are hundreds of reasons for keeping quiet, for trying to remedy the situation on your own, for offering consolation to the children, for trying to protect the family unit and the abuser out of your own need to feel needed, you can't deny that you are witnessing crimes. If you are an enabler and these crimes are taking place in your household, you are actively aiding and abetting criminal acts as long as you don't seek help. Seeking help may involve temporarily relocating to a shelter for battered women and their children, talking to a social service worker, talking to a faceless, nonjudgmental voice at the other end of a confidential abuse hotline, talking to a member of the clergy, consulting your lawyer or therapist, or going to the police or the district attorney's office.

It's tough to stand up in the face of the threat of violence, especially when the threat lives in your home. But the longer you deny the truth, the longer you make yourself an accessory to those crimes through your silence. If you look at the situation as a crime scene where you are a material witness, your responsibilities to yourself and your family will become clearer. You are not the accusatory finger pointing at your defenseless spouse or parent, you are a victim as well as a witness. If you allow the abuse to continue, not only are you endangering your life and the lives of the other people in your family, you are enabling a dangerous person to hurt other people. You do not need to protect the abuser. You need to protect yourself.

Therapists at women's shelters agree that one of the surest ways to stop violence in your home is to leave it. If you and your children are not there to be hurt, you are out of immediate danger. As crime victims you may qualify for community funds for temporary shelter and food. The shelter or community agency may be able to relocate you or, in the event that the abuser is arrested by the police, you may be able to go back to your own home. Courts have the power to restrain the abuser from returning home and place you and your family under an order of protection. These court orders are enforceable by the local police, and the abuser can be arrested and kept in custody for not obeying them.

Intervention

Your situation may be too complicated for the straightforward solutions that I've suggested. Perhaps you perceive that because of your job, your spouse's job, your finances, your children's situations in school, your responsibilities to other members of your or your spouse's family, your relationship to the community, or any one of a hundred reasons that may be unique to you, you can't simply walk out of the house. You may still be enabling, but you are looking for ways out of the problem. In these situations, I strongly recommend an intervention structured by a *certified* licensed therapist who is either a psychologist or a psychiatrist. The therapist may recommend that you consult with a medical doctor because you or your children may benefit from treatment to recover from long-term trauma or stress. We have described interventions elsewhere for drug abusers and alcoholics, and these types of interventions for abusers are no different in principle, even though they may have a different spin on them because they may or may not carry the threat of legal intervention as well.

An abuse-oriented intervention is designed to bring a case of domestic violence and abuse or threatened domestic violence and abuse to a screeching halt by confronting the abuser with the ramifications and consequences of his or her behavior. Most people, even those seriously out of control, do not want to harm the ones they love. I have known brutal parents who spent years in the throes of remorse because they did not know how to control their behavior. In their own ways, they called out for help even while the enablers in their families assumed they were providing the help. These were tragic cases of missed communication. Interventions are designed to make the communication as clear as possible while presenting the abuser with an unmistakable picture of the consequences he or she faces as a result of the abusive behavior. They can be conducted privately in the home or in the therapist's office and are designed to bring about an immediate change in behavior.

Those interventions that I facilitate—where victims confront abusers and abusers and enablers confront each another—are often structured around principles developed from those expressed in the Twelve Steps of Alcoholics Anonymous. The abuser is made to understand that, first, his or her life is out of control; second, that because of an addiction to chemicals or to violence, his or her life has become unmanageable and requires an outside intervention to bring it back under control; and, third, that in order to bring it back under control, the victims will help the abuser take a fearless and objective moral inventory of his or her life. These are drastic steps, but they tend to work because they're not as drastic as the consequences that would follow if the abuser were allowed to hurt or kill someone.

In some cases, abusers recognize the need for a form of hospitalization to allow their systems to detoxify under supervision. In other cases, abusers may acknowledge that the stresses they face in their lives have become unmanageable as well. In these instances, abusers may check themselves into some type of residential convalescent facility for therapy. A substance abuse clinic is another option addicts or alcoholics may choose if they feel that the addiction has deprived them of a structure and meaning to their lives. But in all cases, the intervention serves notice on the abuser that he or she is now under close scrutiny. The spotlights have been turned on, behavior patterns that have been enabled to continue are now no longer acceptable, and the consequences of the abuser's behavior are brought into the open.

INTERVENTIONS AND ENABLERS.   The intervention serves a dual purpose. On the one hand, it allows enablers to bring the abuser's behavior out from behind the cloud of denial. On the other hand, the enabler's behavior is also revealed. Thus, both the abuser and the enabler are able to see how they've interacted and how each has provided for some need in the other. Usually, the enabler discovers the extent to which he or she has contributed to the dysfunctional family situation and is able to enter recovery as well. Therefore, if you opt for an intervention in your circumstances, don't be surprised if you are seen as part of the problem as well as part of the solution. Don't blame yourself or judge yourself, even though others in your family may find fault with you, but accept the extent to which your needs dictated your actions. That level of acceptance is the foundation of recovery and healing.

Overcoming the Enabling of Emotional Abuse

Emotional abuse is generally a more insidious and longer-running problem than physical abuse, even though it can be just as devastating to its victims. In some cases, emotional abuse is a foreshadowing of the physical abuse to come. In others, it smoulders just below the surface of an otherwise socially correct family situation, diminishing the natural optimism of the children and inflicting pain on anyone who comes into contact with the abuser. As the enabler, you may bear the brunt of emotional abuse more than anybody else in the family. Even when it's not directed at you, you can feel its deadening effects on others and see the hopeless look in their faces when they realize that there is no pleasing this abuser. Emotional abusers seem to saturate their environments with a very special type of venom. Their unhappiness permeates the atmosphere of the household and colors every event with their disdain and pessimism. Emotional abusers dislike themselves so intensely that they inflict it on those around them. Consequently, when an abuser tells a child that he or she can't do anything right, the abuser is really expressing the opinion that he, himself isn't worth having someone do any right for him. This is a roundabout way of saying that emotional abusers are ultimately abusing themselves. This might be the key to undoing the effects of emotional abuse.

Enablers routinely allow their abusive spouses, children, or parents to traumatize those around them by showing the abuser that his or her behavior works, that it is having the desired effect. Enablers take the abuser's negative behavior seriously without trying to defuse it or deflect it. As a result, the abuser is told, "If you are trying to hurt me and the rest of the family, you are succeeding." More than likely, this is the only real success the abuser is having in life, hence he or she continues. You have to show this abuser that he or she is not succeeding, that you will no longer enable, allowing him or her the negative pleasure of inflicting pain. You need to employ a counterstrategy that will protect you and the rest of your family by neutralizing the effect of emotional abuse and showing the abuser that he or she has to change.

Here are some quick techniques to dismantle emotional abuse, overcome your enabling of it, and possibly turn the abuser around at the same time. These have worked for some of my clients; they might work for you. The premise of these techniques is that abuse that doesn't work is eventually turned off. Abusers inflict pain on others because the effects of the abuse confirm their negative attitudes about themselves. If there are no effects, there is no echo, nothing is confirmed, and the abuse dries up at the source. You must begin by telling yourself that even if you have to play-act at it, you are worthwhile. You do not deserve the abuse, you've done nothing to warrant the abuse, and the abuse itself makes no sense. This may be a form of denial, but I prefer to call it "counterdenial," a denial of the false premise that you're worthless. By denying that falsehood, you act from strength. Therefore, you can:

- Ignore emotional abuse by figuratively turning off the hearing aid. You will hear no evil.
- Pretend you absolutely don't understand what the abuser is saying.
- Step away from the abuser emotionally so the words fall short.
- Refuse to respond to anything that even sounds like abuse.
- Play dumb and keep on smiling.
- Play rope-a-dope until the abuser expends all of his or her energy. The abuser will see that it's fruitless and give up.
- Respond to all forms of emotional or verbal abuse with a torrent of affection.

- Tell the abuser in a straightforward way that you know what he or she is doing, but it will have no effect on you or the children because you won't respond.

In prototypical forms of emotional abuse, these techniques usually call attention to the abusive family member by isolating the abuser and his or her behavior. As long as the abuser continues the abuse, he or she is ignored. When the abuser responds in positive ways, he or she is rewarded with the warmth that comes from trust. These techniques may even have the same effects as a structured intervention because the entire family conspires to challenge and confront the abuser.

You can also, and probably should, seek some form of counseling for yourself and the children. The abuser will likely have done some damage to the developing personalities of the children, and you will need to talk to someone about your enabling. It is likely that your therapist or counselor will have other suggestions. Remember, you want to show the abuser that his or her abuse has no effect while at the same time protecting yourself and your children against the danger of escalating violence. In order to be able to do this, you should familiarize yourself with the myths of abuse that are pervasive in society.

Myths about Domestic Abuse

The first myth we have to get rid of—fast—is that a man's home is his castle and what goes on there behind closed doors, is shielded from the law by a constitutional right to privacy. Nothing could be further from the truth. Wherever physical abuse takes place, it's a criminal act. If you or your children have been abused or threatened with abuse, you are victims and entitled to the protection of the law. The way our society works, however, a crime must be committed before the legal system can prosecute the abuser, but if you've been *threatened*, there are steps you can take to seek protection. Seeking some sort of protection is an important step because as long as you allow the threats to continue, even if you're deathly afraid of retribution for speaking up, you are acting in the role of enabler. That may seem unduly harsh—as if I'm saying that enablers are responsible for becoming victims. But I don't mean it to be harsh. I'm suggesting you examine the ways in which the abuser thinks you're allowing him or her to perpetuate the abuse, even if it's simply because you're a frightened victim who doesn't know where to turn for help.

The second myth follows from the first: Most spouses who are victims ask to be victims. If they didn't want to be victims, they'd leave. We know from thousands of hours of research into the psychology of victims and abusers that this couldn't be further from the truth. Most victims are simply too scared to know what to do. They are afraid to blow the whistle precisely because they are afraid of being stigmatized by the police or local authorities.

Even in the cases of purely emotional abuse, where there are no incidences of physical violence, most victims are too scared to speak up because the *threat* of violence is always present. Janet, one of my clients in therapy asks herself,

> If a small child hears her mother constantly complain, "You're my worst mistake, I should have gotten rid of you when you were a baby"—how much do you think that child will feel her life is worth? That litany played throughout my entire childhood: "They told me I should have had an abortion but I was afraid. Now look what I wound up with!" My father, who I never even met until a few years ago, was always the villain and she was always the hero. But she wanted to kill me.

Janet grew up thinking she was worthless and even today has an extreme overreaction to the threat of violence. "If someone stares at me from across the street for too long, I run back to the apartment and stay there. Sometimes I don't leave again until the next day, and even then I have to work up to it." Janet's fears have played havoc with her life, not to mention her self-esteem. And they were mostly the result of a parent who emotionally traumatized her.

In Janet's case there was no actual enabler, nor was there another parent to act as a buffer. Janet had to face her mother alone. But in many homes, the other parent is an active enabler who would rather just keep a lid on things than confront his or her abusive spouse. This describes what happened to Corinne who grew up in an affluent suburb just outside of Columbus, Ohio, and remembers how her father stood by helplessly while her mother made her feel worthless with her sarcastic humor. "Even today I can't stand sarcasm," Corinne confesses. "I was dating a guy who I liked, but his sarcasm about other people just wore me down." Her father, who visited me to talk about Corinne, filled in the blanks about his wife that Corinne only vaguely remembered.

Jean was a very special, very talented woman who was brought up in a very proper Midwestern Republican family. She could play by all the rules, but she was happy about it. When Corinne was born, I guess I treated her like the heir apparent in the royal family. I loved her to pieces, told her how beautiful she was, and how she was my favorite girl. Jean didn't like that one bit.

The more I doted on Corinne, the more Jean felt she had to take her down a few notches. Problem was that I wasn't at home during the day. It was just Jean and Corinne. By the time I'd come home at night, Corinne would be complaining about how mean her mother was and all the awful things Jean had said, but I just laughed it off. Kid stuff! All kids hate their moms! It's a phase they go through, or so I thought. And even when I saw Jean and Corinne going at one another in the evenings, I didn't step in. Not a man's place to get between a mother and her daughter, I thought. Had Corinne been a boy, you bet I would have said something. But I was also afraid of Jean. I knew how mad she was that when the war was over she had to give up her job and have children. She must have been taking it out on Corinne, too. I certainly wasn't going to be the one to fight with her. It was more important to keep the family together. It wasn't until after Jean died that Corinne and I ever talked about it. Now, it's probably too late.

Corinne's father enabled his wife to continue abusing their daughter. At first, he told himself he didn't do it out of fear, but out of a misunderstanding that girls were raised one way and boys another. Ultimately, however, he realized that he was afraid of his wife's deep anger at being relegated to second-class citizenship while watching her daughter receive the love she felt she was not getting. By not confronting his wife, Corinne's father perpetuated the kind of emotional abuse that left Corinne with scars that may never heal.

The Abuser

The stereotypical sex abuser is a male who has himself been a victim of child abuse. More often than not, the abuser has a problem with other addictions and has been at risk with the criminal justice system at some point in his life. Men have no exclusivity in this area, however. Women are fully capable of abusing children, other women, or even men. The most frequent form of child abuse by women is a covert form: emotional incest.

The stereotypical victim of child abuse is a female child who, if she survives the abuse, will most likely grow up to become a child abuser or an enabler. A startling 25 percent of *all* women have encountered some form of abuse during their lifetimes, but we would be negligent in not citing the 10 percent of all males who reported having had at least one incidence of abuse in which they were the victims. These are incredible numbers because they point to the overwhelming prevalence of child abuse in our society. The reality is that both men and women are victims and both are abusers.

Child abuse in families is so much a cyclical function that therapists regard it as a multigenerational dynamic. That's psychological jargon meaning victims of child abuse have a very high probability of becoming child abusers themselves. The chances are so great, that we can look right down a genogram and follow a pattern of child abuse from parent to child to child to succeeding generations thereafter, just as with alcoholism. Regardless of the form of abuse, once it infects the family of origin, the individual who was victimized goes on to victimize others unless he or she receives treatment. For instance, the person who as a child was subject to violent outbursts from a parent on either a regular or infrequent basis tends to display similar behavior as a spouse and parent. Once the normal, natural boundaries are broken, there is little emotional understanding, especially in times of stress, of where one person's boundaries end and the other person's begins. If abusers could articulate their mind-set they might say:

> I learned about relationships from the way my parents treated me. From early on I came to understand that people intrude in my space at will. Regardless of whether it's my body, my feelings, or

my thoughts, people can come whenever they want and take what they want. This makes for a dangerous world. As an adult, I look at other people in the same way. If I want what they have, I'll just take it. If I don't do for me, no one will. There's absolutely nothing wrong with using others in order to attempt to gratify myself. I may take their body. I may manipulate them with guilt to get them to do what I want. I may invalidate their feelings and thoughts. Only mine are important. The focus must be on me.

There are only two kinds of people in the world: the powerful and the powerless. I therefore need to act out on others because if I don't act powerful, I won't be powerful. If I'm not powerful, then I'll be powerless. And powerlessness is the very feeling I had as a child. I don't ever want to face that again.

Unfortunately this mind-set does not lend itself to conscious articulation. Only after abusers work on themselves in psychotherapy do these insights begin to come to the surface. Because their own sense of powerlessness is so frightening, a very slow and gradual process of understanding follows.

In the process of the abuser's acting out his or her violent script on a child or spouse, the boundaries of these significant others are routinely broken. Regardless of the nature of the abuse, it always involves an actual incursion into the other's physical or emotional territory. In cases of spouse abuse, a basic bond of trust between individuals is broken. The partner, the mate, becomes a predator. If the victim participates by not confronting the abuser, the victim becomes an enabler. The moment the victim seeks help, breaks out of the enabling pattern, leaves the physical space where the abuse takes place, or challenges the abuser, the relationship will shift.

The Three Forms of Abuse

The abuse of a child, spouse, parent, or other member of the household can be overt as in the case of physical violence or it may take the form of a covert act, such as casting guilt or otherwise manipulating a loved one. Throughout these acts the enabler often acts overtly or covertly in complicity with the abuser. Sometimes the enabler may only have a dim awareness of these actions.

As the case of Hedda Nussbaum shows, when a person is so overly invested in another so as to ignore her own internalized set of values, she may act as if she is in a hallucinatory or dream state. It is important to remember that the ultimate and original purpose of all enablers is some sort of self-preservation and self-protection. While there may be no real threat, enablers perceive it as quite real. As they confuse perception with reality, they become terrorized. Suddenly the enabler must confront his or her own fears of "disintegration of the self," and take whatever steps necessary to protect him- or herself. This is a natural human reaction when you feel trapped into an emotional corner. The problem for the victims is that they feel such an essential need to preserve existing relationships with the abusers, that they allow abusers to continue to act out the abuse on both the enabler and their children. The enabler allows his or her own victimization to continue because of the perpetuation of the psychological myth that "I can't live without him" or "I will fall apart if the relationship dissolves."

There are three main forms that this synergy of abuse and enabling usually takes.

Physical

Physical abuse is usually accompanied by some form of violence and it is usually inflicted on children, spouses, and/or elderly parents living in the household. When physical abuse takes place within the family, it is usually in the presence of an enabler who does not commit the crime but becomes an accessory by perpetuating the behavior. Without the enabler's complicity of silence and inaction, there would soon be an end to the victimization.

Often, enabling, substance abuse, and codependency are intricately connected with each other so that the codependent of the substance abuser becomes a physically abusive parent in his or her own right while the substance abuser becomes the enabler. This may sound complicated, but, as Tom's case will illustrate, it is one of many ways in which the dynamics of chemical dependency and child abuse are interconnected. We cited the example of Tom's family earlier in the book, but the relationships among the issues of child abuse, spousal emotional abuse, alcoholism, codependency, and enabling are so clearly defined, the family situation bears repeating here.

TOM

For as long as Tom knew his father, he could only remember the drinking. Tom's father would come home from work each night, start drinking, and before long he would wind up in a dull stupor. Tom's father wasn't the abuser in the family, that was the role his mother assumed. And because his father was already starting to pass out by mid-evening, he was in no position to intervene when she began to assault the children.

> Talk about abuse of power. Once my father got drunk enough he would do what he became famous for among the kids: turning into the invisible man. I'm sure it affected us as kids, but we didn't really notice what we were missing because we had nothing to compare it to. We didn't know what really having a father was all about. The problem was that when dad faded out, the monster in my mother seemed to take over.
> It was just awful the way my mother abused us. I'm sure she had plenty of reasons to be disappointed and angry, what with the way my father drank, but to take it out on us! I remember on more than one occasion her literally sitting on my chest with my arms pinned back under her legs, flailing away at my face. No wonder I have problems dealing with my own anger now. But at least I'm nowhere near as bad as her!

Tom needed his father to intervene on his behalf. Unfortunately for him and his siblings his father just faded into the background, oblivious to the assaults going on around him. To the extent that his mother did not demand that his father quit drinking she was his enabler. But to the extent that he tolerated her abuse of the children, he was her enabler. Tom's mother was out of control. Tom is quite right in thinking that she had more than her share of disappointments with his father. She compensated for her frustration and rage at his father by beating the children. Then, when she was full of guilt, she compensated for the guilt by beating the children some more. But regardless of her feelings

of powerlessness, guilt, and frustration, these issues had nothing
to do with her children, even though the children never understood that when they lived in the household. It would take Tom
years to come to that conclusion.

Tom, along with his brothers and sisters, was also the victim of
arbitrary discipline that rarely bore any relationship to his behavior. The children were repeatedly subjected to harsh and insult-
ing punishments, oftentimes coming right out of the blue for no
apparent reason. Furthermore, this kind of abuse from the only
parent who functioned in the household served to plant the seeds
of distrust and fear that have ruined the marital relationships of
Tom's brothers and sisters. It is noteworthy that the sensitivity
and insight that sprang from his hurt and betrayal led Tom to
become a psychologist. It is not at all surprising for helping professionals to be initially drawn to the field as an expression of their
desire to better understand and heal themselves.

Sexual

The sexual abuse of children is an extension of physical abuse that
breaches the psychological boundaries between adult and child.
Where the abusing adult is a parent, the crime is incest and it
distorts the expectations of the child as well. Incest becomes a
cruel mockery of the nurturing and care the child instinctively
expects from his or her biological parent and creates an emotional
scar tissue that can be treated but never removed. Left untreated,
the adult will almost always abuse children in turn. Once treated,
the adult will usually have to think about or intellectualize any
sexual fantasies about young children that might spring up. The
fantasies might never go away, but an adult victim who has been
through therapy will understand that those fantasies are simply
reactions to the violence of the past. They are harmless in and of
themselves as long as the adult victim recognizes the importance
of talking about them openly to a certified licensed therapist if
they threaten to overwhelm him at any point in his life.

Sexual abuse also distorts the young child's sense of power and
perception of control. For the rest of the victim's life, power and
control and the senses of trust and distrust will wage war for
stewardship of his or her spirit. Sexual abuse can be one of the

prime components in the life of an enabler. Many enablers developed their patterns of behavior as coping mechanisms to keep themselves from being emotionally destroyed or overpowered by the abusive adult. Enabling was the way in which the abused child learned to manipulate his or her way out of compromising situations by rechannelling the normal anger and hostility he or she felt. To display that anger might have meant that the child would have become a victim of even greater violence.

VICTIMS WHO BECOME ENABLERS. It is no surprise, therefore, that children who are victims of abuse discover that if they can earn the approval of those who abuse them, the level of abuse tends to decrease. Further, if the abuser can be made to feel that the child victim is an ally instead of an enemy, he or she will leave that victim alone and find a new victim. In this way, the child learns how to deflect threats by becoming an accomplice of the abuser. If there are other children in the family, those who become allied with the initial victim—usually the eldest child— can learn the process of deflecting threats and will be protected. Eventually, all children in the family will learn the game and participate in a dynamic of shifting alliances while enabling and deflecting the abuser.

KIM

My client Kim is a twenty-five-year-old woman who has been in counseling for several months, initially because she is an ACOA. During the course of her sessions, she became aware of the extent to which she shared many of the same characteristics that other adult children of alcoholics described. In particular, Kim was disturbed by her constant attempts to seek approval, her tendency to second-guess herself, and her tendency to overreact. She bent over backward to enable other people by wringing approval out of them. She complained about the negative impact all of this was having on her attempts to form meaningful relationships with men.

It quickly became apparent in treatment how different Kim felt from others. As she began to trust herself and the therapeutic process more, it began to dawn on Kim that her alcoholic father had also sexually abused her. Because she was a victim of abuse, she learned to enable others to deflect what she perceived as threats to her health and welfare. This is typical of adult enablers who were also childhood victims.

First there were the vague feelings, then the dreams, and eventually she began to remember actual memories of assault. This, of course, terrified her, but it could only be one-tenth of the horror she actually experienced as a nine-year-old when the abuse first took place.

> I didn't think it was possible at first. But then I kept having these feelings. For a while I wanted to get hypnotized so I could find out about my past without having to feel the feelings. But I kept on coming to counseling and all the pieces started falling together: the weird way I always remember feeling around my father, my distrust of men, and my anger.
>
> Knowing I am a victim of sexual abuse has helped me. I feel like I'm not so much hiding from myself like I had been. I just wish my mother had done something. I've thought about it again and again. She must have known something was up, but just didn't want to see it. She's still like that. It makes me feel sad. I feel like my childhood was taken from me.

Kim is quite right. So much of the innocence and trust that can be so much a part of childhood was ripped away from her. And while the responsibility must fall on her father for abusing Kim, her mother must also be considered in the picture.

Before Joan got married and gave birth to Kim she had been, as she puts it, "protected from the outside world in Catholic schools." She still describes herself as a "hopelessly" naive Pollyanna. Joan was clearly invested in having the picture-perfect marriage and family and seemed intent on achieving it, even if she had to fabricate the illusion herself. Accordingly, Joan was particularly dependent as a young wife and mother and would do anything for Dick. Apparently she even went so far as to block out of consciousness any awareness of his impropriety with Kim and her sisters. Joan was an enabler. Her perceived need that Dick always be there for her compelled her to see only what she wanted to see. She is by no means a bad or malevolent person, but in reality she sacrificed the emotional and physical welfare of her daughters in order to feed her insecurity. In doing so she enabled Dick to continue to sexually abuse his daughters.

Kim, in turn, became an enabler who, out of a perceived need to obtain the approval of others, allowed people in relationships with her to act irresponsible or even abusive. However, because of Kim's experience as a victim of child sexual abuse, she also brought to any relationship distant, but distinctly unpleasant, memories concerning physical and sexual contact. Her instinctive attempts to win approval through enabling ran counter to her almost primitive abhorrence of sex. This conflict informed most of Kim's relationships and shows what can happen to adults who are both enablers and victims.

Kim's mother presented a different picture. Enablers like Joan are usually very nice people, however they oftentimes give their control over to the sense of emptiness that they carry within. When this happens they tend to abdicate both their value systems and the responsibilities of their roles as caregivers. As we will see, this pattern not only plays out in instances of sexual abuse, but is the hallmark of all forms of emotional abuse.

Emotional Abuse

Victims of emotional abuse must eventually confront one of the most difficult challenges of adulthood: the recognition that something wrong but almost imperceptible took place during childhood. They can't tie it to a specific event, to a physical scar, but it keeps creeping into their perceptions of things. People and situations remind them of the abuser. They have reactions to seemingly innocuous events that seem to spring out of nowhere. Typical of enablers in other situations, they cannot give over their trust. And also typical of most enablers, they cannot relinquish control and remain vigilant at all costs: stereotypical adjusters. They often abuse their children as a matter of course, yet, they cannot pinpoint a cause. Their inability to acknowledge that there is a problem keeps victims of emotional abuse chained both to their abuser—whom they enable—and also to a life of disappointments and unfulfilled expectations.

We might wonder how it is that an individual who had been scarred by a parent wouldn't realize what had happened. It is no less a wonder that the victim doesn't understand what the ramifications of its occurrence are for his or her adult life. The answer lies both in the nature of the enabling and in the nature of the abuse itself, a trauma so subtle and pervasive that the victim hardly even realizes it occurred at all. Victims usually grow up in families where this is practiced on a regular basis. Sometimes all the children are treated in an emotionally abusive way, while in other families one child seems to be singled out for the assault. After years of being subjected to these attitudes and behaviors a scar develops. It's real, but the individual tends not to notice it just as someone tends not to notice a birthmark except on those occasions when it is pointed out and brought to our attention.

After years of negative scripting, inappropriate personal criticism, defeatist self-images, and pessimistic attitudes, these victims venture into the world with their eyes on the ground. They are prepared to fail. They become young adults whose unconscious expectations are that the dynamics of their families will be replicated in the outside world. What this usually amounts to is a perception of the world as an unsafe place where one must constantly be on the lookout for defeat at every turn as opposed to striving for success. With an I'm-afraid-I-can't-really-do-it attitude these adult children of dysfunctional families suffer from loneliness and dissatisfaction in their love and work lives. The one thing they know is that something is wrong, although they don't know the real origins. Most people end up attributing their string of disappointments to a sense of inadequacy inherent to them. They feel they are to blame and that there is little they can do with the fact that they simply aren't good enough.

PARENT-CHILD. The most common source of emotional abuse lies in the relationship that develops between a child and parents. Kathy's situation is a classic example of emotional abuse, its consequences, and the role the enabling parent played in perpetuating the abuse.

Kathy has a Pakistani father and a British mother, both now American citizens. Her childhood might be accurately described as the product of the rigid sexism of fundamentalist Pakistani culture and the staid reserve of British Victorianism. Had she been raised in Pakistan, Kathy might not have been affected with the residue of emotional abuse, but given her awareness of how her other friends were treated by their much more traditional American families, the scarring began.

> I used to think my father hated me. Looking back on it now I can see that he had his share of problems and unhappiness that had nothing to do with me. But he took it out on me. Boy did he take it out on me.
>
> My brother was treated like royalty. When he did something wrong my father was always so understanding of him. And he was only charged with having to do about half of the chores I was responsible for. I was even told to make *his* bed!
>
> I wish it was as simple as the inequities with chores, but that only scratches the surface. I wasn't allowed to have feelings and be a little girl. I remember when I was about eight being silly and laughing one night at dinner and my father responded by quarantining me in the garage to eat my dinner for a week.
>
> As I grew he seemed to adjust the level of abuse accordingly. My father always used whatever would get to me. When I was fourteen he told me that no man would ever want to marry me, that there was nothing that I had to offer. I felt unlovable and hopeless and carried these feelings into my adult life.

After a crisis with her boyfriend brought Kathy into therapy, she began to unravel the labyrinth of her emotional abuse. She found that because of her childhood as a victim of emotional abuse, she because an enabler who was incapable of standing up for herself, representing her legitimate gripes in intimate situations, or forcing a lover or friend to act responsibly. Instead, Kathy acted on behalf of others and allowed them to act irresponsibly toward her. As this same pattern of failed relationships recurred again and again, and as each failure enveloped Kathy in waves of self-retribution and the despondency of failure, Kathy realized that she was locked in an endless loop of self-defeat.

In fact, Kathy was using the years of self-doubt and put-downs at the hands of her father both positively and negatively. On the one hand she took up his challenge to her worth as a person by using her natural intellectual gifts to earn a Ph.D. in chemistry. But on the other hand, she suffered through her adolescence and young adulthood by dealing with a great deal of disappointment in her relationships with men. When confronted with the possibility of a relationship, the old scripts of "You're not good enough" and "No worthwhile man would want to marry you" still haunt her. Kathy either involves herself with irresponsible men who don't respect her or she falls in love with married men who are unavailable. She somehow always seems to find a way to make sure that relationships with good and emotionally available men never work out. As is the case with many adult children of emotional abuse, Kathy is lonely, self-deprecating, and very unhappy. Even though she is currently hard at work reestablishing her emotional strength, it's too bad that she has spent so much of her young life dissatisfied.

The questions that remain are: Where was her mother when all this was going on? Couldn't she have done something to prevent this damage from taking place? Kathy's mother certainly could have exerted a positive influence, but unfortunately she was not available for her daughter. She was too busy being an enabler.

Kathy's mother was demure and, in Kathy's words, "typically *veddy* English." She didn't express herself emotionally, but she was always there to provide the family with a meal, a Band-Aid, a little parable about having a stiff upper lip, and a bedtime story. In many respects Kathy was lucky to have a mother who offered her tender caring and focus. This is probably what helped to prevent the consequences of her father's emotional abuse from being even greater. Yet Kathy's mother could have done more. She could have stopped the abuse from continuing. But she didn't.

My mother never said much. And certainly not to my father. Only during my teenage years did she finally begin to stand up to him. In fact after I went to college she actually divorced him. But she just wasn't there for me when I needed her. Sure she'd come to me later and attempt to comfort me, but telling me that "You have to understand your father means well" just didn't cut it! I needed her to get me out of the doghouse and the garage, literally. I didn't need her after the fact, I wanted her to do something about it. Through my tears I remember holding myself back from telling her to do something about Dad, because deep down I knew she wasn't strong enough. Sure, I'm angry about that now, but really I'm mostly sad.

Kathy's mother enabled her husband to be an abuser and Kathy to be the victim because she, herself, had a low self-image. Even as a ten-year-old, Kathy's assessment of her mother as a woman who didn't feel strong enough was right on the money. When Kathy's mother eventually mustered the strength to confront her husband and divorce him, the damage had already been done. Because of her lack of faith in herself, Kathy's mother inadvertently enabled Kathy to be emotionally damaged by her father. The quiet support in the background was helpful, for sure, but it was not enough. Kathy not only grew up to believe she was not worthwhile, she, in turn, became an enabler of irresponsible men. This is the emotional residue of an enabler as parent.

In Linda's family the emotional abuser was her mother. But, unlike Kathy, she did not have her father to perform damage control. He was a part of the conspiracy of silence that so often punctuates enabling relationships.

> Now I know my mother was a very sick woman. But I didn't know it as a kid. She would say the most God-awful things to me and put me down, but the worst thing of all was that she would say one thing to me and then in almost the next breath deny that she had said it. It would make me crazy.

Linda's mother acted out one of the most powerful forms of emotional abuse. Like Kathy's father, she treated Linda in a manner that imparted a great lack of self-worth and esteem. This was enough abuse to cause harm. But in giving double messages she also challenged Linda's internal sense of perception and judgment. She taught her to not trust herself. Often, during these bouts of abuse, Linda would look for help and ask the question most abused children ask about the other parent: "Where was Dad?"

> Perhaps the thing that got me the most upset was that my father would go along with her fantasy. I'd turn to my father right after she'd tell me to do the opposite of what she just said and he'd say, "Don't talk back to your mother." I would know that he heard differently but he didn't want to get into it with my mother so he just went along. It was so disappointing to me. It was like going to court full of faith in the system only to the find that the judge was

Julius Hoffman from the Chicago Seven trial. There was just no chance at justice.

Sometimes Linda found herself terrified at her mother's behavior. As a bright and rather precocious child, Linda's curiosity often got the best of her and would get her into trouble with her mother. The incidents were nothing monumental, in fact they were the typical things we would expect from an active nine-year-old. Regardless of whether she was caught climbing the apple tree, placing pennies on the railroad tracks to flatten them, or inadvertently breaking some water glasses as a result of an experiment to see how many she could carry, her mother reacted with the same fury. Linda's mother didn't have the insight to understand that all children have to explore their world if they are to learn and grow. For that matter, her mother didn't have much understanding for children at all or sympathy for their funny attempts to experiment with their surroundings. In fact it seemed as though she felt in some way threatened by her daughter's actions. Not only was Linda taken to task for breaking the rules, but she was given one of the most powerful of sentences for a child: isolation and guilt.

> I was generally a good child. Despite the fact that my curiosity would occasionally get me into trouble, I really never did anything awful. I certainly never hurt any animals, friends, or even my younger siblings. But when my mother would catch me breaking a rule she didn't take any of my inherent "goodness" into consideration.
>
> I can still remember the most cruel punishment she ever used on me. On more than one occasion she would lock me in the attic and tell me she would never let me out. I remember screaming in absolute terror as she would scold me from outside the locked door on what I had done wrong and how I was a bad person. I would plead with her to let me out, but to no avail.
>
> The attic was unfinished. It was too cold in the winter and too hot in the summer. When she put me up there, I could never go past the bottom step. It was there I would sink into my tears and wait for my mother to let me out. Although it was only for an hour, it always seemed like forever. And each time I was afraid that something evil up there would get me and I would never get out.

Linda's mother reacted to her daughter's childhood folly as if her world were spinning out of control. Her punitive treatment of Linda seemed to be a desperate and distorted attempt to absolutely eliminate the spark of independence that shown so brightly in Linda. It was as if she could not emotionally tolerate the sense that Linda was separate from her, and she saw it as a critical threat. Fortunately, Linda's will and strength of character helped her to keep herself from breaking under the severe stress. But the fact is that some cracks did form in her personality that might well have been prevented had she had a father who could have intervened on her behalf. The isolation and emotional assault in the attic occurred on numerous occasions. Surely her father was aware of these goings on at least once or twice. Yet he stood away from what was taking place in his family, and by his inaction condoned and contributed to this abuse.

Linda's father was timid about the world and terrified of his wife. When she got angry with him she wouldn't let him off the hook for days. Consequently he did whatever he could to avoid any confrontation with her. In his efforts to achieve peace at all costs, he enabled his wife to live her life as if there were nothing wrong with her. He denied what he saw and left her free to terrorize her child. By not having her distortions of reality brought into check by her husband, Linda's mother was out of control and repeatedly savaged her daughter's emotional boundaries. Years of having her perceptions regularly challenged planted the seed of self-doubt in Linda. Considering the nature of her father's complicity in the abuse, it is remarkable that the damage done was not more severe, for these very double-message signals have been attributed as a major factor in some cases of schizophrenia. Like all survivors of abuse, Linda was victimized both by the abuser and the bystander. In the typical pattern of domestic violence, one parent was the aggressor and the other could only stand and watch.

EMOTIONAL OVERINVOLVEMENT AND ENABLING BEHAVIOR. Another form of parent-child abuse occurs when a parent is emotionally overly involved with the child. This type of relationship can occur with the same- or opposite-sex parent. When the latter occurs, it sometimes even takes the form of emotional incest. Although there is no sexual or inappropriate touching going on, it's almost as if there might as well be considering the intimate nature of the relationship. Whether emotional incest takes place or not, the inappropriate involvement almost always turns the child into an enabler who believes he or she must take care of his or her parent. It is for this reason that emotional involvement and emotional incest are like molding machines that fabricate victims of this form of abuse into adult enablers who will eventually become overinvolved with their children.

Emotional overinvolvement and emotional incest are very insidious and subtle. Because they have marked the parent-child relationship from almost its inception, neither the abuser nor the victim are consciously aware that it is taking place. The one thing they both know is that the relationship is very special and very important. Usually neither is very much aware of the potentially destructive impact this type of relationship could have on the child, whatever the age. The consequences range from a six-year-old shying away from involvements with potential playmates to a sixteen-year-old or twenty-six-year-old having difficulty establishing emotionally satisfying relationships with potential life-mates.

Child therapists still do not fully understand how it is that a child can have difficulties in adulthood because of a relationship with a parent. It isn't just that the child learns to emulate a faulty model, it goes deeper than that. We expect that children "grow" their personalities in ways similar to how their bodies grow and develop. Whatever they are fed, they use as nutrients. If parents feed their children healthy personality "food," such as positive reinforcement and a positive self-image, children develop one way. If parents feed them negative self-images, they develop another way. If children receive attention and love, they think they are worth being loved and deserving of success. Without love, they think they are worthless. However, attention and doting that are inappropriate, that violate the space that the child will later on reserve for peer relationships, skew the child's normal abilities to form those relationships and intimate relationships with mates. Children will not know what to do with their feelings for their parents who violate these spaces; they feel uncomfortable but can't reject their parents out of hand. The child conflicted in this way does not learn to express his or her emotions properly and enables others as a way to fill up that void of unknowing.

Social relationships with their peers are important, but the basic personality work is already in place by the time a child steps into the playground. Peers can have a dramatic effect, to be sure, but no one can possibly offer the child the singular and special focus of the parent. Therefore, when the special trust between parent and child is breached by emotional incest, the results can be devastating.

Jill is a twenty-seven-year-old client who came for counseling at the insistence of her husband Bob. Here are some excerpts from the first few sessions:

BOB

I don't know what it is with her. She seems to be more married to her father than to me. I know the relationship between a father and daughter is supposed to be special, but this is ridiculous! They call each other every morning and she confides in him, not me. I've tried to be honest and as open with Jill as I can. When I complain, she just looks at me like I'm crazy. And ever since we've been married, our lovemaking has gone down the drain. I want to do something about it, but she says she doesn't need sex as much as I do. We used to make love all the time when we were dating, now maybe it's once a month at best. She even told me I should be more of a real man like her father. I'm at my wits end. My father and sister never acted like this!

JILL

I just came to appease Bob. I'm satisfied with the relationship the way it is. And frankly if he wants me to be more open with him or wants more sex, that's too bad. We just don't have that kind of relationship. He always complains about my father, but at least my father understands and cares about me. Bob is so self-centered, he doesn't even see it.

Bob and Jill only remained in couples counseling for about two months. It became very clear that both were very sincere, but were not in a position to have more of a relationship with each other. Despite Jill's perceptions, Bob was not so self-centered. He merely longed for the intimacy it appeared they were heading toward during their courtship. He was feeling alone, rejected, and undesired.

Through some individual counseling sessions the history of Jill's emotionally incestuous relationship with her father came to light. Their relationship became so overly involved over the years that it seemed that each felt that the other was an extension of themselves. They were so psychologically enmeshed that several years earlier Jill asked and her father agreed (he was a psychotherapist) to conduct her psychotherapy with her. Not only was this in violation of his professional ethics, state law, common sense, and even common decency, but neither of them saw this as a problem! It was no wonder that Jill's father felt very dissatisfied in his marriage. He was clearly looking for his fulfillment from his daughter. In response she lapped up the attention.

The fact is that such distortions of the parent-child relationship and the subsequent distortion of the child-peer relationships are entirely preventable. Children are not responsible for these relationships, and it is the duty of the parent to make sure they do not occur. The only two people in the domestic household who can intervene are the perpetrator and the enabler.

At its root, the problem of the parent's becoming too emotionally involved with a child is innocent enough. We all want and need to feel emotionally fulfilled and satisfied. The problem is the parent who looks to his or her child as the source of satisfaction. There may have been a death of the other spouse and perhaps both parent and child have turned to each other out of their mutual grief. Or, as is most often the case, the relationship between the parents is strained and distant. Out of either a fear of being continually rebuffed or simply out of a fear of intimacy one parent may look to a child for the fulfillment of emotional needs. That the child responds in kind is understandable. Children love their parents and want to help if they can. Children also crave parental love and attention and bask in it. All the seeds are there for the development of an intimate emotional relationship between parent and child.

It's at this point that either parent can intervene. If there is no severe pathology in the parent, he or she can come to an understanding of his or her unfulfilled needs and make plans to address the problem by either working on the marriage or by getting out. Greater attention can then be given to maintain an appropriate amount of emotional and personal space for the child. Should there be a lack of awareness, the other parent has a duty to bring this problem to the attention of the child's over emotionally involved parent. If, as if the case of most parents, the child's best interests are the primary concern, the parent can then make adjustments in the relationship to reform a healthy emotional boundary with the child.

The other parent is in a unique position to see these goings on by virtue of his or her vantage point. That parent becomes an enabler, however, by deciding, for whatever reason, to not take any appropriate action. The enabling parent may be indifferent or angry at his or her situation, but, because of the inappropriate intimacy between the child and the abusive parent, the enabler fears intimacy with the child most of all. To be intimate with the child/victim, means that the enabler is violating the territory of the abuser. Thus, the child/victim, while becoming inappropriately attached to one parent, becomes inappropriately distanced from the enabler. In seeking to compensate for the extreme asymmetry in his or her parental relationships, the child/victim learns to cope by developing enabling behaviors. The child learns, first, to take care of the parent who is inappropriately close by satisfying the parent's need for comfort and, next, to take care of the parent who is inappropriately distanced by staying out of harm's way and smoothing over every situation so that the distanced parent finds the child blameless.

The distanced parents, the original enablers, may choose to withdraw because they have their own personal inabilities to participate in intimate family situations. They probably didn't want to become involved in being in a family in the first place, and see the relationship between the emotional abuser and the child as a way to "nonparticipate" in their own families. The abused child is a handy way to deflect the intimacy of the family away from the enabler because the child serves as the perfect distraction. The abusing parent is focused on the child and the enabler can remain safely out of contact. Neither parent in the family is subject to the reasonable demands that emotional intimacy with another adult requires. This is not unlike the way it often works in families where children are physically and sexually abused, although in those cases the pathology is much greater in both parents, as is the fear of violence in the nondirectly abusive parent.

Most cases of emotional incest are instigated by parents who are at the outset well-meaning and otherwise normal. They didn't have children for the express purpose of violating them. Their emotional reactions toward their children were most likely completely unforeseen. The abusers would say it just "happened." This is why emotional overinvolvement and emotional incest are so prevalent. For the enabler, however, it's a completely different story. The enabler is looking for an out, a way to distance him- or herself from the family without confronting the issue of his or her own unhappiness. The enabler wants it both ways: being in the family without committing emotionally to the marriage. When the enabler notices that the spouse is making inappropriate advances toward the child, the enabler sees that as an out and stands away. The abuser actually makes it possible for the enabler to have the emotional distance he or she craves without having to pay the penalty for it. The child pays the penalty.

It's in the enabler's best interest to perpetuate the abuse. The perceived danger of the enabler parent is that if the abusive parent regains and maintains appropriate boundaries with the child, then he or she will look to have a real relationship with the enabler parent. In the event that the enabler feels ill-prepared to deal with the prospects of a relationship, he or she may attempt to shift the focus back onto the child in the hope that the child will again become the center of an inappropriate relationship. The child, being none the wiser, is often glad to receive such lavish attention. The enabler doesn't realize that the child already feels uncomfortable but has no direct way of expressing it. Unfortunately, the victims pay a high price for the special attention they receive when they become adolescents and young adults and attempt to establish their own love relationships. There is often a great sense of dissatisfaction and disappointment as relationship after relationship fails. As is Jill's case, the mates never seem to measure up in providing the focus and self-centeredness to which the child has grown accustomed. The enabling parent holds the key in preventing this kind of damage from occurring.

ADULT-ADULT.   Adult-adult emotional abuse is the exploitation of one adult in a relationship by the other. It takes two forms, one of which is an aggressive assault on the victim's personality and the other an inappropriate closeness, an absorption of the victim's personality into the abuser's.

In the former case, the abuser exploits the victim by using him or her as personal whipping post, a target for the abuser's rage and hostility. The abusive partner vents frustrations with life and work and projects this onto the victim as if the victim were the true source of the problem. Abusive partners can't face the reality that they are responsible for their own problems. They find it convenient to think that if they are not responsible for what goes wrong in their lives, then they are also incapable of success. Accordingly, they are never satisfied and blame the victim for all their woes. The more one partner becomes abusive, the more the enabling partner becomes compliant in the hopes of meeting the needs of the abuser. But it's a trap; the emotionally assaultive partner can never be satisfied, no matter what the enabler does. In fact, enabling only makes it worse. You can see this type of relationship in many families where an abusive person is usually attacking his or her spouse in conversation while the victim is trying to be overnice.

The symbiotic form of emotional abuse is very much an extension of emotional incest, although in this case the object is the other adult partner. As with emotional incest there is a definite aggression across personal boundary lines that ranges from "We don't like butter on our potatoes" to "We just don't feel that Jeffrey is the right man for you to marry." In the case of symbiotic abuse, one partner starts it and the enabler decides to go along until after a while we can't really tell who is who. That is the very nature of this form of abuse. There is an attempt to merge the two selves into one. Usually one partner is "taken over" by the other. In actuality the enabling spouse agrees to submit. What is lost in the process is all that can enrich a relationship: individuality and intelligence, separateness and boundaries, and all that can allow one to truly respect and value the other.

The tragedy of the assaultive and symbiotic relationships is that we can give freely only when we are separate. Similarly, we can only appreciate the other when we see him or her as a separate person. In the case of these relationships, both the abuser and the enabler are usually motivated out of a fear of being emotionally intimate with the other. Because of the ever-present fear of being either taken over or being abandoned, both parties cling to the neurotic but familiar pattern of relating to each other. Because of the use of this unhealthy glue to keep the relationship together, there is usually little satisfaction felt by either partner.

The Philadelphia Syndrome

I didn't invent this term, but it's an apt description of a form of abuse often inflicted on children of relatively affluent WASP or WASP-manqué families. In these situations, the child is forced to bear the burden of the family's mantle of leadership, a form of noblesse oblige in which children are trained to live within a very restrictive set of rules. True displays of emotion are often forbidden, parents communicate with children in very rigid or pro forma ways, family problems are often swept under the rug, the family lives behind clouds of denial, and parents rarely engage in meaningful discussions with the children. Family members learn to distance themselves from their feelings, to experience them from behind the veil of a corporate or third-person demeanor, or to deny that painful emotions can ever affect them at all. The result is an ingrained sense of denial of reality that affects every area of the family's life. The Philadelphia Syndrome is a very real and very painful form of abuse in which, as a Princeton University student once described, you are continuously beaten with a velvet glove. These victims almost always become enablers both inside and outside of the family or worse yet become involved in a dysfunctional relationship or engage in other forms of self-destructive behavior such as chemical dependency or sexual promiscuity.

Hazlet James first described the Philadelphia Syndrome in *The Nemenema Song* as an adapted pattern of behavior and attitudes taught to children by parents of well-to-do families and passed on down from generation to generation like a bank trust. The behaviors and attitudes are best characterized by the old British notion of a stiff upper lip in the face of all adversities, even those that would normally involve some form of emotional reaction. Philadelphia Syndrome WASPS always feel good and look good, but at the cost of becoming alienated from themselves and from other people. I have had clients who have even become alienated from their own bodies. They have a sense that they can't really participate physically in the world. It's as if they've become abstractions. Consequently, in those affected by Philadelphia Syndrome there are high incidences of somatic diseases and other attitudes toward health involving a denial of pain.

Sufferers believe one must keep feelings and thoughts inside rather than share them, except under the obligations of formal or ceremonial situations. The Philadelphia Syndrome is progressive: the younger a child is, the worse the child is at playing at it. The older a person is, the more entrenched he or she is at playing at it. It is reinforced by the social structures of prep schools and Ivy League colleges, the hierarchies of executive management structures of well-established corporations, the rules of social engagement at law firms and investment banking houses, and the social rituals at resorts or vacation enclaves.

Individuals who have the Philadelphia Syndrome have very impaired abilities to share intimate thoughts and emotions, and don't know how to relate to other people or to communicate in ways that make other people feel worthwhile. At its very worst, sufferers cannot even communicate meaningfully with their own spouses and children and become distanced from the families they are trying to protect. They have denied that which is human and only react to the external symbols of their existence. Fourth- and fifth-generation children who've grown up in these families become so alienated that they have no sense of direction or purpose, no ability to react to the humanity of other people, and no ability to love or appreciate being loved. Once in recovery or therapy, they describe themselves as having been emotionally sterilized. Yet, like other forms of dysfunction, people who have it deny that there is anything wrong with it.

The Philadelphia Syndrome can bring with it much pain because the burden of carrying it can't ever be communicated. That pain and its suppression and denial enables the dysfunction to be perpetuated from generation to generation. Even talking about it is a social taboo. People enable themselves, enable their families, and enable their colleagues from similar families. The result is a conspiracy of denial and silence whose most obvious victims are the alienated children. This is like the alcoholic family, except there is not obvious substance abuse.

BEVERLY

Beverly, a client in a psychotherapy group, is a good example of someone who has been victimized by the Philadelphia Syndrome and who can now talk about it in therapy. She effectively used the group therapy process to deal with her tendency, a result of her upbringing in an affluent, socially established family, to swing from maintaining very rigid boundaries in her life to having almost none at all. These wild swings were very destructive and upset her entire equilibrium.

> When I listen to the people in group I just get too emotional. I love them all and I do identify with their histories, especially the ones who come from neglectful families like mine. But all of a sudden it happens. It's as if I lose all perspective. Their problems become mine and it all gets to be too much. I start to think that I shouldn't only not be in group, but I start feeling that I shouldn't be with any people. When this happens the feelings begin to get out of control and I think that the only way I can stop it is to die.

Beverly's experience in group reveals the reason she has kept her distance from people all her life: She doesn't have a clear sense of where she ends and the others begin. She is an intelligent young woman who is *intellectually* aware of the difference between herself and others, but who *emotionally* cannot make that distinction. When she allows herself to become too close to another person, her personal boundaries become blurry and begin to disintegrate. She identifies so closely with others that she enters into relationships in which she always ends up taking care of the other person. Beverly is really attempting to take care of herself, but she is incapable of doing that on her own. As a result, she tells herself that once she is able to fix the other, then she will be all right. This is a nice try, but healing can't take place through another. It can only happen within ourselves.

Beverly was raised in a particularly abusive household in which there was no overt violence, alcoholism, or substance abuse. From the outside her household looked perfectly normal: stable family, four children, parents who supported their community, three cars, well-cared-for pets, well-maintained lawns, and even a little apple orchard. But inside this well-to-do household there wages an intergenerational battle marked by the quiet violence of emotional neglect and psychological burden that is sometimes heaped upon the children in our more affluent communities. It is the trauma of collective silence enforced by parents who would rather deny emotion than confront it. They tend to lapse into their individual roles and bury their frustrations under the make-work responsibilities of social obligations. I often see the consequences of this obsessive demand to look good when, as adolescents, the children of these families attend prestigious Ivy League colleges like Princeton or Penn. It is at college, in their struggle to find a clear identity, that there are disturbing involvements with alcohol and substance abuse, sexual promiscuity, other manifestations of self-destructive behavior, and long series of unhealthy relationships.

These adult children are victims. They have spent a lifetime learning to look good on the outside, have lovely manners, look resplendent at their eating club galas in black tie or gowns, but are often fractured on the inside. Beverly never learned to respond to her own valid emotions. She denied them and thus denied a part of herself. Her parents always spoke to her and to one another in hushed voices, subtly teaching her to hide her emotions, and cautioning her never to express her opinions in opposition to the majority will. There was little tolerance in Beverly's household for any ruffling of feathers. The emphasis was on being well-behaved and proper. Although this was true for all the children, the demands were focused with righteous indignation upon the girls in the family. There was much more tolerance for "boys being boys" and as such they were given far greater latitude in expressing themselves.

As a consequence, Beverly learned to operate with grace and deftness as she maneuvered through her life. She was pretty and carried herself very well. She practiced in prep school how to gracefully fend off her admirers. Just as in a romantic novel she would grant them a kiss, subtly flirt, and then make a memorable exit. But although she had mastered the art of the wonderful performance, she had no idea how to maintain and share in a relationship. She did not know how to express her true feelings, to listen to someone else express true feelings, or how to trust another person. She lived in a family that taught her mostly how to hold her real emotions inside while maintaining a rigid boundary against all potential intruders.

Beverly became an enabler in order to cope with her situation. She had to protect the status quo of the family. She had to protect the myth that because of its emotional reserve, her family was uniquely special and above many. Although she didn't realize it at the time, she was a very lonely girl. Soon thereafter Beverly arrived at Princeton. She began to become aware that something felt very wrong. She still maintained very good grades and continued her work as a classical pianist; however, there were disquieting rumblings within.

> I started feeling like Dr. Jekyll and Mr. Hyde. I would dress in a gown to give a performance only to party like a factory girl afterward. I began to be attracted only to the wild men on campus. The ones who had had many women. They would drink and I'd laugh. It was so exciting. That second semester in college I slept with five men. I was out of control. It just felt so good to finally be free. Then the pregnancy and abortion brought me right back down, only lower. I had no idea who the hell I was. So I went back and tried to play the part of the "proper" I had learned so well, only now it was harder to pull it off.

Beverly was doing what all adolescents do in the process of growing up: struggling to find an identity. Unfortunately for her, she was only trained to be a nice girl, one who adhered to the value systems of an older generation. She had not been taught to love herself and listen to her own needs. It was not as if she wouldn't have chosen to adopt the values that were forced upon her, but she never got a chance to express her wants and needs. She never had an opportunity to choose. In her attempt to find herself, Beverly swung from acting the part of the rigidly proper young lady to that of a carousing vamp. She didn't know what her personal boundaries were so it was to be expected that she would open herself to others without reasonable discretion. In adolescence, which should be a time of experimentation and discovery, Beverly suffered because she went too far. She is now in the process of learning who she is and how to experience her true feelings. As she explores emotions for the first time she is often amazed by them. She is acknowledging limits and boundaries and finding out that these boundaries can be a source of freedom rather than sanctions that are imposed from the outside. Now, through her use of group psychotherapy, Beverly is beginning to do the work on the inside that had been neglected for so long.

Help for Adult Victims of Abuse

There are many different ways a child's boundaries may be damaged or destroyed. Beverly's fell as a result of parents who lacked a clear sense of themselves and relied on rigidly defined social protocols and rules of etiquette as a means of defining themselves. Childhood boundaries are also compromised by the unpredictabilities, role reversals, and the gross dysfunctions of the alcoholic household. In households where there is incest or other forms of violence there is an actual breaking of physical boundaries. Generally speaking, victims from these families will either become enablers or abusers in their own right or a combination of both. They tend to carry the dysfunctional script into the next generation and perpetuate a cycle of negative behavior.

Victims of these families can find help even after they've become adults. My five-step program stressing acknowledgment of the truth, understanding the dynamics of one's family of origin, practicing sets of new behaviors, looking for support from people with similar problems, and looking at the cycles of behavior that normally trip you up are positive ways to map out the pitfalls of your life. Recovery is a process that begins with understanding and acceptance. We understand what happened to us as children, confront the truth, and overcome denial. Then we accept what happened for the reality that it was. It need not inform our futures for the rest of our lives. You will find that, despite what you may have believed about the inevitability of your reactions, you have a lot more control over your life than you think. If you practice making decisions about what you want and give yourself the space to make mistakes without penalizing yourself overmuch, you'll find that change will be easier and the results more easily measured.

Be vigilant to recurring patterns of behavior. Be aware of your feelings—they will never lie. Don't be afraid to listen to those who challenge your structure of reality but don't necessarily surrender your structure of reality to someone else. Recognize that you might have been in denial throughout your childhood and that you might still be in denial even now. Most important, however, empower yourself to change. It is your right as a human being and your responsibility as a parent, friend, and lover.

9

The Enabler in the Workplace

"It's like I never left home," Jane confessed to the rest of the group. "I'd only been working at SE for a couple of months when it was just like a déjà vu thing, the exact same feelings. I was as uncomfortable and doing the same things at the office that got me in trouble at home. When I knew I had fallen into the exact same pattern, that's when I knew the gig was up." Jane complained that as soon as the people in her new office became accustomed to her presence, they began dumping paperwork on her desk as if she were the office slave. "They'd be off having a late lunch at the Newsroom or John's Doggie Shop while I was doing their overflow work. Then they'd get the praise and I'd just sit there. I knew if I quit and went somewhere else, they'd still keep their jobs and I'd go through the same thing I was going through now. The pattern never ends."

As the eldest daughter in her family, Jane shouldered all the work of raising her younger siblings. When something went wrong, it was Jane's fault. When extra chores had to be done, Jane did them without complaining. When her mother had to go into rehab, Jane made all the arrangements. It was always Jane. Finally, she realized there was no way out until *she* stopped the machine. She was ice-cold with fear at first. But she had gotten to the point where the pain of shouldering all of the abuse, even though it was pleasantly familiar, was just too much. That was when she stopped, turned off the internal voice that kept giving orders, and refused to carry the burden. She felt guilty at first, but she compressed it into a ball and stuffed it into her pocketbook. She let it out in group, but by then we were all able to shine a light on it. Jane was able to talk about her problems without guilt staring her in the face. You can do the same thing.

When enablers, adult children of alcoholics or others who were raised in dysfunctional families leave home to enter the work-place, they often find that they inadvertently play out the same roles that they played in their families of origin. If a person was a rescuer or an adjuster in the family, chances are he or she will act out that role at work. Everyone will soon learn that in a pinch you can always count on Jane. She might even be so reliable that she'll let people take advantage of her, all the while smiling. Similarly, a person who served as the family victim is likely to play the boss's victim at the office. And once the boys at the office find a victim, they heap on the abuse until he or she is out the door. No matter how hard the victim tries, he'll keep on finding ways to fail the very people who count on him. Eventually people dismiss him as a deadbeat, and from job to job he keeps fulfilling those expectations.

Work, as substance abuse therapist Janet Woititz has said, is just like a home away from home. Regardless of the type of family we come from, we either seek out or replicate the same conditions at work that we grew up with at home. If you are fortunate enough to come from a relatively healthy family, then you will find yourself equipped with enough of the emotional and inter-personal tools you may need to make your experience at work a success. On the other hand, for most of us who were not so lucky, work can become as confusing and frustrating as we found life to be in our families, as my thirtyish-year-old client reveals below. She is just beginning to understand the connection between her role in her dysfunctional family of origin and her experience on the job.

> In every job I've had I always end up feeling disappointed. It just seems so important that I please my boss and my co-workers
> . . . everybody! No matter where I work the same things keep happening. I'm always feeling as if I have to do more, yet nothing

ever seems quite good enough. I've seen it enough now to know that it's me.

Many people have recognized the importance of work in an individual's life. In our working class society, our lives are defined by our careers and our days by the types of jobs we do. For people who are satisfied with their time at work, their existence seems purposeful, and they are healthy and satisfied. On the other hand, when work becomes a frustrating, endless series of chores, people suffer from stress, physical ailments, and churning angst. Freud so valued work that he attributed one half of life's importance to it. (The other half was love.) Indeed, work is a potential source of great meaning and satisfaction. One can easily see how fragile this satisfaction can be, if as a result of a co-worker's dysfunction, a once satisfying job has become a dreaded daily burden. Usually it takes more than just a co-worker with a problem to breed dissatisfaction at the office; it also takes at least one enabler.

As a licensed employee assistance practitioner, I've consulted with corporations about chemically dependent and otherwise troubled employees for over eight years. During that time I've been a part of the implementation process of employee assistance programs that cover over fifty thousand employees and family members all over the United States. Much of what you'll see in this chapter is based on my experiences in helping supervisors, employees, and their family members at work sites that range from the office to the assembly line, from urban to rural, and from the mailroom to the oak-paneled boardroom.

Teamwork

Teamwork is the key to fitting in. Part of the requirements of almost any job is that individuals subordinate themselves to the greater good of the company. If people perform their mutual tasks well, all benefit. Accordingly, American workers are re-markably cooperative in pulling together to get the job done, even though our society is informed by the mystique of the high-plains drifter, the loner who refuses to conform, gets the job done, saves the day, and moves on into the horizon. From the barn raisings of the 1700s and 1800s, to the mobilization of industry in World War II, to the bailout of the Chrysler Corporation, our real collective history is marked by a spirit of working together. A function of this kind of cooperative working together is reciprocity, workers picking up the slack from someone else on the team. This can be called "good" enabling.

All co-workers have an investment in making sure their project is a success. Whether we're working together to launch the space shuttle or to stock a row of shelves down at the A&P, we have a mutual interest in making sure it goes well. Because of my interest, I may at times fill in for you if, for whatever the reason, you are not up to it. And because of our reciprocal relationship, I may do so quite willingly. In this sense, my tendency to enable is built right into my job and our work relationship. In fact, if I choose to not act as a team player, I may feel both a pressure from my peers to conform and a coercive influence from my supervisor to pitch-in with all the rest. The problem only arises when one of us repeatedly chooses not to carry his or her fair share while another tends to do too much in order to compensate. This is where healthy cooperation leaves off and dysfunction and covering up take over. This is also when the familiar family dynamics of enabling kick in.

It is only natural to do what feels familiar and comfortable. This is oftentimes the way it is when we begin to enable at work. Let's not forget that the origins of all enabling lie in altruism. Therefore, if you see yourself acting out the part of an enabler at work, you first have to stop beating yourself up over it. Forgive yourself! You are simply doing what you learned in your family. Second, allow yourself to recognize the fundamentally benevolent nature of your actions. The only problem is that your behavior has gotten out of control. Enabling at work, like all forms of enabling, is basically an obsessive and compulsive pattern. If you grew up in a family that required this behavior and attitude it is only understandable that, unless otherwise brought into check, you will continue to replicate this pattern.

Out of Control

When people fall into patterns of enabling at work there is both good news and bad news about it. The bad news is that the enabling behavior tends to be out of control. There may be a peer who, for whatever reason, never seems capable of following through on a task. You might end up doing it and saying, "It's easier if I do it myself." Or you might find yourself acting the role of the fireman, always putting out the brush fires and other crises that tend to crop up. When people enable, it eventually becomes a habitual pattern that is usually never questioned. We get up, go to work, and slip into our enabling mind-set as soon as we cross the office threshold. The good news is that despite the insidious nature of enabling, when it is done at the workplace it is much more easily seen than in either our family of origin or in our nuclear family and love relationship. The best news is that when it comes to enabling, having *any* perspective is helpful. The structure of the workplace allows that opportunity. My client Jane shares some of her insights about her tendency to act out a pattern of enabling she originally learned by growing up in her family.

I guess I've always been a bit of a star. I've always liked the recognition that it gave me. I mostly like it at work, but that wasn't always the case in my life.

When I was a kid I *had* to come through in a big way for my family. My mother was alcoholic and I had to raise my younger sisters virtually myself. My father was a caring man, but he was always working, so that left only one person to take care of the house: Me. I washed, cleaned, cooked, and even made sure my sisters had done their homework. Sure, I felt good that my father was proud of me, but I really felt that I had to come through. I had to be a star, otherwise I was afraid that the family would fall apart. It's no wonder that I have absolutely no interest in having children, I already raised an entire litter by the time I was fourteen!

These days, however, I find myself being a star at the office. If anybody needs a project followed up on, they call Jane. If anybody needs something in a hurry, they call me too. I even have managers from other areas coming over to ask for my help. Actually, it's very flattering. But I've been coming to realize that I'm there for everyone else, but no one ever seems to be there for me at work or at home. Not when I was a kid, not in my first marriage, and not at work. It gets me angry. I wish I would find it easier to come through for myself!

Jane's pattern of enabling has dictated how her work habits, life patterns, and personal relationships spool into one another. She has truly been out of control of her life for as long as she can remember. By virtue of her actions and her father's inactions, Jane's mother was allowed to let her alcoholism go unchecked. To this day her mother is still an active alcoholic. Through her family experience Jane developed a perception of the world as a dangerous and ever-changing place in which, unless one was hypervigilant and always in control, everything might crumble away. Jane feared that her family might disintegrate and consequently did whatever she could to keep it intact. Although she kept things very much in control, inside Jane felt quite the opposite. Keeping a family together is a monumental task and tremendously unfair for any twelve-year-old. But when the twelve-year-old learns how to do it well, it becomes her job for the rest of her life unless she decides to change.

In addition to seeing the world as unsafe, Jane learned to see herself as vital to any situation or relationship. It got to the point where she would only feel good about herself if she were in the position of being essential. She became what is commonly called a "control freak." When she was courting and found herself in a relationship with an equally competent man, invariably Jane would find a reason for the relationship not to work out. At times she would feel bored, sometimes generally dissatisfied, and eventually would dismiss these feelings as indications that he was not the right guy. What Jane realized later in therapy was that she always felt not good enough when she was with a man who was her equal. She had to improve some loser's life in order for the relationship to work. Without a problem to be solved or an inadequacy to be rectified, she simply didn't feel needed or worthwhile. It was not surprising therefore when Jane married a man who eventually turned out to be emotionally unexpressive, physically unfaithful, and generally irresponsible. This marriage was an enabler's paradise.

Interestingly enough, it wasn't until she came in for counseling to remedy her general dissatisfaction at work that Jane began to see the pattern of enabling in all the areas in her life. Because Jane was receptive to looking at herself, she was able to see the origins of her tendency to enable in her family. She also allowed herself to face the guilt, shame, and general feelings of low self-esteem that she carried. Like many enablers in the workplace, Jane was using her status as "Ms. Reliable" as an attempt to compensate for these feelings of not being good enough.

It is much easier to leave work issues at work than to leave home issues at home. Whether it's the upset from just having had an argument with your spouse before getting on the train or the much longer-term upset from being raised in a dysfunctional family, we tend to carry the perceptions of ourselves that we learn at home to all our relationships outside the family. And that includes work.

Double Checking

You might be asking yourself, "How can I tell for sure if I'm setting myself up for failure at work?" "What are the signs that I might be carrying a dysfunctional pattern of relating to people into the office?" Or "How do I know if I'm enabling at the office, when I'm basically a helpful person?" These are very reasonable questions to ask. All by themselves, these questions indicate you are willing to examine your work relationships and have a willingness to be open. That's essentially all you will need in first understanding your pattern of enabling and eventually getting a handle on it.

The chances are that if you've known yourself to take on the role of enabler in your family and other significant relationships, it would be very surprising if you did not also do so at work. This is entirely expected because it is basic human nature to transfer our perceptions of our place in the world and in our relationships to all the contexts in which we find ourselves. Because the one sure common denominator in all your relationships is you, it's only reasonable to expect the same patterns to play out wherever you go. The question is how do you recognize the manifestation of enabling behavior and attitudes at the office? Fortunately, work settings almost always provide a wonderful opportunity for observing your enabling behavior. The reason is that unlike our romantic, sibling, parental, and other significant relationships, there are clear expectations of what constitutes appropriate and responsible behavior and performance on the job.

When we sign our employment contracts and agree to perform a specific job in return for specific compensation, we make a commitment that is measurable and holds us accountable for our performance. Because the work contract is written in behavioral terms, we may sit down with our supervisor during our annual review and have an objective method of determining whether the terms of the agreement have been fulfilled. Under routine circumstances, the agreement is clear, the supervisor has defined standards of evaluation, and we even have specific grounds for recourse if the boss tells us we've not been fulfilling the requirements of the job. These same standards can also tell us whether we've been asked to do something that is beyond the scope of our job descriptions.

This is the way it should be in all normal relationships. There are certain expectations that govern how we will behave toward each other and how people respond to us. We establish social contracts with friends and acquaintances that may change within a range of behaviors according to the dynamics of the relationships, but we know what to expect. If the relationship is healthy, chances are that any misunderstandings in expectations will be addressed by either person. If the relationship is dysfunctional the lack of communication will increase in direct proportion to the degree of dysfunction. But these are social relationships that do not and should not govern us when we are faced with examining our mutual expectations on the job. Yet they inevitably do. And when they form a long-term pattern that follows us from job to job and makes us feel as if we can never escape our dysfunctional families, we know that we are enablers at work just like we've been enablers at home. We have to stop the enabling behavior.

In the workplace we have the opportunity to see whether performance matches expectation. If we are an employee who has not been performing up to standard, then we hope we may be subject to the feedback from a supportive and objective boss. This gives us the opportunity to make whatever adjustments are necessary in order to address the problem. If we are to some degree impaired by an emotional problem or by the use of alcohol or other drug and are resistant to addressing the personal problem that is the cause of the work problem, then we will do whatever we can to get the boss not to make demands about the work problem. However appropriate the supervisor's expectations may be, oftentimes in order to perform adequately on the job, the personal problem at the root of the performance problem must first be addressed. An employee in this case is likely to employ one or more of the following avoidance strategies: attempting to become invisible by just getting by at work, denying that there is a problem in the first place, or if confronted, distracting the boss away from the real problem by either acting like this is really the boss's problem or by attempting to elicit the boss's sympathy by telling tales of disappointments and upset with problems outside of work. This last is one of the oldest and most effective strategies for eliciting enabling tendencies from a boss. It makes it especially difficult for the boss to then confront the employee on the basis of poor performance. It would be tantamount to saying,

> I am your overly demanding and insensitive boss and despite the fact that both your parents are dying of cancer and your child is about to undergo a liver transplant and you can barely make it as a single parent on this pitiful salary, I nevertheless have the nerve to put forth the heartless demand that unless you shape up today, I'll ship you out tomorrow!

No boss wants to be seen as a heartless bastard, and consequently, if he or she has been sucked into a dialogue with the employee about the employee's personal problems, the boss's effectiveness as a manager will inevitably begin to wane. When the supervisor's legitimate expectations and ability to set and enforce limits are taken away, the person quickly becomes one of the dysfunctional employee's many enablers. This disarming of a supervisor is a particularly effective skill that impaired employees hone to a fine science. This pattern of avoidance and denial is especially likely in the presence of a chemical dependency problem.

Chemical Dependency

It has been well established that *at least* 10 percent of the general population will at some time in their lives have a problem in controlling the use of alcohol, cocaine, or some other drug. This is a very conservative figure and it helps to make the point that even if only 10 percent are impaired in their abilities to fulfill their obligations to their job, spouse, children, health, finances, and adherence to community standards, it's an awful large number of people who are walking around without being fully functional. Furthermore, it is a fact of life that the vast majority of chemically dependent individuals hold down positions of responsibility in the community, including significant duties in the workplace. The reality is that when these individuals are active in their addiction, they can't help but be somewhat dysfunctional at work. Different people manifest their impairment differently, all the way from being drunk at work to missing deadlines and shirking responsibilities, to using too much sick time and reducing the productivity of the organization. A chemically dependent employee almost always negatively impacts on the work environment. It's merely a question of when and how.

Three Phases of Chemical Dependency

When employees are chemically dependent, they tend to pass through a series of three phases of the chemical abuse cycle that have corresponding signals at work.

PHASE 1. In phase one of the cycle, the employee tries to get relief from the building tension. Initially, there is an increased tolerance to the effects of the drug. Later on in the phase, the individual begins to experience occasional blackouts and fabricates the real truth about his use of the substance. At work, the employee comes in late or leaves early, is present at the workplace but disappears from his desk, begins to experience tension or conflict with co-workers, routinely misses deadlines, loses productivity because of poor judgment and inattention, and complains of physical problems or illness.

At the beginning of this phase most supervisors would tend to not notice the employee's emerging pattern of declining job performance. Supervisors usually express the natural human trait to give a person the benefit of the doubt. As a result, the first indicators that something may be wrong are either not observed or are dismissed as merely the case of someone's having a bad day. Everyone has a bad day once in a while; however, what the supervisor can't know at this point is that these signs are only the tip of the iceberg. For a normal supervisor who is competent in assessing the level of declining performance of a subordinate and confronting it if warranted, this period of being understanding and humane is admirable. It reflects an understanding of her responsibility to keep things moving, but at the same time cues her to watch for the time to "shake things up." She knows that her job performance is on the line as well and that she's measured by the productivity of her subordinates.

The supervisor who is prone to enable is a different story. The enabling supervisor is perceived by both peers and subordinates as vacillating between being a nice person and being a wimp. The person may very well be humane, but as is the case with all enablers, there is more to it than meets the eye. Remember, all enablers have a vested interest in preserving the status quo. They are afraid of upsetting the apple cart, even if there is a job to be done. With this in mind, we can see how easy it is for such a supervisor to think that everything is perfectly fine in the first phase. However the supervisor who enables inadvertently allows a problem that at first may be solvable, to get worse.

PHASE 2.   When the employee enters the middle phase of the abuse cycle, he really starts to go downhill. He is in denial about the extent of his abuse and consciously conceals the evidence of his habit. In fact, much of his energy during the day is spent planning when he can next medicate himself. Paradoxically, at the same time he experiences twinges of guilt because deep down even he knows how bad he is getting. He tries to control the frequency and quantity of alcohol or drug used, but fails at this time and again. By the end of phase 2, the user is isolated from friends and loved ones and spends a great deal of time infatuated with his new love: alcohol and drugs.

During the middle phase, all of the initial indicators rapidly intensify. The complaints of illness lead to frequent absences for a wide range of infirmities. By now his word, trustworthiness, reliability, and competence have given way to the general rumor on the employee grapevine that he's become undependable. Along with this general deterioration in work performance is an increased difficulty in getting along with co-workers. He's defensive, and when confronted refuses to discuss any problems or makes matters even worse by laying the blame on them instead of taking responsibility for his now obvious difficulties at work. This causes dissension, forces his former friends and allies to take sides, and raises issues of loyalty.

At this point in the disease process and declining job performance, co-workers and supervisors who had once been members of the employee's entourage of enablers—denying the truth while hoping for the best—realize they're on a roller-coaster ride they cannot stop. Where at the beginning of this phase his co-workers might have resisted the idea that they were enabling, by its end they are forced out of denial. It is now obviously clear that the dysfunctional employee is pulling all of them down. Co-workers who once covered for their friend are now frustrated and frequently angry over having to do more work. There is also an increase in grim humor and other forms of cynicism that attempt to mask anger and frustration. Co-workers who were former allies now turn to the boss with complaints. They might now even perceive their boss as a wimp who let everybody down by not addressing the problem earlier. The supervisor who had acted as a primary enabler of the chemically dependent employee is now faced with the fact that *her own* job is now on the line. She is now aware that her attempts to "save" the employee by giving him personal space and time to work out problems have done nothing more than serve as a veiled cover for continued poor performance.

PHASE 3. In the last phase of the cycle the employee is now more of a full-time user than a full-time worker. Through his actions and attitudes people can see that his job is interfering with his substance abuse habit rather than the other way around. This results in unpredictable absences on the job. By now the physical deterioration is obvious as the totality of problems involving his job, family, health, financial, and legal affairs collapse unrelentingly upon him. During his final phase the chemically dependent employee is generally considered to be a pitiful joke among co-workers. There is also a general feeling around the office that "Someone should do something to put this guy out of his misery." At this point even the most liberal and permissive of supervisors can't help but face the reality that it's time for the final warning. At the end, the enabling supervisor who tried to protect him is forced to admit that the employee is beyond help.

Larry is a middle-level manager in a large corporation with about twenty-five professionals and support staff working under him. Larry originally came for counseling because he longed for a more intimate relationship with his wife, but felt incapable of getting what he wanted from her. He loved her but didn't know how to either ask her for what he wanted or confront her when she seemed to run away from him. After a while it became clear that he felt the same powerlessness at work as at home. As he explained,

> I would have never thought that I would think this, no less admit it to anyone, but I feel like I'm a real wimp. I've felt this my whole life and I hate that about myself.
>
> Before I came for counseling I used to think that my wife thought I wasn't good enough in bed. She never said anything and always seemed satisfied, that's what I thought. I even started feeling that my penis wasn't big enough and that she didn't tell me the truth because she felt sorry for me.
>
> Then I realized that this is the same way I had been feeling about myself at work. I wasn't strong enough and I let everybody take advantage of me. I'd try to be fair and a nice guy to my people, but then later think that they laughed at me behind my back. Between the bedroom and the office, I felt that I couldn't do anything right.

What Larry started to face in counseling was his sense of not being good enough. It was understandable that he came to see himself that way given his background. He grew up a black child in a southern community that was a stronghold of the Ku Klux Klan. Furthermore, Larry's father ruled the family with an unyielding and unforgiving iron hand. In childhood he developed a coping mechanism that got him by. He learned to do whatever was necessary to make people like him. He became so adept at being all things to all people that by his early adult years he got himself elected to his town's governing council. The problem was that in developing this coping skill, he lost sight of what he wanted out of life. Concurrently, he began to question and doubt people's motivations whenever they seemed to like him or did something nice for him. This inevitably interfered with his life both at home and at work.

Larry was diligent at work. This helped him get recognition and numerous promotions. But he also behaved as if he were in a popularity contest and that his task was to win the "Mr. Congeniality" award. Unfortunately, this is exactly what prevented him from dealing professionally and forthrightly with John, a formerly outstanding employee who gradually became addicted to cocaine.

> I still feel responsible for John. I know I didn't make him take the drug, but I can clearly see how I made it easy for him to continue.
> Looking back on it now I can see many times over a period of months when he just wasn't himself. Not in personality or in quality of work. He started being out a lot and all I did was hint at my want for him to be in more. Then when his reports started getting shaky, I even ended up rewriting parts for him. I know now I was the perfect boss for his addiction. I was his enabler. Thank God I was in counseling and saw this in time to refer him to the employee assistance program. I think it might have been *the* thing he needed in order to save his life. And to think he almost lost it because I was too afraid of him not liking me and risking me losing the popularity contest I had been playing my whole life.

Fortunately for John, Larry came to understand and see his pattern of enabling in the larger context of his life. With this insight, Larry was then able to change how he acted even in the face of an old internal voice that told him more often than not to get along by going along. He was much more accustomed to that attitude of enabling because it felt familiar and brought him a certain kind of comfort while keeping him bound to the same unsatisfying treadmill. It is indeed hard to stop enabling, but as Larry can attest, having your own life back is worth it.

The enabler cast in the role of supervisor does not want to disappoint or hurt other people's feelings, even if it means that the product doesn't get out, the project isn't completed, or the job is compromised. Like Larry, enablers always have an ulterior motive for their seemingly "nice guy" actions. There is almost always a sense of feeling some kind of deficit and all actions spring out of a want and felt need to either fill the void or at the very least attempt to cover it up. Again, when we talk about a supervisor who is also an enabler, we are not condemning or criticizing him as not being good enough. If we were to do that it would only serve to underscore the perceived need and impulse to enable. The fact of the matter is that when a person enables there is always a good reason for it. That reason doesn't justify the harm that results, but it can explain the underlying causes. The point is that enabling behavior in the workplace tends to feed off itself. One almost always feels justified in acting it out. But once we start to have the insight as to its origins, we begin to arm ourselves in arresting the old pattern of behavior. Similar to controlling addictions, addressing the enabling behavior and attitudes is not a matter of sheer willpower, it's a matter of self-awareness and honesty. One needs to understand its origins, surrender to its presence in our life, and, in the case of a professional manager, develop the awareness that will allow a nonjudgmental observation of oneself in action on the job.

The bottom line is that wherever there is a troubled employee, there is always a troubled supervisor. All of us who have supervised others know that whenever we're not confronting a problem head on, we're juggling, shuffling, and maneuvering to adjust to it. There is, in fact, an old saying among employee assistance program professionals that goes, "Whatever energy you spend denying and delaying dealing with a problem employee, doubles the energy it would take if you just take care of business today." This is true for many things in life, certainly for enabling, and is worth keeping in mind if you are a supervisor.

One of the most common and potentially destructive types of enabling involves a secretary and his or her boss. Regardless whether the secretary or boss is male or female, as long as the two are different sexes, their professional relationship parallels a marital relationship. Moreover, because we already know how much a spouse can inadvertently perpetuate an addiction by not challenging the addict, we can extrapolate to the situation at the office when the boss is addicted to alcohol or drugs.

Assistants have to be the trusted subordinates who are always "there" for the boss when he or she really needs help. Valuable assistants are unquestioningly loyal, tireless in their devotion, and self-sacrificing. The managers I work with have told me time and again that they would kill in order to find assistants or secretaries with these qualities. Managers also know that the general rule of thumb is to take extra special care of a good secretary once you have one, because they're hard to find. You treat them with TLC and protect them from other pillaging managers in the organization. Ironically, though, it's this very "Be there for you in a pinch" kind of loyalty that places secretaries and assistants in a precarious position when the boss is chemically dependent.

One of the things that happens when an executive is addicted is "job shrinkage"; he continues to rely on old solutions to solve new problems. The tried and true techniques that were so helpful earlier in his career suddenly become a set of crutches now that he is no longer operating on all burners. Over the course of time there is a tendency for him to not take on new challenges, and as a result the scope of his job eventually shrinks. When he is flushed into the open, a shrinking executive is sent to the corner to wait for his retirement if he is not fired immediately. His loyal staff members, including secretaries and assistants, want to protect both their boss and their own necks. Therefore, they are apt to cover up for the increasing ineptitude of the boss so as to not go down with the ship and to preserve their own reputations for loyalty within the organization. No manager wants an assistant who will prove to be disloyal even if that disloyalty is a legitimate means of surviving an alcoholic boss. Therefore, the "good" secretary covers for the boss even if he or she knows the boss is an accident waiting to happen. Given the tendency of addicted individuals to fly into a rage because of denial, confrontations or mutinies are out of the question.

There is no universal solution to the dilemma faced by the assistants to an alcoholic boss, but it is worth recognizing that some things are beyond our immediate power to remedy. Once a line is crossed, however, and the addiction becomes destructive and obvious, even the most loyal and enabling secretary finds little choice other than taking action. If a competent and confidential EAP exists, opportunities are afforded for the executive to seek help himself, for management to confront him and offer him a constructive solution to the problem in the form of a referral to

EAP, and, lastly, for the secretary to have access to a confidential source of help.

If you are a secretary or an administrative assistant with a superior whom you know to be an alcoholic or addict, you have to protect yourself without giving him up publicly. If your company has a *confidential* employee assistance program, and I stress confidential, you should find out what it takes to get the practitioner to assess your boss. Usually, you will find the EAP rules in your company's employee handbook, its policies and procedures manual, or its health benefits handbook. Assuming for the moment that you're not an enabler and that you're not going to sacrifice yourself to your boss's addiction, you should be prepared to bring him in for a soft landing if necessary. That means that you're going to make sure that he shows up for his meetings, he signs what has to be signed, and he knows what's on his schedule each and every day. If the other managers know your boss is in a tailspin, they have to be made aware that you as his loyal assistant are taking care that whatever damage he causes is limited.

If you're an enabler, the problem can be a hundred times worse. You will probably start to feel guilty as your boss's performance deteriorates. Recognize that these are old feelings that have been in place since childhood and have nothing to do with your boss. His problems aren't necessarily your problems. Therefore, *it's not your fault!* Worse, the minute you begin to enable your boss, you become his codependent. The minute you become his or her codependent, you will lose all of your objectivity and will become a liability instead of an asset. Everybody in the office will see that you've become a liability and will have to be shipped out along with your boss. Therefore, you have a perfectly valid reason for turning off the voice telling you to take care of the boss and cover up for him at every turn. In order to protect your boss better, you have to remain rigidly routine and professional. You can address your enabling tendencies separately, perhaps by going to your company's EAP on your own behalf, and using the boss's problem as a way of solving your own. Sounds tricky, but it works.

Enabler's Toolkit for the Workplace

Most enablers in supervisory positions tend to avoid confrontations with their employees. Even when the employee is not performing up to expectations, the enabler may often tell himself that the employee's personal problems are none of the supervisor's business. In cases of alcoholism or drug abuse, this excuse no longer carries much weight because companies are enforcing strict rules for alcohol- and drug-related problems on the job. However, for the vast array of personal reasons, enablers believe that they don't have to diagnose a troubled employee because it's not really the employer's business. This is a false perception and it can easily get an enabler into trouble at the workplace because as the employee's work begins to suffer, the supervisor is the one who will eventually take the flak. On the other hand, supervisors who are not enablers may also worry that if they become too involved with an employee, they can be sucked in and become part of the problem. That's why many employees are left to fend for themselves when their work begins to decline.

Therefore, supervisors may ask, "What do you do when the quality or quantity of an employee's work begins to decline?" If you're an enabler, you don't want a confrontation and you surely don't want to get the employee fired. If you're not an enabler but are afraid of getting involved in the employee's personal affairs, where do you draw the line between professional feedback and personal involvement? The answer to both questions lies in determining beforehand the scope of your comments and the range of options you have at your disposal. Whatever comments a supervisor has must be restricted to on-the-job behavior and attendance. These are the only issues that concern you. If he or she has personal problems at home that impair performance in the workplace, you have to be aware of it. You may not be able to do anything about the personal problems directly, but by addressing the issues of job performance and showing how the employee's personal problems affect it, you may encourage the employee to solve them on his or her own.

No matter when you address the issues of your subordinate's declining job performance, you should understand that it began long before you noticed it. Therefore, it's imperative that you be alert and continually observant in the changes in the work behavior pattern of your subordinates. Here is what you need to do:

1. Keep your eyes open for changes in the productivity and attitudes of your employees.
2. Keep your ears open for conversations that may indicate that one or more of your employees are in trouble.
3. When observing a pattern of declining job performance, it's imperative that you intervene early to address the problem by at least letting your employee know that his or her performance is declining.

The problem with most enablers is that they have no scripts for dealing with confrontational issues. Enablers either become hostile because they're afraid of the confrontation, or too passive because they can't face the confrontation in the first place. If you have the ability to put yourself on the employee's side right from the outside, you don't have to be locked into either position. Here's how to address the issue: Be straightforward. Explain that you notice your employee's declining productivity and that you want to help. You simply want the employee to know that you're aware that something seems amiss. Without challenging the employee to argue with your observation, let him or her know that you're available to talk if necessary. You might say, "You've been here but haven't been getting much done of late. Your output isn't what it has been in the past and in fact is below average. Is there anything I need to know?"

If your employee rejects your assessment of his or her performance, point to whatever productivity reports or records you need to establish your assertion. Again, you don't need to be confrontational. Simply remind the employee that you are only going by the paperwork and that if he or she disagrees, you'll be happy to listen to the other side. In the meanwhile, you still have to go by the reports. Reestablish that you're on the employee's side and that you're available for a talk.

If the employee turns down your offer of help, you should simply remind him or her that you're available. "OK I just need you to take care of this" should be sufficient to establish where the responsibility lies. If the employee's performance continues to decline or if it resumes declining after a brief remission, it's incumbent upon you to readdress the problem. A healthy supervisor would allow a brief period of time to elapse to see which direction the employee was taking before raising the issue again. When you raise the issue this time, you should offer such specific constructive steps for remediation as a tailored contract between the employee and yourself regarding specific tasks to be accomplished and when. Use this contract opportunity to make up for work that is backlogged, work that has to be redone because it was below standard, or work that needs to be reassigned to the employee because the department's entire performance has been impaired by the bottleneck caused by the employee. You may also want to refer the employee to your company's EAP. Do this only if you feel it necessary to pass the problem along because you think it will not go away. EAPs are there to help. They are run by professionals specifically trained to address employee problems.

Should the employee's behavior continue to display a pattern of declining or inadequate job performance and you have not already referred him or her to an EAP, now is the time to do so. This is an imperative decision to make because failure to make the referral may be regarded as a serious lapse in your own professional judgment. However, if after a reasonable period of time, despite the intervention of an employee assistance practitioner, the pattern of poor job performance still continues or if the employee's output declines even further, then you must take further action in the form of either suspension, formal disciplinary action, or putting the employee on notice of termination.

This path contains pitfalls for supervisors who are inclined to be enablers. Codependent problems also play out in work relationships. Statements such as "Do I have a right to demand this of this person?" "What if he or she loses his or her job as a result of my demands?" "How will everyone look at me?" are some of the anxieties that will rise up in an enabler. However, remember this: you have a right and a responsibility to demand a reasonable minimum level of performance from all your subordinates. That level of performance requires that they be at work, that they get their jobs done, that their jobs get done on time, and that the quality of their work be acceptable, whether they work on an assembly line or in front of a CRT. All supervisors have a right to an acceptable level of job performance, even if only at a minimum level.

EAP counselors are also available to help supervisors through their own issues when it comes time to confront troubled employees. They can help you sort out your issues of codependency and enabling behaviors, overcontrol or hypervigilance, and work through your tendencies to avoid confrontational situations. No doubt you've managed to reconcile your enabling instincts to the demands of your job for as long as you've been on the job. However, many enablers often encounter job-related situations that challenge them on basic personality levels and threaten their jobs or their careers.

The danger for enablers who are supervisors, like all people who are prone to be passive, is that when they first begin to take action, they often feel an impulse to come down hard. The fear of being so demanding and angry often paralyzes the enabler from making demands that are reasonable. Therefore, my general advice is to intervene early, confront the employee in a supportive way about what you see—after all, you are both on the same team—and remember that it's your right to take reasonable steps to help an employee perform to an acceptable standard. Supervisors who are also enablers consistently overlook that which needs addressing. This is most unfortunate in the case of chemical addiction and severe emotional problems because the problem is often not addressed until the situation reaches critical deterioration. Therefore, once a supervisor sees a pattern of unacceptable behavior or of a decline in productivity, he or she must take action to protect the company, his or her job, and also the employee.

10

The Enabler's Toolkit

By now you realize that enabling is a very pervasive form of behavior that can occur in a wide variety of contexts. At the same time it is also an entirely normal component of most relationships. Being normal, however, does not necessarily mean enabling is particularly helpful or productive. Neither does it mean that enabling is a disease. The fact is that enabling is simply a bad habit. For most people, it is an old, once functional coping strategy now gone awry, a well-meaning attempt to deal with an unhealthy or emotionally destructive situation that is no longer threatening. Whether you learned enabling at home in a dysfunctional family or as a response to the dysfunctional behavior of your partner or spouse, it is now time for you, as well as your partner, to break this bad habit. It is clear that you can't control the actions of your partner, but you certainly can take charge of your own life.

We've seen how enabling develops and how you need to position yourself to overcome it; now it's time for some practical advice for doing so. This chapter is your toolkit. First, it contains a variety of ways to help you identify your specific pattern of enabling. Next, it will prescribe practical remedies for overcoming those patterns.

Forgiveness: Presetting Your Emotional State

Begin by forgiving yourself. That's the first place to start. Take for granted that enabling has caused you pain. For most people, enabling is a very hurtful thing. It's so upsetting that it's often used as justification for continually beating ourselves up. Chances are that whether you know it or not, you are like most enablers and are as mad as hell about it. You are probably angry about how it came about in the first place and are disappointed in the many ways it has interfered with your life. Many people who know themselves to be enablers report carrying around a feeling of hopeless desperation that they are powerless to effect change in the most important areas of their life. They have every right to be angry. Almost all enablers burn with a fuming rage every day of their lives. It's like being on fire and being the fire fighter at one and the same time.

Trusting Yourself

We know with certainty that when and if we are capable of trusting ourselves, things seem to go better in our lives. This is what happens when we allow that natural positive potential that lies within all of us to be tapped. When we allow that great reserve of forward-moving energy to be released, there is almost nothing we can't do for ourselves. The good news is that when we trust ourselves or even act as if we trust ourselves, we are able to succeed.

Assumptions

We start with several assumptions we must make at the outset. The first is that people who are committed to healing and maintain that commitment through adversity will eventually succeed. I've witnessed amazing transformations in the course of my practice: teenage cocaine addicts who would think nothing of regularly stealing from their mothers' purses, alcoholics whose lives and relationships were in complete tatters, and adult children of alcoholics who carried within them a self-hatred and self-doubt that only served to perpetuate their dissatisfaction with their lives and their successive strings of disappointments. All of them were able to transform their lives into rich, satisfying experiences. But this happened only after they mustered the courage to face their pain.

When we allow ourselves to experience and explore our vulnerabilities, our anger, and our seething frustration within a supportive setting, emotional healing begins to take place. As part of this process, the natural tendencies to grow in a healthy and positive direction always unfold. It's as inevitable as the biological mechanism that forces plants to grow toward the sun. This natural healthy tendency is in all people.

The second assumption is that this positive growth potential is ready to operate on its own. In essence we are assured self-healing if we can set aside the negative self-talk and recognize the disappointments and pain of the past for what they are: the past. What interferes? Most of the time, people inhibit their own growth potential because negativism is all they have ever known. They were taught it as children of dysfunctional families where they experienced frustration, sadness, guilt, shame, and disappointment. They were taught very early that their lives were worthless and they were undeserving of any happiness. Therefore, it would only be natural for such a person not to trust in his or her own capacity for positive change. They don't know what it looks like or how it tastes or smells. They only know, based on family history, that if it is good, then it is not for them. It is this very attitude that plagues codependents and other enablers. Listen to the inner monologue of the enabler:

> I don't really deserve to have things better in my life. And even if I was worthy, I'd still probably end up on the short end of the stick. I know I'd like to be happier, have people treat me better and feel more sure of myself, but I can't ever really expect that to happen. So in the meantime I'll just hang on to what I've got. Life's unfair and that's the way it is.

This is the mind-set of a victim. This is what it feels like to have the control of one's life determined by forces from the outside. This is a very powerless feeling. And where there is such powerlessness, there is usually an enormous amount of anger. Most enablers don't often see themselves as angry people, but the fact of the matter is that while in their enabler mind-set they can't even confront their anger and rage, it is so huge. People who live or work around them come to know the signs of that anger and tread very lightly when they sense it's near the surface. That only makes enablers madder, and they turn that fury upon themselves. They realize that their facial expressions, body language, and demeanor are sending off bad vibrations. They also fear that by making people tense around them, they will make people angry around them. But they can't confront the anger of others anymore than they can confront their own. Hence, they are in a roiling conflict that only feeds upon itself. But enablers are controllers who've learned how to clap on the control mechanism. Therefore, the anger rarely explodes to the surface. It only simmers, making normal people steer a wide berth around them, while dysfunctional addicts—those who've come to know and love enablers—are attracted as though they had homing devices. What keeps codependents and other enablers stuck is that this anger is inadvertently directed against themselves. The results are feelings of depression and self-depreciation.

On the other hand, if this personal power were tapped for productive use, there is almost no limit to the positive changes it could spawn. This is exactly why it is so important to allow ourselves to trust that there is a force inside of all of us that is ready to move in a productive, positive, social direction if we only allow it to happen. It's the very life force that was present at birth, but was stunted as a result of encounters with family, school, and church. For a while it became redirected as self-anger and lead to disappointment and upset, but now you perhaps are beginning to recognize the possibility of using it for the enrichment of your life. Maybe you're telling yourself that all of this positive life force and attitude stuff sounds pretty good, but that you have no idea what to do with it. Since you can't tap into it or turn it on like water from a spigot, where do you find it? Who can give it to you?

Here's the big ten-million-dollar tip that every successful person already knows:

In the absence of a genuine sense of personal trust,
act like it anyway.

This does not mean faking it or lying to yourself about your self-doubts. This is not denial. I suggest, though, that in the very face of your personal history of feeling not good enough or ineffective, you must make a choice to act differently. Say to yourself, if I had all the right parenting and I came from a set of perfect parents, how would I behave? Then act that way. Once you do, things will begin to change right away.

When we act as if we trust our inner resources, we give ourselves an opportunity to relearn what trust feels like. When this happens, the successes that are likely to follow will serve to encourage us to continue this experiment in personal change. The self-talk of a person who is struggling to face his or her feelings about his- or herself and at the same time attempting to be different can be expressed in the following affirmations. Apply them to your own situation and repeat them to yourself. Keep repeating them as you are confronted with each situation that challenges your will to succeed. Armed with these affirmations you will succeed:

> I am aware that I doubt myself and have a tendency to want to give up. I have carried a shame and a sense of not being quite good enough inside me for as long as I can remember. I learned to enable others in order to protect myself from losing whatever I had. The easy thing for me to do is to assume that things won't get better. Although it's not very satisfying, I know it's safer that way. But I'm going to try to be different.
>
> I'm going to risk giving up my familiar feelings of disappointment. Instead I'm choosing to act as if I love and trust myself. Without denying my doubts, I'm discovering that when I act as if I like myself, I actually start to feel as if I really do! When this happens it's really exciting, so much so that I feel anxious. I am aware that I feel frightened I might count on this good feeling to last, only to face the usual disappointment.
>
> Most of the time I feel the impulse to give up and resort to my old familiar ways and sometimes I feel I do. But I also realize that if the good feelings occur more than the bad ones, then I'm doing better in the long run. So when I fall back I'm resolved to allow myself to not be perfect and I pick myself up and act as if I trust myself. I'm hoping that at some point the feelings will stick.

Just as the journey of three thousand miles begins with one step, behaving as if we trust in ourselves and in our natural tendencies for positive emotional growth can afford us the opportunity to change one step at a time, one day at a time. As you change your behavior you must also readjust your attitude. A mind-set fixed in worry and doubt will only serve to maximize the probability of failure.

Life experiences, whether they result from a dysfunctional childhood or abusive adult relationships, underscore negative affirmations. "You're not good enough; you're not worth it; and you'll always be a failure" is the kind of negative self-talk that these unhealthy relationships breed. What is required now is to substitute new positive affirmations. Statements such as "I'm a good person, I can learn to trust myself, and I can do fine if I turn my problems over to my higher power" can go a long way in rewriting your personal life script. A conscious effort to incorporate positive self-talk into our daily life is an enormous help in overcoming a self-defeatist attitude. Remember, the negative self-talk has been running on an endless loop inside your head for so long that your conscious and concerted effort to replace it with positive affirmations is required. The reality is that all efforts to overcome enabling behavior will be futile unless a willingness to change our attitude and behavior comes first. What is required is to recognize both intellectually and in your heart that:

1. The natural capacity to grow in a positive direction is within all people, including you.
2. You need only try as best as you can to increase the frequency of tapping your intellectual and emotional resources to enrich your life.

Whenever any of us tries anything new, we occasionally meet with disappointment and failure. The important thing is not to be afraid to fail. It is even more important to resist letting the fear (which is natural) get in the way of doing what needs to be done. Therefore it is important that you also recognize that occasionally failing during your experiment in personal change is not only expected, but it is a valuable source of learning about yourself.

It's OK to lose a battle here and there. As long as we're alive, the war is still winnable. Yogi Berra's "It ain't over 'till it's over" is absolutely true. It is a well-known fact that British novelist John Creasey published over 550 books and that Babe Ruth hit 714 home runs. But what is commonly overlooked is the fact that in the course of accomplishing these feats Creasey received over 750 rejection slips from publishers and that Ruth struck out over 1,300 times. Failing and making mistakes is how we learn. It is how we learn to make adjustments. Although you may feel that failure or mistakes are like death, the fact is that they're only transitory setbacks. They're opportunities to be channeled into personal success. Risking personal trust requires the courage to face ourselves and, while it is the first and biggest step in the process of personal change, we have many opportunities to try it again. One step at a time. One day at a time.

The Tools

Here is the toolkit you were promised. It contains a variety of tools from which you may choose to use in overcoming your enabling attitudes and behavior. It is my hope that, when ready, you will really allow yourself to take an active part in your experimenting with new techniques for transforming yourself. Pretend you are a scientist interested in creating something new: a you unbound from the yoke of enabling. I encourage you to continue the experiment until you find the formula that works best for you.

The Process

This is how to implement the process of change according to the Five Steps to Overcoming Enabling Behavior we talked about earlier in the book.

Recognition

1. There is a general tendency among most enablers to experience the world as a series of either/or events. Either I'm all good or all bad—I'm either doing excellent in recovery or just barely holding my ground. This kind of "two-valued thinking" is characteristic of many adults who have grown up in dysfunctional fami-

lies. It is an old coping mechanism that was originally used to make sense out of a chaotic world that you were powerless to alter. It is commonly seen in some recovering enablers who substitute being aggressive and demanding in place of their previously passive attitude. Regardless of how you manifest this type of either/or thinking in your life, remember, all that's needed is for you to pay attention to the possibility that you may be viewing yourself or the world in black or white. You may be limiting the maneuvering room necessary to express yourself fully. If you notice that you are, forgive yourself and move on. It's all a part of the recovery process.

2.　Many enablers find it helpful to keep a *behavioral stress journal.* This is a private and confidential collection of events and your reactions to them. Journal writing can be very helpful in focusing your thinking about a person or a particular event in which your usual reaction is to enable. I suggest that you begin by writing about one event per day. Be sure to record what you experienced in anticipation of the event, during, and after. Outline the pages in advance if you like so that you are forced to think in terms of before, during, and after. When you write about your encounter with an enabling situation try as best as you can to distinguish between what you feel and what you think as two separate processes. Your journal will serve as a source of clarity that evolves directly from your willingness to make distinctions between thinking and feeling. Many people find it helpful to write in it at the same time every day, but your schedule may not allow that. The times that you write and the frequency of your making entries are entirely up to you. However, you should try to make some space during the day for it.

3.　Part of your journal, or as a separate exercise entirely, is what I call the *enabling decision tree.* This is another tool to help you work through issues so you can take control of your enabling behavior. If you've ever seen the troubleshooting guides in most new appliance or car owners' manuals, then you know what I mean by a decision tree. It is a series of yes/no questions for specific problems such as: "Light on?" "Fan on?" "Paper feed?" "Sound?" and other typical questions you'd answer about your VCR, new television, car, or toaster oven. In your journal, you should create the questions you will answer about the events that trigger your enabling behavior. For example, you should ask yourself whether the person you're feeling overly responsible for reminds you of anybody in your family: an alcoholic parent, a codependent parent, a victimized sibling, your youngest sibling. Ask yourself whether you are playing the role of victim, rescuer, or adjuster. Ask yourself whether you will be blamed if you do not intervene to protect the person you are enabling from failure. Who will blame you? Does the situation remind you of an event from childhood? Do you still expect your mother or father to come marching through the front door to accuse you of a lapse in behavior or of being bad or not good enough? In each case, it would be helpful if you flush out the monsters you're keeping in your closet. You should write up a yes/no series of questions about each event that troubles you. As you begin to change your behavior, keep track of what you're thinking about by rereading your decision trees. You'll be surprised at the amount of progress you'll make in just a very short time.

4. Another way to increase your ability to recognize the personal dynamics around your tendency to enable is to *work backward*. I'm especially fond of this behavioral evaluation tool because it invariably points out where the sources of the problem lie. Working backward simply means that you start right at the most painful behavior and evaluate the events that led up to it. Instead of trying to retrace your steps from the beginning, you do what Sherlock Holmes always does and move backward from where you are.

For example, let's say that you're feeling particularly sick to your stomach—an old and familiar sign—because you let your boss walk all over you again. You watched him screw up, he confronted you about it, and even blamed you for his mistake. You caved in. You swallowed the truth he laid out even though both of you knew it was a lie. You could have just walked away and let him fall on his face, but you didn't. You stood there and enabled him to pin the blame on you so he wouldn't lose face. Then, worst of all, you sacrificed your own weekend by working overtime to bail him out. He knows you bailed him out, and not only does he not thank you for it, he goes out of his way to make you feel bad. You've been a martyr again, the same type of martyr you were during most of your childhood. You hate yourself for letting people walk all over you. You hate it especially because you know exactly what you're doing when you're doing it. You can even relive the moment when your resolve melts and you flatten yourself into a footbridge. You may tell yourself that you can't control how you behave but you also believe that's just another way you've been lying to yourself for years. You'd like to display more backbone, but there's nothing you can do about it. You finally ask yourself: "What is it that turns me into a coward?"

Working backward can help you figure that out. If you think about your behavior with any clarity at all, you know that at some point during the confrontation with your boss you felt something tug inside of you. You know that your boss knew just the right buttons to push to get you to agree to lie. Then, once he had you in a lie, he pushed your face in it. But he knew you well enough to predict that once he got you to assume responsibility for his screw up, he had you by the neck. Where in the entire interaction did you turn left when you should have turned right? By creating a decision chain backward from the point where you caved in, you should be able to see what behavior affected what decision and what decision affected what behavior. Were you afraid of your boss? Did you expect some sort of divine retribution if you didn't cave in? Did you grovel because you thought that by bailing out your boss you would get praise and acceptance? Did you feel that because you are always seeking legitimacy, you have to go the extra mile for other people? Did you feel during the entire confrontation that you were being sucked into some kind of whirling vortex from which you couldn't emerge no matter how you tried?

Now work backward from the confrontation. Did you know your boss was going to screw up? How long was it obvious to you that he was going to fall on his face and require your extraordinary services to bail him out? Did your co-workers also know the boss was going to screw up? Did they make a wide berth around him, knowing that when he fell someone was going to have to stand him up? Did your co-workers know in advance that that person was going to be you? Does this feeling that everyone in the office shares a secret about you feel familiar?

Retrace every event and see what your reactions were. If you do it assiduously in your journal, you will see that you gave off clues to everyone in the office that you were the one who'd pick up the pieces. You've been giving the same cues to your boss for as long as you've worked for him. Now analyze some of the specifics that let people know you can't bear to see anyone fail. Does it start to make you sick? Do you begin to feel revulsion because you've been foolish? These are good reactions. They mean that you're probing close to home. Keep pushing until you can't even face yourself or begin to feel confused. At that point, pretend you're someone else and admit to yourself privately that you acted like a fool and will keep on acting like a fool until you stop. At this point be sure to remember your pattern of enabling probably had its roots as an understandable means of coping, and so forgive yourself. Only in the absence of your harsh judgment will you be able to change.

If you can pinpoint the exact chain of behaviors, write them down. Now use your decision tree to rewrite the script. Try to associate your painful feelings with events from your youth. This is probably one of the most painful parts of the exercise, but it will help you get to the truth. Once you've made the relevant associations with behaviors from your childhood, you're in the position to act out different behaviors. Don't go for the moon in one shot. Just be vigilant to when the same behavior chain starts up. When you see it forming, stop it. Just stop it and look for a different reaction. If you remain true to yourself and don't give in, I guarantee that people will be surprised at your behavior and will not have the same expectations of you that they had before. You will feel better about yourself and that positive feeling will give you even more of an impetus to change.

Taking Action

1. First of all it's important to *give credit where credit's due.* The fact is that you have already begun to change. Your very decision to reevaluate your behavior is but one piece of evidence of the change. You may already be involved with other reading materials, self-help groups, and counseling. Allow yourself to feel good about the fact that to the extent that you have been pondering your enabling behavior, you have allowed a desire for change to emerge from within. That's a very good start.

2. One tool that can be particularly helpful in charting a course for overcoming enabling behavior is to imagine what healthy people act like and then to apply this "What would so and so do in this circumstance" to your particular enabling situations and conflicts. This kind of behavioral rehearsing is very effective in preparing a plan of action if, for instance, you aren't sure what to do when your spouse comes home drunk again or when your best friend forgets once again to pick you up on the way to work.

It's not hard to imagine a healthy set of behaviors. You only have to model your behavior on the behavior of someone else you think is healthy. That person doesn't have to be perfectly healthy or normal as long as you believe that certain of his or her reactions make sense to you and seem healthy. One way to seek out healthy behavior models is on television or in motion pictures. Find someone you like and ask yourself what he or she would do in a particular situation. Even though it's a fictional character, if the character rings true to you, you should be able to predict his or her actions. Try it out. If it works, use whatever you can to build the aspects of your personality you think need work.

Changing

1. *Make allowances for people's reactions to you* when you begin to substitute more positive attitudes and behavior for your old enabling style. People often get anxious in the presence of change, especially family members and those close to us. It may be unsettling to them and cause them to wonder if your relationship will still be viable. Don't let their anxiety inhibit making the changes you need for yourself, but remember these changes are never made in a vacuum.

2. *Keep it simple!* This is one of the guiding principles of all twelve-step recovery processes. Don't get lost in mind games. Don't feel you have to figure out that one key event when your mother first screwed you up. There's no need for psychoanalysis. The task at hand is to act with love and compassion for yourself and to give yourself encouragement as you experiment with new nonenabling behaviors. Just do today what needs to be done today and keep it simple.

3. Use a freeze-frame technique to pause the action in what might otherwise feel to be an overwhelming situation in which you might ordinarily act in ways that compromise you. Call a halt to whatever you're doing and analyze your situation to increase your awareness of your feelings, attitude, and behavior. Do this whenever you feel you are being compromised before, during, and after you enable someone else. Remember to play the imaginary video back slowly and take note of your assumptions, feelings, and thoughts as you go along. When you see things that disturb you, allow yourself to play it back over and over again until you can understand what went on. Because human behavior tends to follow an order, rest assured that you can eventually come to understand yourself and your motivations to enable. This technique works particularly well in conjunction with the use of the behavioral stress journal.

Support

1. We are fortunate enough to be living at a time in the life of the recovery movement where there are different choices for support. The old standby that is guaranteed to be helpful is the twelve-step program. You can choose from Alcoholics Anonymous, Narcotics Anonymous, AL-ANON, Adult Children of Alcoholics, Families Anonymous, and Codependents meetings. These are all free, confidential support groups that follow the Twelve Steps and Twelve Traditions. Their purpose is to provide a place where recovering people can provide support and fellowship to each other. The simple and indisputable fact is that these programs work.

2. Sometimes working solo on your own recovery even with the help of a twelve-step group is not enough. The difficulty is usually the result of being so close to the problem that it's easy to get lost in it. That's when it's time to call in the reinforcements. There are a variety of counseling and psychotherapy approaches from which to choose and many books that explain their differences. Make certain that your counselor is comfortable with and has a specialization in dealing with adult children of dysfunctional families, codependency, and addiction issues. The last thing you

need to do is have to educate your own therapist. Many of my current clients tell of previous counseling experiences in which the "professional" admittedly knew little of these matters. Regardless of whether your decision is to work in a psychoanalytic, behavioral, or humanistic approach, the most important thing is that you are comfortable with your counselor or therapist. As long as the relationship is supportive and you feel free to be honest with the therapist, then the psychotherapy is likely to be helpful.

Asserting Yourself

One of the most time-tested ways of implementing healthy change into your life is through the use of assertiveness training techniques. Assertiveness training, which has been written and talked about in seminars and self-fulfillment groups since the 1960s, is predicated upon the fundamental assumption that directly expressing your thoughts, feelings, or requests is your perfect right. First, it is imperative that changes in your enabling behavior be accompanied by attitudinal changes. You have to convince yourself of the rightness of the demands you will make upon yourself and others. In other words, you have to make attitudinal changes from the inside out so that when you do assert your wants and needs, they are more than ineffectual "wish" statements. This can be easily accomplished by affirming to yourself that you have the power, the fortitude, and the perseverance to get you through this stressful period of change.

Affirmations

Affirmations are powerful statements of purpose and intent that, when repeated over and over again during times of stress, operate like mantras. They focus your mind on the positive, drawing it away from fearing the negative, and actually help you carry out your strategies. Affirmations are a part of athletic training programs, sales motivation courses, executive planning sessions, religious ceremonies, and self-help support groups. Affirmations range from such general statements as "We are number one" and

"Every day in every way I am getting better and better" to specific mind-focusing attitudes such as "I will close this sale" or "I will hit this pitch." Use the affirmations that we talked about in earlier chapters or develop new ones for each situation that confronts you. Make your affirmations positive statements of purpose or about yourself. Tell yourself that when you address an employee's declining job performance you are acting rightly and properly. You are doing your job as supervisor. You are helping the employee do a better job so that he or she does not get fired. You are helping your company's performance. If you are defending your performance to your own supervisor, tell yourself over and over again that you are in the right. If you repeat it to yourself, you will be able to convince others. Do not waiver in your faith in yourself. You can also use some of the general affirmations for enablers that we discussed earlier.

Developing an Assertive Style

Developing an assertive personality style is easier than you might think at first glance when you consider that there are only three modes of behavior—aggressive, assertive, and passive—and two of them are counterproductive.

AGGRESSIVE BEHAVIOR.   Aggressive behavior or statements having to do with angry and oftentimes defensive reactions announce to the world that, "What I want is the most important thing. To hell with everyone else." While you may think these actions reflect a strong and assertive personality, quite the opposite is true. For if I were truly strong and sure of myself, then I wouldn't have to behave in such a hostile manner. Aggressive behavior and attitudes are largely nonsocial actions.

PASSIVE BEHAVIOR.   When people are passive they convey that they are not worthy of consideration by other people. Feigned humility usually reveals exactly what the passive individual often displays: "I am not worthy," "You are more worthwhile than I," "I hold myself in lesser esteem than I hold you," and, most important for our purposes, "Your wants are more important than my wants. Therefore, I yield to you." Simply put, passivity is a collection of attitudes and behaviors that constantly put the wants and needs of other people first because the passive person conveys that he or she doesn't have a right to have valid or worthwhile feelings.

ASSERTIVENESS.   Assertiveness stands in stark contrast to both aggressive and passive behavior. It conveys through action an attitude of self-respect and an intent to have needs and wants addressed in a reasonable manner. Assertive behavior is very social in that it affirms one's own wishes while at the same time respecting those of other people. Assertive statements always convey a clear want or desire in a manner that makes allowances for the other person. "I understand that you want to go to the movies tonight, but I'd much rather stay home and read a book. So if you want to go anyway I'll understand," or "I'm concerned about your drinking and I've decided that the best way I can take care of myself is to not be around you when you indulge. It's your life and you may certainly do what you like, however, I love you and I'm not going to stand around and watch you while you kill yourself." Assertive statements are clear, direct, and inoffensive. They are like extending a hand and saying "I want you to know who I am and I am also interested in you."

When most people initially consider asserting themselves after years of codependent and otherwise enabling behavior, they oftentimes run into trouble when people react defensively and otherwise negatively to their efforts to be different. These reactions are usually attributable to two general truths.

The first is that people generally resist change and are oftentimes threatened by it. This is especially true when the people you might be experimenting your new, more "assertive" behavior with are people who have already gotten used to you covering up, bailing out, or ignoring their irresponsible actions. The people you have enabled will resent and feel offended by the new you. And it only stands as true that they would be resentful, for if you are to take care of yourself by asserting your legitimate and reasonable wants, then the focus falls on them to come through, and that would require a major change in their attitudes and behavior.

The second truth is that enablers usually mistake aggressive behavior for assertive behavior. This is not surprising because it is only natural for someone who has spent much of his or her life behaving passively to swing all the way to being aggressive once there is an opportunity to be different. Most enablers have no real middle ground. Like ACOAs, enablers under pressure tend to see things as either all black or all white. Thus, when passive humility is clearly not an appropriate reaction to a challenge or even a perceived threat, the only alternative is an aggressive statement or action. The aggression might be as futile as the passive reaction, and the enabler probably knows it. There is, of course, no real shame in this because there is a good deal of anger stored whenever someone chooses to be passive instead of standing up for himself or herself. The problem arises when, once the door to change is opened just a crack, most enablers, believing that they could never really get what they want by just asking or asserting themselves end up shoving the door open in an aggressive crash. This results from, first, a combination of a lack of trust in their abilities to articulate their reasonable demands and to expect to have them met and, second, a well of anger that has been stored by years of passivity. Thus, their anger can easily boil over into aggressive and sometimes antisocial behavior.

Choosing the Right Behavior

You might be wondering how to differentiate among these three forms of behavior. It might be easy to remember these simple examples:

- When you're acting passively, you'll feel like a doormat.
- When you're acting aggressively, you'll feel like Attila the Hun.

These two modes of behavior stand in stark contrast to the calm sense of well-being and dignity you'll feel when you're acting in an assertive manner. You almost always will be able to know in which mode of behavior you are by simply asking yourself how you feel. Most people find that by using their feelings as a behavioral cue, they are better able to tune into how they are acting and to make any adjustments in behavior that are warranted. For example, if, in the middle of berating a husband for spending what she feels is too much time with his stepdaughter, a wife might adjust the aggressive behavior to a more assertive stance that might convey, "It is not my intention to attack you like this, it's just that I don't feel that I hold a special enough position in your life's priorities. I would like you to focus more on me and my needs."

In another example at the opposite extreme, a normally passive employee notices that he is once again agreeing to stay late to finish the work that others have been allowed to neglect. He may address his boss by declaring: "I realized that I just said that I would stay late again, but I now realize that this is not my preference. The reality is that I don't mind pitching in, it's just that there are other people in the department who do not follow through on their projects and I always seem to be the one to pick up the pieces. My son is playing Little League this afternoon and I don't want to miss yet another game. I guess I'm so used to complying with any request and feeling as if I have no choice that I was saying yes just out of habit."

By using your feelings as a way to check your behavior, you'll find that your awareness of yourself will increase and as a result you'll be acting more for yourself in a reasonable assertive manner.

Pulling It Together

Taking charge of your life is not as simple as trying out some new behavioral or affirmational techniques, attending twelve-step meetings, going to counseling, reading the right books, and getting the recovery/therapy jargon down so you can use it at lunch or in dinner conversations. In order to take control of our lives we are required to choose to be responsible by the actions (however small) we take in our everyday routine. Even the choice to get up and out of bed and get something meaningful done in the very face of a depression is an action of self-love and personal responsibility.

Sure, there are times when it's OK to lie in bed and not get out. Your concern should be for those times when you continually display a passive approach to life and find it impossible to assert yourself. It's easy to feel as if we're not in charge of our life when we act that way. Most people would find it depressing to feel as if others make our decisions for us. Ultimately, however, we have to make a choice: feel stuck and frustrated with the way things are or choose to be different. Remember, when we try out new behaviors and attitudes we don't pretend that the old feelings and negative thoughts are gone, rather we are making a choice to act differently because we care enough about ourselves.

Finally a comment on true recovery and substitutions for the real thing. Recovery, whether it's from a chemical or from a pattern of dysfunctional relationships, means making real changes in the problematic behavior accompanied by living a sober life. Just as an alcoholic may stop drinking and still not be sober, an enabler may stop enabling and still not be living a responsible, sober life. It's important, of course, to stop the dysfunctional behavior, but in the long run it means little more than that without a change in attitude.

Sobriety is what happens when an alcoholic not only chooses not to drink, but is willing to live according to the principles of the Twelve Steps of Alcoholics Anonymous. It is what happens, for example, when she looks into her heart and accepts herself for who she knows herself to be. It's also the continual process of working the Fourth Step: to make a searching and fearless moral inventory of ourselves and to trust in a higher power to help make whatever changes are necessary in order to live a life in which we're more honest with ourselves and our loved ones.

Just as not drinking is only being "dry," not acting as an enabler doesn't necessarily denote sobriety. Many enablers who have been passive sometimes swing all the way to acting aggressively over the course of their recovery. This sometimes happens as a temporary behavior that is tentatively being explored for its value or usefulness. However some people make a decision to stay in the behavior, assuming that the best defense is a good offense. Sure, shooting arrows at someone is a lot better than being shot at, but this only conveys a different way to cope with a feeling of powerlessness. In this case sobriety is lacking in both attitude (the world is dangerous and I can't trust it, so I'd better get them before they get me) and in behavior (acting out aggressively).

There are no substitutions allowed in the recovery process. Substitutions, whether it be alcohol for cocaine, resentment for alcohol, aggressiveness for enabling, are not what sobriety is about. The choices may at times seem difficult, if not impossible. I want to encourage you to allow the natural healer that resides within us all to direct you. With your support and positive affirmations you can and will have a rich and satisfying life, free of guilt and enabling. One day at a time.

Resources for Enabling and Codependency

Self-help Groups

Most self-help services available today focus exclusively on codependency issues, with few resources focusing on the broader issues raised by enabling in general. Nonetheless, the services and support offered through Twelve Step groups can be enormously helpful.

The main source of Twelve Step support is through meetings of Codependents Anonymous. Meetings are free of charge throughout North America and elsewhere, and they offer support to people wishing to recover from having grown up in an alcoholic or otherwise dysfunctional family, aid in the development of self-esteem, and direction in building healthy, fulfilling relationships.

For a list of meetings in your community, contact the International Services Office of Codependence Anonymous, Inc., P.O. Box 33577, Phoenix, Arizona 85067-3577; phone: (602) 277-7991. They also list CoDA meeting times and places for the following countries: Canada, the United Kingdom, Mexico, Hungary, the Netherlands, Japan, Saudi Arabia, Sweden, Guam, Spain, and India.

Additional support is available through Codependence Anonymous for Helping Professionals. This is an international Twelve Step group for practitioners in a variety of the helping professions to help them learn how their codependency is affecting their working with clients and patients and to help further their recovery. Psychologists, social workers, psychiatrists, physicians, addiction counselors, nurses, and other individuals from the helping professions are welcome to participate. For more information, contact Codependency Anonymous for Helping Professionals, P.O. Box 18191, Mesa, Arizona 85201; phone: (602) 966-5170.

Psychotherapy

Regardless of whether you wish to address a general tendency to enable or a more specific problem with codependency, many people find psychotherapy quite helpful. Even if you choose to enter for only short-term therapy, it is important that you choose a therapist wisely. So much of the value gleaned from the therapeutic process is determined by the training and experience of the therapist and the relationship that is formed with the client. I strongly recommend working with a professionally trained provider of mental health services, such as a social worker, psychologist, or psychiatrist, who has a specialty in dealing with individuals from dysfunctional or chemically dependent families. If you choose to enter psychotherapy with an individual who is trained solely as an addictions counselor, you run the risk of working with someone who may be operating beyond his or her area of expertise. In making your selection you might want to consider your priest, rabbi, minister, or a mental health center as a source of information. You can also try to find help through a referral service provided by your state or county psychological association or office of social services.

Books

The following is a list of readings specifically addressing the issues of enabling and codependence, as well as books for general personal growth.

ENABLING AND CODEPENDENCE

Beattie, Melody. *Codependent No More.* New York: Hazeldon/ Harper & Row, 1987.
Covington, Stephanie, and Liana Beckett. *Leaving the Enchanted Forest.* New York: Harper & Row, 1988.
Cruse, Joe. *Painful Affairs: Looking for Love through Addiction and Codependency.* New York: Doubleday, 1989
Cruse, Sharon, and Joe Cruse. *Understanding Codependency.* Deerfield Beach, Fla.: Health Communications, 1990.
Friel, John, and Linda Friel. *Adult Children: The Secrets of Dysfunctional Families.* Deerfield Beach, Fla.: Health Communications, 1988.
———. *Codependency: An Anthology.* Deerfield Beach, Fla.: Health Communications, 1988.
Mellody, Pia. *Facing Codependence.* New York: Harper & Row, 1989.
Miller, Angelyn. *The Enabler.* Claremont, Calif.: Hunter House, 1988.
Schaef, Anne Wilson. *Codependence: Misunderstood and Mistreated.* San Francisco: Harper & Row, 1987.
———. *When Society Becomes an Addict.* San Francisco: Harper & Row, 1987.

PERSONAL GROWTH

Alberti, Robert, and Michael Emmons. *Your Perfect Right.* San Luis Obispo, Calif.: Impact, 1970.
Bloomfield, Harold. *Making Peace with Yourself.* New York: Bloomfield Press, 1985.
Bradshaw, John. *Bradshaw on the Family.* Deerfield Beach, Fla.: Health Communications, 1988.
———. *Healing the Shame that Binds You.* Deerfield Beach, Fla.: Health Communications, 1988.
Dyer, Wayne. *Pulling Your Own Strings.* New York: Avon, 1978.
Goldberg, Herb. *The Hazards of Being Male.* New York: Signet, 1977.
Harris, Thomas. *I'm O.K.—You're O.K.* New York: Harper & Row, 1967.

Lazarus, Arnold, and Allen Fay. *I Can If I Want To.* New York: Warner Books, 1975.

Lerner, Rockelle. *Daily Affirmations.* Pompano Beach, Fla.: Health Communications, 1985.

Peck, M. Scott. *The Road Less Traveled.* New York: Simon & Schuster, 1980.

Pelletier, Kenneth. *Mind as Healer, Mind as Slayer.* New York: Dell, 1977.

Phelps, Stanlee, and Nancy Austin. *The Assertive Woman: A New Look.* San Luis Obispo, Calif.: Impact, 1987.

Presnall, Lewis. *First Aid for Depression.* Minneapolis: Hazeldon, 1985.

Rogers, Carl. *On Becoming a Person,* Boston: Houghton Mifflin, 1961.

Rosewater, Lynne Brovo. *Changing Through Therapy: Understanding the Therapeutic Experience.* New York: Dodd, Mead, 1987.

Travis, John, and Regina Sara Ryan. *Wellness Workbook.* San Francisco: Ten Speed Press, 1986.

Wilbur, Ken. *No Boundary.* New York: New Science Library/ Bantam, 1981.

Woititz, Janet, and Allen Garner. *Life Skills for Adult Children.* Deerfield Beach, Fla.: Health Communications, 1990.

Index